Abundance Not Capital
The Lively Architecture of Anupama Kundoo

Abundance Not Capital
The Lively Architecture of Anupama Kundoo

Edited by Angelika Fitz, Elke Krasny,
and Architekturzentrum Wien

Architekturzentrum Wien, Vienna
The MIT Press,
Cambridge, Massachusetts,
and London, England

Introduction

Anupama Kundoo's Lively Architecture
Abundance Not Capital

**Angelika Fitz
and Elke Krasny**

**Angelika Fitz
and Elke Krasny**

Imagining Architecture
Otherwise
10

Doing Architecture
Otherwise
22

Reinventing Beauty:
The Abundance of
Differences
82

Crafting Experiments:
The Abundance of
Knowledge
26

Maintenance and Care:
The Abundance of
Generosity
94

Local Economies:
The Abundance of
Materials
42

Climate Healing:
The Abundance of
Nature
106

Beyond Norms and
Standards:
The Abundance of
Solutions
56

Soothing Architecture:
The Abundance of
Regeneration
116

Experimental City:
The Abundance of
Aspirations
70

List of Selected Projects
126

Essays

Modernities, Colonialities, Frictions

Ranjit Hoskote
Unreal City: Utopia and
Its Afterlives
132

Madhavi Desai
The Legacy of Women
in Modern Architecture
of India
147

Peggy Deamer
Anupama Kundoo and
a Post-capitalist Future
161

Capital, Extraction, Labor

Laurie Parsons
Constructing Carbon
Colonialism: The Body,
The Built Environment,
and the Global Politics
of Extraction
176

Charlotte Malterre-Barthes
Architectural
Extractivism in Times
of Post-accountability:
A Restorative Approach
189

Jordan Carver
Drawing and Building:
Architecture and the
Global Building Industry
199

Life, Care, Maintenance

Shumi Bose
Homing as a Verb
212

Shannon Mattern
On Maintenance
229

Rupali Gupte
Feminist Practices and
Architectures of Care
239

Appendix

Acknowledgments
252

About
Anupama Kundoo
254

About the Authors
262

About the Editors
267

Imprint
270

Imagining Architecture Otherwise
Introduction

Imagining Architecture Otherwise

Angelika Fitz and Elke Krasny

Abundance Not Capital. How is it even possible to think this or say this out loud, let alone propose that architecture can create abundance and not be a tool of capital? This book has many aims which converge around our primary motivation for imagining architecture otherwise. These aims include exploring how the study and curation of architecture can contribute meaningfully to reimagining and, ultimately, practicing architecture otherwise. They also reflect a strong commitment to using the traditional monograph format to write the architectural history of the present from anti-colonial and anti-patriarchal standpoints and to develop critical architectural theory that advocates for architecture serving the cause of planetary care, bringing together the rights of humans and the rights of nature. We aim to use the book as a means to open up spaces for learning, exchange, and dialogue with many others.

In February 2024, we, Angelika Fitz and Elke Krasny, together with the architect Anupama Kundoo, visited her built work in southern India. While Kundoo has been teaching at prestigious universities worldwide and is currently operating offices in Berlin, Germany, Mumbai and Puducherry, India, the vast majority of her built work can be found in Auroville and Puducherry. Our embodied experience of Anupama Kundoo's lively architecture made us feel that the spaces created by her make it possible for humans and environments to breathe freely. Her architecture resists the suffocation of form follows money, no matter if it concerns the representation of the wealthy and powerful, the financialization of property, or the bare essentials for the poor and disadvantaged. Kundoo's refusal of form follows money began in the 1990s when she began her architectural career. After studying architecture in Mumbai in the mid-1980s, she moved to the experimental town of Auroville in southern India, where she set up her office Anupama Kundoo Architects at the age of twenty-three. At that time, globalization and urbanization were advancing at an unprecedented pace and scale. Architecture, along with the construction and infrastructure industries, played a significant role in accelerating capitalism. Architect Rahul Mehrotra reflects on how the architectural profession transformed, particularly in fast-growing India during this period, and analyzed sharply that this era saw the emergence of "architecture as impatient capital."[1] It is precisely within this context that Anupama Kundoo chose to practice architecture otherwise: she rejects architecture as a tool of capital and instead embraces it as an embodiment of patient abundance. In the first part of the introduction, we will share how a critical study of the built work of an architect provided us with insights into its underlying philosophy, which we then transformed into a theoretical framework useful for the in-depth exploration of its guiding principles. In the next section of the introduction, we will present the chapters by our contributors and interlocutors, Ranjit Hoskote, Madhavi Desai, Peggy Deamer, Laurie Parsons, Charlotte Malterre-Barthes, Jordan Carver, Shumi Bose, Shannon Mattern, and Rupali Gupte.

Dimensions of Abundance in Anupama Kundoo's Built Work

The first part of the book, written by Angelika Fitz and Elke Krasny, offers an introduction to and reflection on Anupama Kundoo's lively architecture, framed through the concept of abundance not capital. Before presenting the eight chapters on Kundoo's built work, we would like to clarify the "we" behind this text. We are two research curators of architecture and urbanism. We share a profound interest in architecture as a form of "critical care,"[2] despite the prevailing forces of capital. Holding that architecture intertwines the conditions for human livability with the environments in which they exist, and that architects bear responsibility and accountability for planetary care, and ultimately planetary habitability, we do critical research on the present moment through architecture. Our research is shaped by having conversations with architects and the people who inhabit and use their spaces, by spending time in buildings, sites, and environments, and informed by our ongoing engagement with transnational feminist spatial practices, as well as anti-colonial, queer, and environmental theories.

The chapters on "Anupama Kundoo's Lively Architecture. Abundance Not Capital" approach her work through eight distinct facets of abundance: knowledge, material, solutions, aspirations, differences, generosity, nature, and regeneration. What these chapters do not aim to do is provide a chrono-logical analysis of individual projects. Rather, by understanding Anupama Kundoo's architecture as a body of work, we engage with her entire portfolio through a specific facet of abundance discussed in each chapter. Abundance also served as the focus of our photographic field research. By connecting our research photography with architectural images from Anupama Kundoo's

Rahul Mehrotra, Ranjit Hoskote, and Kaiwan Mehta, *The State of Architecture: Practices & Processes in India* (Mumbai: Urban Design Research Institute, 2016), 13.

2 Angelika Fitz and Elke Krasny, eds., *Critical Care. Architecture and Urbanism for a Broken Planet* (Cambridge, MA: The MIT Press, 2019).

studio, each of the eight chapters offers a theoretical analysis while weaving a visual narrative of these dimensions of abundance. Each chapter presents examples from Anupama Kundoo's architecture to show how the concept of abundance shapes her ethics, her designs, and the built work.

The first chapter, "Crafting Experiments: The Abundance of Knowledge," explores how architectural innovation is achieved through persistent experimentation with crafts, viewed as technologies, and technologies, seen as forms of craft. The abundance of knowledge in architecture and construction doesn't rely on expensive materials or industrially perfected products. Instead, it is informed by and helps shape the creative use of locally available materials and technologies. Earth, clay, stone, and craftsmanship are just as central to the architectural ethics of abundance as the process of testing experiments. The *Wall House*, the architect's home in Auroville, served as a testing ground for generating this abundance of knowledge and innovations, which were later applied to her other projects.

The second chapter, "Local Economies: The Abundance of Materials," explores how Anupama Kundoo's approach rejects the practices of the globalized construction industry, which is built on exploitation and resource extraction. Anupama Kundoo's interest in materials began with aesthetic and economic concerns. Over time, however, her perspective on materials became a critique of coloniality. Kundoo rejects the idea that India is a "poor" country needing "development." Instead, she acknowledges, values, and deliberately works with the abundance of locally available building materials and construction techniques. This approach, in turn, fosters and strengthens local economies through architecture and construction.

The third chapter, "Beyond Norms and Standards: The Abundance of Solutions," explains how the politics of anti-colonialism and anti-capitalism converge in the resistance against norms and standards. During colonization, standardization began the process of globalization, erasing local architectural knowledge and Indigenous construction technologies. Today, while norms and standards ensure safety, they often prioritize the global construction industry over local needs. Kundoo argues that using ecological, local, and affordable materials is essential, as is preserving and expanding knowledge about their use to create context-specific and situated solutions.

The fourth chapter, "Experimental City: The Abundance of Aspirations," provides information on the context of Anupama Kundoo's architecture. Much of her work is connected to Auroville, where the vision for a city founded on unity and peace began to take shape in the 1930s. Auroville was officially founded in 1968 with representatives from 124 nations. The city's name means "City of Dawn" in French. Today, Auroville is an international township focused on human unity, with 3,300 residents from fifty-eight nations. Anupama Kundoo views Auroville as a practical, aspirational experiment, where material and spiritual progress coexist, and land ownership is communal, with no private property. Auroville's realization is shaped by historical factors, including the conditions of colonialism, integral yoga, modernist architecture, Western anti-capitalist ideals, UNESCO support, international aid, and the Indian Government. While Auroville's aspirations are not without friction or conflict and colonial entanglements persist, they create fertile ground for architectural experimentation, with architecture playing a crucial role in realizing the city's vision as it continues to be built.

The fifth chapter, "Reinventing Beauty: The Abundance of Differences," highlights how Anupama Kundoo's architecture evokes a beauty that is both subtle and powerful—humble, accessible, and distinct from the overtly spectacular or dominant. Her work imagines and brings to life a different conception of beauty. Building beauty otherwise reveals that beauty is not limited to a single way of building or inhabiting the planet. By blending modernism, traditional methods, and place-based material experiments, Kundoo fosters a new coexistence where elements maintain their distinctiveness, rather than merely mimicking the past. Her work exemplifies a continuous process of cultural negotiation, facilitating the coexistence of diverse influences. Kundoo situates her understanding of beauty within a continuum of diverse architectural influences, drawing upon the design principles of ancient temples, traditional Tamil Nadu dwellings, Laurie Baker's low-tech methodologies, and the modernist innovations of pioneers such as Le Corbusier.

The sixth chapter engages with the themes of "Maintenance and Care: The Abundance of Generosity." Recognizing that all architecture necessitates ongoing maintenance and care while simultaneously shaping the spatial conditions for caring labor and social reproduction, we are keenly aware that capital not only systematically but also ruthlessly exploits care work. While resisting the violence of capital remains essential, it is equally important to develop a more nuanced understanding of how care practices extend beyond the logics of capitalism. We contend that the deliberate creation of spatial conditions for care, coupled with an acute awareness of the requirements for maintenance, when thoughtfully integrated into architectural design and construction, have the potential to materially produce and reinforce an ethos of generosity. Here, we introduce the idea that maintenance and care can cultivate an abundance of generosity, emphasizing that this is not just an abstract ideal but a tangible reality in Anupama Kundoo's architecture. Her work embodies an ethic of care—integrated into both design and construction—that actively reshapes our relationship with the built environment, transforming generosity from an ideal into a lived architectural practice.

The seventh chapter, "Climate Healing: The Abundance of Nature," begins with the recognition that architecture is deeply embedded in the ways humans have historically shaped and transformed both the planet and its climate. We argue that architecture is the built manifestation of Man's relationship with nature, embodying its profound and often catastrophic impact on the climate. Anupama Kundoo approaches architecture as a form of climate healing, requiring a fundamental reimagining of humanity's relationship with nature. This entails recognizing that nature is neither an inexhaustible resource nor a commodity for profit maximization, but rather a living system that requires restoration to recover from the violent destruction of capitalism and to regenerate its inherent abundance.

The eighth chapter, "Soothing Architecture: The Abundance of Regeneration," is perhaps our most personal reflection, while also introducing new terminology to foster a more nuanced architectural discourse and theorization. Spending hours in the *Wall House*, we felt a profound sense of renewal and tranquility. During our visit to the *Wall House* and other works in Auroville and Puducherry, we searched for the right words to describe how her spaces made us feel. We soon realized that architecture lacks a nuanced vocabulary for describing environments that are *soothing* and regenerative—a telling absence that reflects the field's historical emphasis on power, capital, and spectacle. In contrast, we chose soothing to characterize Kundoo's architecture—not as a claim to define an era but as a recognition of the bodily, emotional, and even spiritual experiences her spaces create. This final chapter of the book's first part invites reflection on architecture and the built environment as spaces for pause, recharge, and presence, exploring how Anupama Kundoo's work cultivates peace, restoration, and emotional well-being—qualities often overlooked in architectural discourse.

Anupama Kundoo's lively architecture generates abundance without catering to the interests of capital. Although she rarely employs explicitly anti-capitalist, anti-colonial, or anti-patriarchal language, we, as research curators, argue that her built work exemplifies how architecture can be imagined, designed, constructed, inhabited, and experienced differently. Her built work reimagines and redefines the "power"[3] of architecture—challenging its conventional hierarchies, reconfiguring its agency, and demonstrating its capacity to operate beyond dominant capitalist, colonial, and patriarchal structures.

3   See: Elke Krasny, "Architecture Builds Power: Ending Domination, Practicing Life-Making, Finding Response-ability," in *On Power in Architecture. From a Materialistic, Phenomenological, and Post-* *Structuralist Perspective*, ed. Mateja Kurir (London: Routledge, 2025), 191–201.

On the Essays

The act of envisioning—and indeed materializing—architecture otherwise inevitably confronts the hegemonic structures that define our contemporary neoliberal, neocolonial, neoimperial, and neopatriarchal realities. The second part of this book critically examines the systemic conditions that have led many, if not most, architects to perceive the possibility of practicing architecture otherwise as unattainable. As editors, we have commissioned a series of original essays and contributions from a diverse group of architectural practitioners, public intellectuals, activists, theorists, and scholars. These contributors and interlocutors critically engage with a broad spectrum of urgent and complex issues, situating their analyses within the wider discourses of architectural theory, the analysis of capitalism, social justice, environmental sustainability, and decolonial feminist thought. In doing so, they establish meaningful connections between these broader concerns and the work of Anupama Kundoo, illuminating the ways in which her practice both responds to and challenges prevailing architectural paradigms. By offering this critical contextualization, the essays and email conversations position Kundoo's architectural approach within intersecting socio-political, economic, and ecological frameworks. Through this lens, the contributors interrogate the historical and structural forces that have shaped dominant architectural ideologies while simultaneously exploring the possibilities for alternative, more just, and regenerative ways of building. In doing so, this collection aims to challenge entrenched narratives, expand the critical discourse surrounding contemporary architectural practice, and foreground the transformative potential of architecture in shaping different futures. The three sections—"Modernities, Colonialities, Frictions"; "Capital, Extraction, Labor"; and "Life, Care, Maintenance"—clearly illustrate the challenges of truly imagining and creating architecture otherwise, and of building abundance. We invited architects, scholars, theorists, and activists to reflect on the questions and concerns raised by Anupama Kundoo's architecture, while critically engaging with the historical and present conditions shaped by capitalist, colonial, and patriarchal violence seeking to understand how architecture can support un-building, un-settling, and un-doing this violence.

The section entitled "Modernities, Colonialities, Frictions" brings together three essays by Ranjit Hoskote, Madhavi Desai, and Peggy Deamer. Cultural theorist and poet Ranjit Hoskote, co-author of *The State of Architecture: Practices & Processes in India*, follows the aspirations and realities of utopian urban planning projects in India. In his essay "Unreal City: Utopia and Its Afterlives" he explains that if planning is to be socially and ecologically farsighted, it must deal with what is there, whether natural or man-made, because we can build neither dreams nor clouds. Architect and researcher

Madhavi Desai, a founding member of the Women Architects Forum and the author of *Women Architects and Modernism in India: Narratives and Contemporary Practices*, sheds light on marginalized but immense contributions to the diverse modernities of the twentieth century by looking at the career paths of several significant first-generation women architects in India. Architect and theorist Peggy Deamer, who argues that one could say that the history of architecture is the history of capitalism and who critically examines how architecture is entangled in the construction of a neoliberal world, links the practice of Anupama Kundoo to the notions of a post-capitalist future.

The "Capital, Extraction, Labor" section examines how architecture is implicated in and responsible for climate destruction, widespread material extraction, and exploitative labor conditions. These represent some of the most complex and difficult challenges in both imagining and actually constructing an architecture of abundance. This section brings together three contributions from architect-activists and scholar-activists, focusing on climate politics and labor conditions, with particular attention to the economies and politics of extraction and exploitation. Laurie Parsons, the author of *Carbon Colonialism: How Rich Countries Export Climate Breakdown*, writes about the actual construction of carbon colonialism by focusing on the bodily dimensions of construction. Charlotte Malterre-Barthes, the driving force behind the initiative and provocation of "A Global Moratorium on New Construction,"[4] offers an analysis of post-accountability and introduces the possibilities of a restorative approach that honors the connections between people, places, and the materials we use for habitat needs. Jordan Carver, a core member of the interdisciplinary advocacy group Who Builds Your Architecture?, differentiates architecture from building and critically examines the role of drawing in relation to the global construction industry.

The third section, "Life, Care, Maintenance," addresses key concerns in architecture that, despite architecture's clear indispensability to human life and well-being, have long been sidelined in architectural history and theory. After introducing the concept of "critical care" in architecture in 2019, we present three conversations conducted by Elke Krasny with key thinkers on care in architecture, foregrounding feminist thought traditions. Architectural writer and historian Shumi Bose, in past conversations with Anupama Kundoo, has rejected being confined by labels and stereotypes such as female, Indian, Global South, or traditional crafts and Indigenous

---

4   Charlotte Malterre-Barthes, "A Global Moratorium on New Construction," https://www. charlottemalterrebarthes.com/ practice/research-practice/ a-global-moratorium-on-new-construction/.

techniques. She turns home into a verb form, homing, and, in dialogue with Elke Krasny, thinks about the question of home in architecture through feminist theories of liberation and Anupama Kundoo's own home, the *Wall House*. In Krasny's research conversation with Shannon Mattern, an interdisciplinary scholar focusing on media theory, urban studies, and information infrastructures, who has written extensively on "Maintenance and Care"[5] in architecture and cities, maintenance is framed as sustaining architectural abundance by resisting the capitalist speed of construction and destruction cycles. The dialogue with architect, educator, and urbanist Rupali Gupte, conducted via email by Elke Krasny, begins with a shared interest in feminist practices and expanding the understanding of care in spatial and material terms, moving beyond Western-centered ethical traditions and theories. It highlights approaches that challenge compulsory neoliberal capitalism, with an emphasis on inhabitation, land rights of Indigenous communities, and responses to monsoon conditions and climate change across South Asia.

In the contexts of accumulation and scarcity, profit and deprivation, extraction and exploitation, critically described in the aforementioned essays, it becomes evident that abundance is not a concept that can be taken for granted, nor is it easily attained. Spatial, environmental, cultural, social, and epistemic abundance is never simply given; it must be actively created, sustained, and carefully nurtured. An architecture of abundance refuses to give in to the profit-driven commoditization of everything. Robin Wall Kimmerer, a plant ecologist and an enrolled member of the Citizen Potawatomi Nation, whose work is dedicated to restoring our relationships to land, questions capital's mindset of commoditization: "Why then have we permitted the dominance of economic systems that commoditize everything? That create scarcity instead of abundance, that promote accumulation rather than sharing? We've surrendered our values to an economic system that actively harms what we love."[6]

Abundance is not simply anti-capitalist. Much rather, practicing abundance embodies lively and life-making economies that are based on a different world view altogether. Candace Fujikane, an English professor at the University of Hawai'i, speaks of "flourishing Indigenous economies of abundance." For Fujikane, "mapping abundance is a refusal to succumb to capital's logic that we have passed an apocalyptic threshold of no return."[7]

Shannon Mattern, "Maintenance and Care," *Places Journal*, November 2018, https://doi.org/10.22269/181120.

Robin Wall Kimmerer, "The Serviceberry: An Economy of Abundance." *Emergence*

Magazine, October 26, 2022, https://emergencemagazine.org/essay/the-serviceberry/.

7 Candice Fujikane, *Mapping Abundance for a Planetary Future: Kanaka Maoli and Critical Settler Cartographies in Hawai'i* (London

and Durham, NC: Duke University Press 2021), 4.

This refusal to surrender to capital is an act of solidarity with life-making, continuity, and futurity. Building abundance, then, is the refusal to buy into believing that architecture can only follow the interest of capital.

Capital is operating on the violent logic of "never enough," which political economies of power exploit to govern through greed and fear. Greed and fear are poor companions, the antitheses of life-affirming practices. Greed and fear thrive on exploitation, extraction, and deprivation, amplifying competition, injustice, and authoritarian, patriarchal violence. Abundance challenges the notion of "not enough" and fosters a mindset of plentitude that resists the dogma of either-or binaries. In particular, Anupama Kundoo's lively architecture refuses architectural binaries of inside/outside, technology/craft, modernity/tradition, nature/culture, beauty/function, resourcefulness/generosity. Abundance is cultivated and becomes spatial and material by transcending the either-or mindset. This expands the discourse on what architecture can and should be.

An architecture of abundance focuses on the idea that there is enough to go around when resources are shared responsibly, and that beauty and functionality can coexist while meeting the needs of people and the planet. According to the black feminist writer and researcher Lola Olufemi, the author of *Experiments in Imagining Otherwise*, "imagination is central," imagination "enables resistant acts to take place by dismantling hegemonic notions of what is permissible under current conditions."[8] An architecture of abundance begins by imagining architecture otherwise and builds architecture that brings this imagination to life, regardless of the constraints imposed by capital. It is an architecture dedicated to lively planetary care, creating spaces that demonstrate the reality that there is, in fact, enough. We firmly believe in the power of words, and that terms like "abundance," which we offer here, can serve as crucial theoretical allies—not just in writing, but in the very act of imagining and doing architecture otherwise.

8 Lola Olufemi, *Experiments in Imagining Otherwise* (London: Hajar Press, 2021), 35.

Anupama Kundoo's Lively Architecture
Abundance Not Capital

All quotes by Anupama Kundoo,
unless otherwise noted,
originate from conversations
held with Angelika Fitz and Elke
Krasny during their curatorial
research in 2023–24.

Architecture has become an engine in the service of globalized Capital.
Mumbai, 2019, Photo: Javier Callejas

1 Rahul Mehrotra, Ranjit Hoskote, and Kaiwan Mehta, *The State of Architecture: Practices & Processes in India* (Mumbai: Urban Design Research Institute, 2016), 13.

Doing Architecture Otherwise

Why "abundance not capital?" Visiting Anupama Kundoo's built work in Auroville and Puducherry together with the architect in 2024, we came to understand how her work embodies lively economies and ecologies, as well as care-full practices of inhabitation and maintenance. We learned about the robust material architectural experimentation and felt how her built work generates beauty and soothing. This led us to want to provide a framework that captures both the refusal of capital-centric architectural production, as well as the insistence on reinventing beauty in architecture.

In the 1990s, when Anupama Kundoo first started becoming an architect, globalization-cum-urbanization took command at unprecedented speed and scale. Architecture and the concomitant construction and infrastructure industries played a huge role in this acceleration of capitalism with its rampant growth, technological advances, and heightened extraction of natural resources and exploitation of laboring bodies. Architect and educator Rahul Mehrotra analyzes how the profession of architecture changed globally and specifically in the context of fast-growing India in this decade as follows: "Since the liberalisation of our economy, architects are pandering to Capital in unprecedented ways — creating what we could call the architecture of Impatient Capital."[1] It is precisely in this context that Anupama Kundoo insisted on practicing architecture otherwise: Kundoo refuses "Architecture as Capital" and insists on architecture as abundance.

Writing Architecture Otherwise

Abundance can neither be naively assumed nor easily achieved. The following eight chapters approach Anupama Kundoo's built work from 1990 to 2019 and its context in Auroville and Puducherry through differentiated notions of abundance: the abundance of knowledge, the abundance of materials, the abundance of solutions, the abundance of aspirations, the abundance of differences, the abundance of generosity, the abundance of nature, and the abundance of regeneration. What the following eight chapters are not: We do not write about individual or single projects in a chronological order. Understanding Anupama Kundoo's architecture as a lively body of work, we use the eight chapters to speak with and to her entire body of work through the specific notion of abundance discussed in each of the chapters. Abundance was also the focus of our photographic field research. Connecting the

Anupama Kundoo refuses "Architecture as Capital" and insists on architecture as abundance. Kundoo in front of her first home *Hut Petit Ferme*, 1990 (left) and in conversation with Angelika Fitz and Elke Krasny at the *Wall House*, 2024 (right), both in Auroville.

Photos: Andreas Deffner (left); Angelika Fitz (right)

Anupama Kundoo grew up in Mumbai, where she studied architecture in the mid-1980s. She moved to the experimental town of Auroville in southern India in 1990, where she set up her office Anupama Kundoo Architects at the age of twenty-three. While she has been teaching at prestigious universities worldwide and is currently operating offices in Berlin, Germany, Mumbai and Puducherry, India, the vast majority of her built work can be found in Auroville and Puducherry, India.

research photography with the architectural photographs from Anupama Kundoo's studio in each of the chapters provides a visual narrative of the dimensions of abundance.

Our curatorial and scholarly approach refuses to reduce buildings to single or stand-alone objects. Both the capitalist economy of buildings and the canon of architecture history embrace the notion of the single building, at once a singular entity valued for its style in the market and in the canon. Much rather, our approach insists that lively architecture never stands alone, but is deeply entangled in an abundance of social, ecological, material, and immaterial relations.

Crafting Experiments:
The Abundance of Knowledge

The built environment is the largest collective undertaking in all of human history. While building had been collective work for the longest time, the modern division of labor separated architects, designers, builders, and users from each other, thereby leading to a disregard for the actual building process and the wealth of knowledge arising from experiments carried out during construction. "Making" types of knowledge, often associated with physical and reproductive labor, were disdained. Anupama Kundoo opens her manifesto "Time as a Resource: Twelve Strategies for Re-Thinking Urban Materiality"[1] with this assessment.

Under petro-capitalism, the construction industry became one of the leading CO_2 emitters and the largest waste producer in the world, without fulfilling the promises of modernity such as affordability, well-being, and health for all. In financialized capitalism, more is being built than ever before. Yet, many people can no longer afford their homes, which become tools of finance and products for investment, and the city skylines are becoming interchangeable. This obvious economic, ecological, social, and cultural failure should prevent us from rolling out these global construction industry standards in previously less industrialized regions, Kundoo maintains.

In Anupama Kundoo's buildings, wealth does not lie in expensive materials and perfected industrial products; variety does not result from the standardized construction industry, but from the innovative use of materials and techniques that are locally available in abundance. Earth and clay are part of this, as is the knowledge of craftsmanship. Kundoo developed a series of roof structures using terracotta elements that save on steel and cement as well as formwork resources. All of these were tested on the *Wall House* and employed in a variety of projects. In her baked in-situ houses, the earth house itself becomes a kiln, and ferrocement experiments radically minimize material consumption. The constructions are exceptionally beautiful, but it is above all a matter of reappropriating the art of engineering.

Wall House, Auroville, 2000
Photo: Javier Callejas

1 Anupama Kundoo, "Human Time as a Resource: Twelve Strategies for Re-Thinking Urban Materiality," *The Plan Journal 6*, no. 2 (2021): 305–22, https://www.doi.org/ 10.15274/ tpj.2021.06.02.1.

"I don't have a nostalgic view of craft. I see questions and opportunities in this that we have ignored for too long," claims Kundoo. "We need to develop this knowledge before we lose the capacity to make things."

Fighting Heat with Air
Vaulted Ceiling Made of Terracotta Cones

Roofs and ceilings headed Anupama Kundoo's list of experiments right from the start. Common RCC (reinforced cement concrete) ceiling constructions use a lot of cement and steel, needing expensive formwork, which increases a building's carbon footprint. And if roofs are not well-insulated, they entail a lot of expenditure on building services and air conditioning technology, which could be avoided in the best-case scenario. Her self-supporting vaulted ceiling made of hand-made terracotta cones does not require any structural steel and keeps the buildings cool.

Cone-shaped terracotta elements, custom-made locally by hand, are the basic components for the vaulted constructions.
Photo: Andreas Deffner

Southeast view of the *Wall House* (top). The picture on the left shows the construction of one of these terracotta roofs in 1996.

Wall House, Auroville, 2000
Photos: Javier Callejas (top); Andreas Deffner (bottom)

Use of the climate-friendly vaulted ceiling in social housing
Sangamam, Auroville, 2003
Photos: Javier Callejas

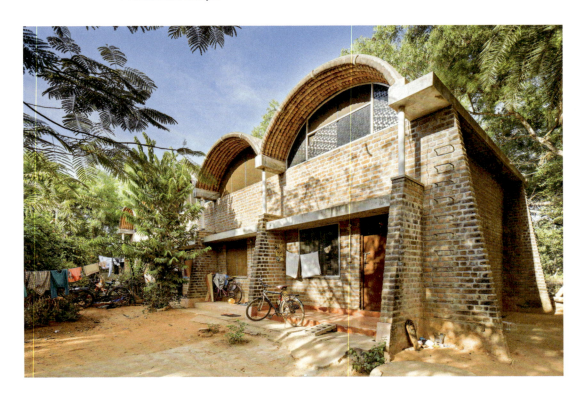

In these private holiday homes, the terracotta cones span the communal living areas and terraces.

Shah Houses, Brahmangarh, 2016
Photos: Javier Callejas

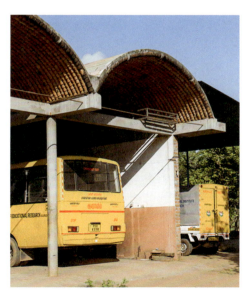

The public bus garage benefits from the cooling effect of the hollow terracotta elements and shows the wealth of possible applications.

Abri Transport Service, Auroville, 2003
Photo: Deepshikha Jain

Nothing Is Lost
Filler Slabs with Terracotta Pots

Another experimental ceiling construction is based on the reinterpretation of the principles of the filler slabs and lost formwork. Recesses with terracotta pots reduce the dead weight of the ceiling and therefore the steel consumption. The elements are not "lost," however, but appear as decorative ceiling components, without high-quality formwork wood, which is rare and expensive in India. The use of clay mortar guarantees a balanced surface, even when working with waste wood. The construction was developed anew at the *Wall House* and then transferred to other residential and public structures.

Traditional clay pots, placed upside down, are the most important elements of this new type of ceiling construction.
Photo: Andreas Deffner

Almost parallel to the testing in the *Wall House*, Kundoo uses the ceiling construction with terracotta pots at another experimental construction site, a pottery workshop that is part of the *Residence Spirit Sense*. This project is also the first time she has built a baked in-situ earth house—see the dome construction in the background.
Construction site of the *Residence Spirit Sense*, Auroville, 2000–2001
Photo: Andreas Deffner

When wood is scarce and cheap leftovers are used for formwork, as is common in India, the surfaces remain uneven and are then usually plastered and painted. Kundoo levels the formwork with clay mortar, which can be easily removed after it dries. This makes plastering unnecessary.
Wall House, Auroville, 2000
Photo: Andreas Deffner

The space for communal eating and spending time in the *Wall House* is spatially and atmospherically shaped by the structure and materiality of the terracotta elements. Kundoo developed the terracotta filler slab for intermediate floors that do not need to provide thermal insulation as compared to the catenary vaults made of conical tubes.
Wall House, Auroville, 2000
Photo: Javier Callejas

The coffered ceiling that is thicker than a conventional reinforced concrete ceiling provides a bigger effective slab depth, thereby reducing steel consumption. The recesses formed by the terracotta pots make it much lighter and lead to further economy.

Creativity Co-Housing, Auroville, 2003
Photo: Elke Krasny
Drawing: Anupama Kundoo Architects

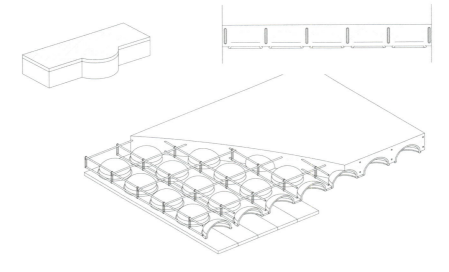

With larger spans, such as the common room of the *Sangamam* social housing project (top) and the seminar room of the *Village Action Center* (left), the steel savings become economically and ecologically significant.

Sangamam, Auroville, 2003
Village Action Center, Auroville, 2000
Photos: Andreas Deffner (top), Elke Krasny (left)

Brick Technology Reloaded
Jack Arch System Made of Hollow Terracotta Bricks

Parallel to the increasing use of reinforced concrete ceilings, the roofs of simple houses in India are made of thin terracotta tiles supported by wooden rafters. With these thin tile elements, the rooms heat up, especially since the room heights have become lower and the roofs are no longer built in two layers. Wood is short in supply. As an alternative, Kundoo developed well-insulated roofs made of extruded, hollow terracotta trapezoids and thin, prefab, reinforced concrete beams that resemble jack arch systems. Such systems were often used for commercial buildings in the nineteenth and early twentieth centuries. Kundoo employs them in a flat, walkable version, as well as in an arched version.

Hollow terracotta bricks on the construction site and in the guest room of the *Wall House*

Wall House, Auroville, 2000
Photos: Andreas Deffner (left);
Javier Callejas (right)

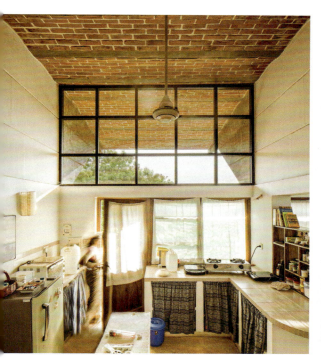

Hollow brick ceiling in a residential building (left) and in a school (right)

Creativity Co-Housing, Auroville, 2003;
Auroville Institute of Applied Technology, Auroville, 2001
Photos: Javier Callejas (left); Angelika Fitz (right);
Drawing: Anupama Kundoo Architects

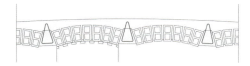
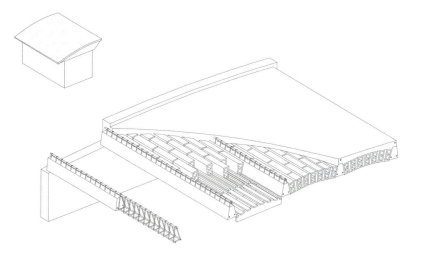

37   Crafting Experiments: The Abundance of Knowledge

House as a Kiln

In the baked in-situ houses, houses made of earth, a building material abundantly available everywhere, become kilns themselves. A construction made of mud bricks and clay mortar is filled with unfired bricks or pottery and then fired. During firing, the walls of the kiln absorb a large part of the heat. This technique makes use of this excess to fire the contents and the building at the same time. In the 1970s, the Iranian-American architect Nader Khalili experimented with firing earth houses as a whole to make them more resistant to natural forces without using cement. The ceramic artist Ray Meeker, who lives and works in Puducherry in southern India, developed the technique further, successfully firing several test structures and some residences. He guided Kundoo and provided technical support on the baked in-situ projects

In 2000, Kundoo worked for the first time with the baked in-situ technique on the central living space for the *Residence Spirit Sense*. The house is fired for three to four days. The bricks for other parts of the building are also fired inside, thus offsetting the cost of fuel. To reduce wood consumption, Ray Meeker also experimented with mixing coal dust into the clay mass so that the bricks baked due to their self-contained fuel.

Residence Spirit Sense, Auroville, 2000–2001
Photos: Anupama Kundoo Architects

Ten years after the first experiment, Kundoo used the baked in-situ technique to create an ensemble for a non-profit organization that offers a home to homeless children and their foster parents. The project included a collaboration with students from the TU Berlin, ETH Zurich, and TU Darmstadt, and was again advised and technically supported by Ray Meeker. Kundoo already worked on this technique in her dissertation at the TU Berlin, where she is currently a professor.

Volontariat Homes for Homeless Children, Puducherry, 2008
Photos: Javier Callejas (top); Anupama Kundoo Architects (bottom)

Material-Saving, Self-Made: Ferrocement

Praised as a "wonder" in the 1970s because of its lightness, ferrocement was quickly replaced worldwide by reinforced concrete, even though the latter uses much more CO_2-intensive materials. The prototypes built by Kundoo are a reminder of the ecological, economic, technological, and design potential of extremely thin ferrocement elements that can be manufactured locally in the backyards of masons' homes using chicken mesh or other types of netting instead of rebars.

Kundoo has been experimenting with ferrocement elements since 1991 with the aim of finding solutions for locally manufactured, easily implemented, and affordable housing through prefabrication. As part of her international university teaching, she also experiments with natural fibers as an alternative to wire mesh.
Photo: Andreas Deffner

In this quickly deployable sanitary unit, the shower and toilet are connected to a covered platform. The construction consists of six prefabricated ferrocement elements that can be assembled in a very short time.
Easy-WC, Auroville, 2015
Photo: Javier Callejas

Full Fill Homes, Auroville, 2015
Photos: Javier Callejas (top, middle)

The wall systems as built-in furniture elements were developed for quickly available temporary housing. The element thickness is reduced to 25 mm by material and geometry, which saves CO_2 and money. In six days the prefabricated ferrocement elements can be assembled. The users can lend a hand and choose combinations. The need for furniture is minimized and the houses can be dismantled again within a day.

A series of load tests, conducted at the TU Berlin's Chair for Conceptual and Structural Design headed by Mike Schlaich, confirms ferrocement's ductility and potential load-bearing capacity that the thin ferrocement elements gain through folding.

Photo: Blas Llamazares

Local Economies:
The Abundance of Materials

The mining, production, transport, and processing of materials have led to the exploitation of nature and workers in the globalized construction industry. This catastrophic abuse continues to this day, but is less often debated publicly than, e.g., the production conditions in the textile industry. Therefore, the realities of migrant construction workers, for instance, who produce glossy architecture under terrible circumstances, and the effects of their absence, often for years, on their families and social contexts in their places of origin are still little discussed. However, there are some initiatives at universities[1] that bring the construction industry and its overexploitation into architecture education. During the design process, it is important to take into account which supply chains, material extraction, profit distribution, and working conditions the architecture will produce. But is an architecture that does not exploit nature and people even possible under the asymmetrical conditions of our economic logic? To what extent are local economies that operate in a place-based manner possible, producing for local needs with the materials and skills that are available, where the profit is not accumulated but remains with the people in the region?

Anupama Kundoo's interest in materials was initially of a particularly aesthetic and economic nature: What gives me new design options? What can I achieve with a small budget? Gradually, the question of materials took on postcolonial and anti-colonial dimensions. India is not a "poor" country that needs to be "developed." This perspective led Kundoo to appreciate the wealth of locally available building materials and production techniques. It is only the wrong choice of materials that makes things unaffordable, says Kundoo. It must be pointed out, however, that the abundance of labor that flows into her architecture is based on low labor costs, which in turn are based on social hierarchies. This contradiction remains unresolved in the local economies. When deciding on individual materials, Kundoo interweaves design, ecological, and social issues. It's not about building materials that

Granite quarry near Puducherry
Photo: Elke Krasny

Such as WBYA? (Who Builds Your Architecture?), founded in association with Columbia University, the research on non-extractivist architecture by Space Caviar and by Charlotte Malterre-Barthes at the EPLF in Lausanne —see also the contributions by Jordan Carver, Charlotte Malterre-Barthes, and Laurie Parsons in this book.

are certified as "good" or "bad," Kundoo maintains, but rather about maximizing what lies around in abundance through creativity, working relationships, and local cycles.

Stone

The region around Puducherry in southern India features rich granite deposits. Granite blocks keep cropping up in the clayey soil between the rice fields and are used as small-scale horizontal quarries. Anupama Kundoo prefers to work with stonemasons to find suitable stones that require little processing. The design can also be based on the material. There are large basalt stone deposits in the area around the *Shah Houses* that were used as the main material for the project. It is important to Kundoo that the stones, as a part of the architecture, must look at least as beautiful as they do in nature.

Granite stone pillars are used in her first home, the *Hut Petite Ferme* (left), as well as in the *Wall House* (right).

Hut Petite Ferme, Auroville, 1990;
Wall House, Auroville, 2000
Photos: Andreas Deffner (left); Angelika Fitz (right)

In Brahmangarh near Pune, basalt stones dominate the terrain. Solid stone walls are the main element of these holiday homes and potential retirement residences when the owners want to escape hectic Mumbai. Vaulted ceilings consisting of locally made terracotta cones span the spaces in between.
Shah Houses, Brahmangarh, 2016
Photo: Javier Callejas

Anupama Kundoo searches together with the experienced stonemason Kumar for suitable stones for a new project.
Photo: Elke Krasny

Long-standing relationships with local craft businesses make unique results possible.
Photos: Vimal Bhojraj (left); Elke Krasny (right)

Earth

Earth is a ubiquitous and nearly no-cost building material that has dominated construction for centuries and is currently experiencing a small renaissance. Anupama Kundoo uses earth both for her structural terracotta elements and handmade bricks, as well as rammed earth, where she has added five percent cement to stabilize it. This addition, which many clay building purists would reject, has pragmatic reasons with regard to the tropical humidity, on the one hand, and aesthetic reasons on the other. Kundoo herself is no longer convinced of mixing cement into earth.

The red color is characteristic of the soil in Tamil Nadu, where Puducherry and Auroville are located.
Photo: Angelika Fitz

47   Local Economies: The Abundance of Materials

Due to its properties (high compressive strength), rammed earth is particularly suitable for walls. During the *Creativity* housing construction, the earth from the excavation is processed on-site.

Creativity Co-Housing, Auroville, 2003
Photos: Javier Callejas (top);
Andreas Deffner (bottom)

Kundoo also uses rammed earth in social housing. The *Sangamam* project is located in an area on the outskirts of Auroville characterized by ecological and social problems. High unemployment and a lack of housing are negatively impacting the people. Drought and salinization are making the soil increasingly infertile. But the local earth is very suitable for load-bearing walls.

Sangamam, Auroville, 2003
Photo: Javier Callejas

The entire foundation of the *Wall House* was made of cement-stabalized rammed earth. The building pit contains red soil with some laterite pebbles, a mineral weathering product that occurs primarily in the tropics and is also used as a building material when dried. Mixed with five percent cement, the excavated soil was then transported back into the pit; the walls of the pit served as formwork.

Construction site of the *Wall House*, Auroville, 1998
Photo: Andreas Deffner

Terracotta

Terracotta pots are traditionally made from the abundant clay. Competition from mass products such as metal cooking pots and plastic storage containers causes a decline in the potters' order situation. The production of architectural elements made of terracotta, such as those developed by Kundoo for her roof structures, generates new income.

Photos: Andreas Deffner

Filler slab ceiling with a lost formwork made of terracotta pots in a communal residential building
Creativity Co-Housing, Auroville, 2003
Photo: Javier Callejas

Rice Farmer and Brickmaker

Between the harvests, the rice farmers make bricks from the damp mud. Since they need fuel for this, they plant casuarina trees between the fields, which they harvest periodically. The harvested material is used as fuel, but also as scaffolding and temporary constructions. "What would happen if no one bought these handmade bricks anymore? Would rice become more expensive?" Kundoo wonders.

Local brick production in synergy with
rice fields in Tamil Nadu

Photos: Andreas Deffner (top, bottom right);
Angelika Fitz (bottom left)

During her first years in Auroville, Kundoo roamed the surrounding villages on her motorbike and observed the finely coordinated production cycles.

Photo: Andreas Deffner

Recycled Wood

High-quality wood is a rare material in India. The trade in used wooden elements is omnipresent. And there is something else that fascinates Kundoo when she explores the regional cycles: the degree to which plants and trees are utilized. If someone has a coconut palm, they cannot only harvest the fruit, but they can also sell the folded leaves there and the coconut shell somewhere else. Coconut fibers are processed into ropes, which in turn are used to tie together the casuarina, the round logs for scaffolding. Kundoo uses these scaffolding materials to build the actual structure of her first house, the *Hut Petite Ferme*.

Trading in used wooden elements on the outskirts of Puducherry
Photo: Angelika Fitz

Kundoo builds her first house with cheap, "inferior" casuarina wood normally used for scaffolding.
Building site in Puducherry, 2024 (left); Construction of the *Hut Petite Ferme* in Auroville, 1990 (right)
Photos: Elke Krasny (left); Anupama Kundoo (right)

In the *Wall House*, Kundoo uses wood that has been repurposed several times. Here is a ceiling beam from a historic Chettinad house that she employs as railing.
Photo: Angelika Fitz

Beyond Norms and Standards: The Abundance of Solutions

The standardization of units of measurement and unit sizes was central to colonial and imperial economies, as they streamlined production and trade relations. Today, global production networks and supply chains are pushing for the standardization of building materials and construction methods. The construction industry promises that standardization is to make building safer, faster, and more affordable. But what if norms and standards support the market for industrial products rather than smart local production? What if they displace place-based solutions and instead establish expensive and exploitative supply chains?

All regulations need to work with generalizations and are therefore necessarily not responding to the specifics of local contexts and knowledge. Kundoo calls them "broadband antibiotics." To be able to incorporate ecological, local, and affordable materials into architectural production, it is not enough to take their materiality into account. It is decisive to maintain and expand knowledge about their use. Why, for example, do all bricks have to be of the highest quality, even though they are therefore oversized for many applications? Kundoo's collaboration with terracotta experts made her aware of the economic, social, and ecological price of standardization. The cheap, locally manufactured, and often inconsistent brick, disregarded by the colonial rulers and brought into disrepute, becomes a design element in her buildings. And why do historical granite ceiling structures survive in temples, even though, according to engineering knowledge, stone can only withstand compressive forces and not tensile forces? Structural engineering is too focused on the combination of concrete and steel and neglects other solutions, Kundoo points out. Her work builds upon centuries-old knowledge stored in historic buildings, and her projects produce new built knowledge—both for regions in which there is an urgent need for cost-effective and sustainable construction to ensure basic supplies, and for regions where the focus is on tasks such as conversion and repair—keyword: We need a "conversion code" that enables other solutions than the building

The house as a kiln (baked in-situ earth house)
produces bricks of varying quality inside.
Volontariat Homes for Homeless Children,
Puducherry, 2008
Photo: Andreas Herzog

code. "I have always thought it foolish to ignore the building occupant and the craftsperson, and instead design for the component manufacturer and building inspector," states Kundoo.

Celebrating Irregularity

Not only the bricks produced in baked in-situ earth houses during firing are irregular. The bricks made locally in the fields, on uneven ground, with varying clay qualities, and fired with twigs and brushwood, have also been considered inferior since colonial times. Kundoo appreciates the so-called achakal bricks, which are only 2.5 centimeters thick, for their variety and because they fit well in the hand—"like an iPhone"—and are therefore easy to work with. "All of this made me celebrate the fact that the bad brick is actually the good brick." Even a material experiment that does not go quite right can produce beautiful results, as the floor on the upper story of the *Wall House* shows.

The bricks fired in the baked in-situ earth house are sorted for different applications.
Volontariat Home for Homeless Children,
Puducherry, 2008
Photos: Alka Hingorani

The brick wall which gave the *Wall House* its name: Consisting of locally handmade achakal bricks laid with lime mortar, the wall requires far less energy to produce than with factory-made bricks. The irregularity of the bricks characterizes its appearance.

Wall House, Auroville, 2000
Photos: Javier Callejas

The brickwork forms a long, two-story wing with a width of just 2.2 meters, which accommodates the more private rooms of the house. Functions such as the bedroom are formed in the shape of projections to the northeast. In the southwest, the experimental ceiling made of terracotta cones spans the open living area and connects to the single-story guest wing.

Wall House, Auroville, 2000
Drawing: Anupama Kundoo Architects, drafted by Alejandro M.

In the *Wall House*, Kundoo was her own client and contractor. She took advantage of this fact to make a series of experiments with craftspeople. The unusual floor finishing resulted from a mixture of white and gray cement.

Wall House, Auroville, 2000
Photo: Javier Callejas

Pragmatic Approaches

Not every project and not every detail has to be high-end. "I have also made many very simple buildings that are hardly worth anyone writing about," says Anupama Kundoo. As an architect, it is often simply a matter of achieving a subtle improvement in everyday life. At the *Keystone Foundation* campus, she leaves a lot up to the local craftspeople and at the *Village Action Center*, she reacts with ease to static objections. Even in the *Wall House*, there are incidental solutions that contribute to the relaxed atmosphere in this icon of architectural history.

In the *Wall House*, water and electrical cables are visible in many places where it makes sense or where subsequent adjustment was necessary—such as when the 12-volt solar photovoltaic energy was switched to centrally supplied 220-volt energy from renewable sources in Auroville. The openable ferrocement screen panels are secured with bicycle locks; oil containers under the kitchen cabinets create a barrier for ants and the like.

Wall House, Auroville, 2000
Photos: Javier Callejas (top left);
Angelika Fitz (top right, bottom)

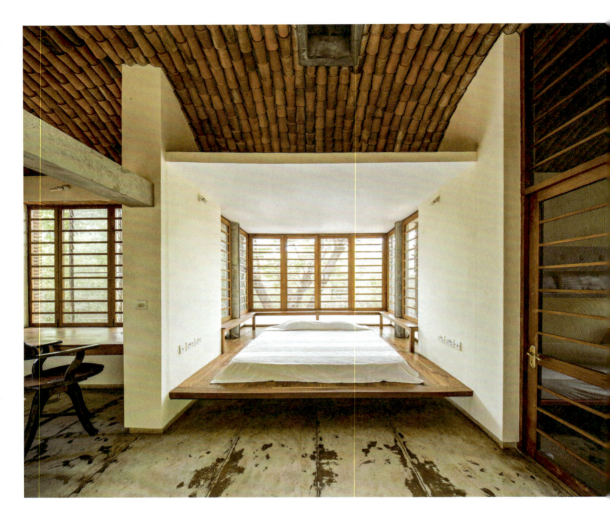

When good wood is scarce, the highest quality does not always have to be used, Kundoo explains. For the window struts in the *Wall House* she uses low-quality and recycled wood. The bed platform consists of mango wood, which is not considered very durable and therefore not used for building. "But decay is only a problem if you can't see it. Here everything is visible and, by the way, still immaculate after twenty-five years," Kundoo stresses.

Wall House, Auroville, 2000
Photo: Javier Callejas

Based on her studies of traditional temple buildings, Kundoo is convinced that granite lintels work. Because the engineering habits contradict this, she simply combines the local granite stones with brick arches at the *Village Action Center*, while also serving as sunshades. The center is one of several facilities of the Village Action Group in Auroville, which runs participatory programs in the areas of education, health, business, and crafts in the surrounding villages. The villages have multiple interrelationships and dependencies with Auroville. Several families have sold or contributed land to Auroville; many work as service providers or day laborers.

Village Action Center, Auroville, 2000
Photos: Angelika Fitz

The *Keystone Foundation* has been working in the mountains of Tamil Nadu for over thirty years at the interface between biodiversity and human livelihoods, together with the Indigenous Kota population. In the Nilgiri Biosphere Reserve, Kundoo is supporting the NGO in integrating the growing campus into the landscape. The small buildings for coffee and honey production, as well as the library and guest houses, follow the slope inclination and are grouped around a central communal meadow. They were built by local craftspeople according to plans by Kundoo. The walls are comprised of rammed earth with five percent cement for monsoon resistance, while the foundations and plinths consist of local stone. The traditional roof systems are made of wood and terracotta tiles.

Keystone Foundation, Kotagiri, Tamil Nadu, 2000–ongoing
Photos: Javier Callejas, 2018

Saving Resources

In-depth knowledge of materials and construction opens the architectural design to a wealth of constructive solutions. The circular *S.A.W.C.H.U.* hall leads to considerable savings in CO_2 and cost-intensive materials. The *Town Hall Complex* shows how urban densification can be thought of in a tropical context. Lightweight housing experiments moreover create prototypes for temporary accommodation that save time and material using a combination of high- and low-tech.

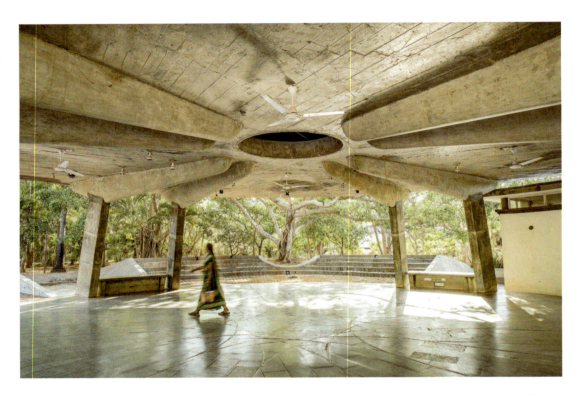

The *S.A.W.C.H.U.* (Sri Aurobindo World Centre for Human Unity) is an airy meeting place and a multifunctional event location for the residents of Auroville. The circular hall is supported by eight columns that are leaning inwards at angles to reduce the spans and thus the material consumption. They are reminiscent of a banyan tree, with the central trunk replaced by an opening.

Informal seating and water basins filled by the waterspouts of the roof slab connect the structure to the surrounding trees.

Multipurpose Hall S.A.W.C.H.U., Auroville, 2000
Photo: Javier Callejas

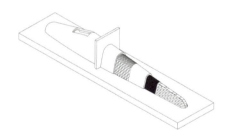

The radial beams that support the round ceiling slab are cast with a lost formwork made of ferrocement, which forms organically soft edges. The corners of the slabs are reinforced with diagonal steel rods for bracing, which allows the support point of the slanted columns to be shifted inwards. All decisions together reduce the volume of concrete from 125 to 75 cubic meters.

Multipurpose Hall S.A.W.C.H.U., Auroville, 2000
Photo: Javier Callejas
Drawings: Anupama Kundoo Architects, drafted by Alejandro M.

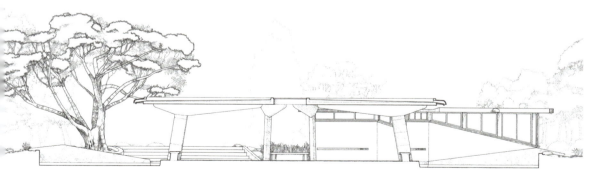

A series of smaller structures form the provisional administrative center of Auroville. Walkways, bridges, and ramps featuring ferrocement handrail elements provide shady connections between the buildings. The harvested roof water is used as drinking water for the cafeteria and the wastewater is treated in a root zone system and used for irrigation.

Auroville Town Hall Complex, Auroville, 2005
Photo: Javier Callejas

At this library in Puducherry, a delicate thin concrete slab roof sits on the walls made of locally produced bricks. Shaped like an open book, the roof also shades the roof terrace, which creates a public space in the residential area.

Library Nandalal Sewa Samithi, Puducherry, 2018
Photos: Javier Callejas

Temporary Housing

How temporary and makeshift can a home be? Influenced by a tight budget and the search for lightness, Kundoo used the simplest locally available material, unprocessed, round scaffolding wood, for her first own house in Auroville and constructed a complex geometry from it.

The *Light Housing Prototype* basically consists solely of a roof structure and does not have conventional walls, supports, or beams. It was inspired by origami folding patterns, in which the folds give extremely thin paper strength and rigidity. The prototype could become temporary accommodation in various contexts with different foundations.

Kundoo did not treat the wood used for building the *Hut Petite Ferme*. "I knew that these termites or insects would eat it, but I observed them. It's a long way to get there. So no rush." She lived in the poetic makeshift shelter for nearly ten years.

Hut Petite Ferme, Auroville, 1990
Photos: Andreas Deffner

During her first decade in Auroville, Anupama Kundoo lived in the *Hut Petite Ferme*, which she designed. The round wooden structures of untreated casuarina trees were tied together in place with coconut ropes and stood on rough-cut granite stilts that prevented termites from reaching the wood. The triangulated geometry was inspired by thatch "capsules" developed by the Australian architect Johnny Allen in Auroville. Natural ventilation, solar-powered electricity, and the use of non-potable water for the vegetable garden enable a resource-saving life. This poetic simplicity was to shape Kundoo's further work: "What is the point in doing efficiently things that need not be done at all?"

Hut Petite Ferme, Auroville, 1990
Photo: Andreas Deffner

To develop the *Light Housing Prototype*, paper forms were first produced, and scale models were then fashioned from reused corrugated cardboard.

Light Housing Prototype, Auroville, 2013
Photos: Marta San Vicente

Made out of ferrocement and chicken mesh, the prototype is resistant to seismic loads.

Light Housing Prototype, Auroville, 2013
Photos: Marta San Vincente

Experimental City:
The Abundance of Aspirations

Anupama Kundoo's built work is largely situated in Auroville, which is fifteen kilometers north of Puducherry on the southeast coast of India. Kundoo first got to know the experimental city of Auroville during her architecture studies. Deciding against practicing architecture for the interests of capital in rapidly urbanizing Bombay/Mumbai, at the time a city of twelve million people, Kundoo moved to Auroville in 1989, when she was in her early twenties. She was attracted to Auroville's aspiration to build a city for the realization of human unity, with building not a metaphor but an architectural experimentation.

During our curatorial research visit to Puducherry and Auroville in February 2024, Kundoo states that the impact of French colonialism is still present, as she points out the spatial division of *Ville Blanche* (White Town or French Quarter) and *Ville Noir* (Black Town). Pondicherry, today Puducherry, was part of so-called French India. Five different enclaves, geographically separated from each other, made up *l'Établissements français dans l'Inde*. The French administration of Pondicherry began in 1763. French India only became part of India in 1962, when the treaty between France and India was signed.

When we stand in front of Mother's House together, Kundoo tells us that residents and visitors flock to visit her residence in Puducherry to celebrate the birthday of Auroville's spiritual founder on February 21st. The Mother is Blanche Rachel Mirra Alfassa, a Sephardic Jew from Paris, who came to Pondicherry in 1914 to join the mission of the freedom fighter, poet, journalist, yogi, and spiritual leader Sri Aurobindo. Recognizing her as a spiritual equal, he named her "The Mother." Already in the 1930s there was a vision for a new city based on human unity and peace. On February 28, 1968, representatives from 124 different nations gathered under a banyan tree in the center of the future experimental township to celebrate Auroville's official founding ceremony. Local villagers had sold and given the land for the future city and some families joined the experiment. The name of the city

People practice yoga on the roof of the
Mitra Youth Hostel in Auroville, with the
dome of Matrimandir in the background.
Mitra Youth Hostel, Auroville, 2005
Photo: Javier Callejas

shows its origins in the French language: *Aurore* means dawn, *ville* means city, hence the City of Dawn.

Since 1988, the township has been under the control of the Ministry of Education of the Government of India, which states on their website that Auroville "is an international cultural township […] where 3300 people from 58 nations including India, live together as one community and engage themselves in cultural, educational, scientific and other pursuits aimed at Human Unity."[1] Land and assets of Auroville were transferred to the Auroville Foundation, whose secretary is appointed by the Indian Government. Recent publications study the alternative economies of this planned city, but also its colonial entanglements. Social scientist Suryamayi Aswini Clarence-Smith, who lives in Auroville, writes about the community's utopian aspirations and how spiritual, social, and economic ideals are put into practice.[2] Historian Jessica Namakkal, who lives in the US, uses a decolonial framework to trace the afterlife of colonialist structures and relations in the experimental city of Auroville.[3] For Anupama Kundoo, the vision of Auroville is far more concrete than utopia, and yet far more aspirational too: "Auroville, envisioned as a city dedicated to the future of human society, is based on a charter and real commitments. For example, no private ownership of land, a site of unending education and constant progress, material and spiritual researches, where 'money is not the sovereign lord' and where the automobile radically makes way for an intimate pedestrian-centric life. In short, laboratory instead of utopia, where experiments are not only encouraged, they are compulsory."

1 Ministry of Education, Government of India, "Auroville Foundation," https://www.education.gov.in/icc-auroville-foundation (accessed August 22, 2024).

2 Suryamayi Aswini Clarence-Smith, *Prefiguring Utopia: The Auroville Experiment* (Bristol: Policy Press, 2023).

3 Jessica Namakkal, *Unsettling Utopia. The Making and Unmaking of French India* (New York: Columbia University Press, 2021).

The City as a Laboratory
Aspirations, Realities, Contradictions

The Mother initiated Auroville as a planned city. In 1965, The Mother appointed French architect Roger Anger as Auroville's chief architect. Anger collaborated closely with The Mother and after several concept presentations she finalized the "galaxy plan" for the "City the Earth Needs" in 1968. A satellite settlement called Auromodele was proposed at the outskirts of the city as The Mother wanted to avoid any compromise on the ambitious city plan. During the early years Anger produced a number of path-breaking experimental buildings and set the bar for the spirit of Auroville architecture. The Mother passed away in 1973, and organic developments led to the formation of several segregated communities on the scattered lands procured for Auroville while residents continued their applied research in a wide range of areas.

According to Suryamayi Aswini Clarence-Smith, Auroville is the largest and one of the most long-standing intentional communities. Such intentional communities are characterized, as critical architecture theorist Keller Easterling put it, by withdrawal and aspiration. Yet neither withdrawal nor aspirations prevent intentional communities, some of which are based on utopian, anarchist, or spiritual ideals, to overcome conflicts and contradictions. Aspirations turned into realities are entrenched in the historical conditions of their creation. In the case of Auroville, these conditions specifically include the lasting impact of colonialism, the teachings of integral yoga, the formal language of modernist architecture, the aims of Western anti-capitalist communes and hippie culture, the support of transnational organizations like the UNESCO, international development aid, the public funding, as well as the appointment of the secretary of the Auroville Foundation by the Ministry of Education of the Government of India, and a structure of self-governance with a residents' assembly, a governing board, an international advisory council, a working committee, and a number of working groups.

Auroville continues to attract visitors who are in search of spiritual frameworks, alternative modes of doing politics, and organizing the economy outside of the paradigm of capital. Even though the master plan has remained unfinished, with only a small part of it realized so far, many of the visitors drawn to Auroville are architects.

"Galaxy plan" of the "City the Earth Needs," 1968
Photo: Dominique Darr

Photographs of The Mother and Sri Aurobindo are omnipresent in Auroville and Puducherry. We saw this photograph displayed at the offices of stone mason Kumar.

Photo: Elke Krasny

Sri Aurobindo's Ashram, with the tombs of Sri Aurobindo and The Mother beneath a frangipani tree, is a center of spiritual tourism.

Photo: Angelika Fitz

Both The Mother and Roger Anger are credited as the architects behind the Matrimandir, the "Soul of the City" of Auroville. Dedicated to the practice of integral yoga, the temple is not only frequented by Aurovilians, but open to visitors who arrive by bus for their pre-booked time slot and participate in the highly choreographed ritual of ascending inside the geodesic dome to the top floor, where they are invited to participate in silent meditation around a giant crystal.

Photo: Elke Krasny

In the last several years the Auroville Foundation has come forward to accelerate the realization of the approved master plan through funding support. This has met with mixed reactions among the residents, and some local residents are currently protesting the construction of the original master plan's Crown Road. "In a country as populated as India, the idea of idealizing low density without paying the price of the land is a very elitist battle, with colonial echoes, and far from best practices" says Kundoo, making a stand in this debate. "The Auroville experiment is a high-density prototype of an exemplary community life based on low land consumption and therefore compact, pedestrian-centric, and car-free."

Photos: Angelika Fitz (top left); Elke Krasny (top right)

Auroville has a long-standing practice of engaging with local communities of villagers. International development aid is used to establish infrastructures for education, training, and collective learning. The *Auroville Institute of Applied Technology*, partly designed by Anupama Kundoo, was sponsored by the Federal Ministry of Economic Cooperation and Development of the Government of Germany.

Photo: Angelika Fitz

People in Auroville explain that it takes three villagers and two tourists per inhabitant to make Auroville's alternative economy work. "This contradicts the fact that Auroville was planned to be an equal society where all would partake in the work," says Kundoo.

Photo: Angelika Fitz

Working Outside of the Conditions of Capital

The Auroville Charter, which was written by The Mother, states that "Auroville belongs to nobody in particular. Auroville belongs to humanity as a whole."[4] Consequently, there is no private land ownership in Auroville. The aspiration of the spiritual framework for Auroville is an alternative, moneyless economy, which not only includes land as commons, but also in which basic needs are met through community services, to which everyone contributes through their work. Working within and from these alternative economic realities was central to Anupama Kundoo's aspirations of working outside of the conditions of capital and of turning architecture into a way of actually transforming the economy. Today, these aspirations, which formed the basis for Anupama Kundoo's ways of doing architecture, are tainted by capital with people demanding a transfer fee for their houses in Auroville or renting them out individually rather than giving them to the community in times of their absence.

Blanche Rachel Mirra Alfassa, *The Mother on Auroville*, ed. Madanlal Himatsingka (1977; rpt., Pondicherry: All India Press, 1999), 30, https://motherandsriaurobindo.in/sama_pdf_viewer.php?page_name=The-Mother/books/compilations/the-mother-on-auroville.

Contributing to using land as commons through architectural experimentation as an alternative means of building with the land and its resources is at the core of Anupama Kundoo's practice.

Hut Petite Ferme, Auroville, 1990
Photo: Andreas Deffner

Experimental City: The Abundance of Aspirations

The ontology of property is deeply inscribed into capitalist relations to the ownership of land, of houses, and what it means to inhabit them. Using one's homes, first *Hut Petite Ferme* and then the *Wall House*, as laboratories for contributing to developing how architecture can be practiced otherwise follows this spirit of the commons. The *Wall House* is characterized by its finely composed porosity with its surroundings, its nuanced degrees of openness to be with others, and its possibilities for retreat.

Wall House, Auroville, 2000
Photo: Javier Callejas

Early on, Anupama Kundoo, who collaborated with the city's chief architect Roger Anger on the urban design and planning, developed a deep commitment to the urban as the form that fosters civic coexistence and collaboration.

Photo: Dominique Darr

Hut Petit Ferme, Anupama Kundoo's first home in Auroville, as well as the *Wall House*, are located in an area outside of Roger Anger's master plan designated for testing model solutions for the experimental city. The *Wall House* is not only a home, but also serves as Anupama Kundoo's place of work, where discussing details of construction with her team are as important as thinking about new forms of urban density in the majority world and the nature of the urban in times of planetary climate catastrophe.
Photo: Angelika Fitz

Committed to creating the spirit of the urban in the context of Auroville, Anupama Kundoo is invested in exploring how varying scales of density can be used to create hierarchies of clusters ranging from social spaces for various group sizes to intimate spaces to accommodate facilities for collective use, while still enjoying privacy. This co-housing is a prototype for urban low-density with different types of apartments for diverse residents who share the common courtyard, as well as facilities like a kitchen and a laundry.
Creativity Co-Housing, Auroville 2003
Photo: Javier Callejas

Finding spatial solutions to balancing privacy and collectivity is central to Anupama Kundoo's approach to a civic understanding of urban coexistence. Providing single and double rooms for youth who come to visit Auroville for the short- or medium-term, the *Mitra Youth Hostel*, which is very close to the *Town Hall Complex*, also creates spaces for different scales of sociality. Small groups can gather on the terraces or in the courtyard, while the entire roof can be used as a space for large gatherings of all the residents.

Mitra Youth Hostel, Auroville, 2005
Photo: Javier Callejas

A town hall is an important building for any municipality, as it symbolizes and materializes the political intent of governance and administration. Even though the current dimension of the town hall is only considered an in-between stage, an annex to the larger one already designed by her, until the actual realization of more civic infrastructures, the 2005 *Town Hall Complex* by Anupama Kundoo is an important step for the experimental city, which has been in the construction process since 1968. Shaded walkways, squares, and places to sit in conversation with each other offer opportunities for civic and public life, and, with only three buildings constructed, it demonstrates the potential of interconnectedness and urban lifestyle envisaged for the city to come.

Town Hall Complex, Auroville, 2005
Photo: Javier Callejas

Reinventing Beauty:
The Abundance of Differences

Architectural history has long been and, in some cases, is still being written along historic periods, styles, and cultural differences. Anupama Kundoo's architecture eludes such classification. Her work brings together elements of modernism, traditional building methods, and place-based material experiments. Not in the sense of postmodern citations and collages but rather by creating a new coexistence in which things intertwine and at the same time retain their distinctiveness.

In his 1994 book, *The Location of Culture*, Homi K. Bhabha introduced the terms "hybridity" and "Third Space" into postcolonial discourse and thereby lastingly repudiated notions of "cultural purity." In a world shaped by old and new colonialisms, there are no self-contained cultures. "Cultural difference" is a constant process negotiated in the "Third Space." Anupama Kundoo's way of working is based on such processes of negotiation, which she designs spatially, materially, and aesthetically. These processes are alive and can clearly be felt in her architecture. Different elements and influences can be experienced and establish new cultural relationships and a beauty that does not ossify into an icon.

As an architect, Kundoo does not regard herself as a master who annihilates the existing to create a tabula rasa for building the new. Rather, she sees herself as part of a continuity of differences that has produced a wealth of outstanding buildings, bold experiments, spiritual material relations, and deep everyday knowledge. The ancient temple complexes in Hampi and traditional houses in Tamil Nadu inspire her just as much as the low-tech brick buildings of Laurie Baker. In modernism, she particularly likes Le Corbusier, but other modernists have also left their mark. And she has greatly admired Charles Correa since her formative years.

The juxtapositions in this chapter illustrate how Anupama Kundoo transforms modernist principles into a place-based modernism and expressivity into unspectacular matter-of-factness, as she at once continues and transforms the existing by understanding culture and nature as a continuum. All of this enables a lively beauty to emerge in which differences are recognized in their own beauty.

all House, Auroville, 2000
hoto: Elke Krasny

From Utopia to Place-based Modernism

The ideology of modernization in India was part of both colonial rule and the postcolonial nation after 1947, when Le Corbusier and Louis Kahn, among others, received commissions in India and realized iconic works of modernism there, such as the government district of Chandigarh in the 1950s or the campus for the Indian Institute of Management in Ahmedabad in the 1960s. Both Le Corbusier and Kahn collaborated with the later Pritzker Prize winner Balkrishna Doshi, who revamped architectural education at the CEPT University in Ahmedabad. Modernism was not a one-way street, but a reciprocal process that produced multiple modernisms. While the British architects Jane Drew and Maxwell Fry propagated a "tropical modernism" that responded to the climate with elements of passive cooling, shading, and natural ventilation, but otherwise designed universally valid solitaires, architects such as Balkrishna Doshi, Charles Correa, Parvina Mehta, Anant Raje, and Raj Rewal interwove the languages of modernism with local typologies, structures, and contexts.

Closely linked to the concept of a universalist architectural modernism was the idea of the "New Man" who was to emerge from their buildings. For the founders of the Aurobindo Ashram and especially for Blanche Rachel Mirra Alfassa ("The Mother"), architecture constituted a tool for the implementation of their vision of a future society from the very beginning, and not just when Auroville was founded. Two decades before Chandigarh, the ashram, working with the Czech-American architect Antonin Raymond, the Czech architect František Sammer, and the Japanese-American architect George Nakashima, built the first modernist reinforced concrete structure in India: *Golconde*, a dormitory for the rapidly growing community of the Aurobindo Ashram, named after the gold mines of the sponsor and Prime Minister of Hyderabad, Sri Akbar Hydari. The architects came to Puducherry

(Pondicherry then) from Japan. Raymond had accompanied Frank Lloyd Wright to Tokyo in 1919 to build the Imperial Hotel, where he stayed for nearly two decades and planned numerous embassy buildings. Sammer worked in Le Corbusier's office before starting to work for Raymond in 1937. Nakashima started working for Raymond in 1934, supervised the *Golconde* construction site, and became an Ashramite himself.

Antonin Raymond, František Sammer, and George Nakashima: *Golconde*, Puducherry, 1935–1945
Photo: Elke Krasny (left page)

Movable slats form the facade grid of the *Golconde* building. An optimal orientation to the sea breeze supports natural ventilation. A Zen-like atmosphere characterizes the perfectly preserved dormitory, which is still in use today. "In Raymond's outwardly rationalist/International style, the ashram represented the re-destillation of the original 'Oriental' germ in the pioneering early work of Wright, from which the radical new conception of space that had driven modern architectural experiment in the early twentieth century had probably been born."[1] This is how Peter Scriver and Amit Srivastava describe the ambivalence and historicity of modernism in their book *India: Modern Architectures in History*.

Antonin Raymond, František Sammer, and George Nakashima: *Golconde*, Puducherry, 1935–1945
Photos: Elke Krasny (left); Angelika Fitz (top)

Peter Scriver and Amit Srivastava, *India: Modern Architectures in History* (London: Reaktion Books, 2015), 119.

At the *Golconde* (left), most of the materials, especially structural steel, had to be imported until the Second World War prevented this. The Ashramites' dishes and jewelry were melted down for the brass fittings. The slats contain asbestos. Kundoo realizes her brise-soleil in the *Wall House* (right) with recycled wood.

Photos: Angelika Fitz (left); Elke Krasny (right)

Facade elements return as furniture in the *Golconde* (left) and in the *Wall House* (right).

Photos: Angelika Fitz (left); Elke Krasny (right)

Air-permeable, pivoting concrete elements shield the service wing and thus the house-work in the sunken ground floor of the *Golconde* (bottom). Related ferrocement elements make the boundaries between private and public alterable in the *Wall House* (top).

Photos: Javier Callejas (top); Angelika Fitz (bottom)

The French architect Roger Anger was commissioned by Blanche Rachel Mirra Alfassa in 1966 to plan the experimental city of Auroville. Anger, forty-five years old at the time, had already completed over one hundred projects in France.

Roger Anger, Mario Heymann, and Pierre Puccinelli:
67 rue Barrault, Paris, 1958
Photo: Javier Callejas

Anger developed his penchant for sculptural modernism into organic forms in Auroville. Anupama Kundoo progressively developed urban design projects within Auroville as tasks given to her by Roger Anger from the 1990s until his death in 2008. She developed the administrative zone, the habitat area near the *Town Hall Complex*, and eventually the whole city center, which he approved. She also played an instrumental role, among other things, in shaping the Master Plan Perspective 2025 in 2001 under Roger Anger's supervision. "I was greatly inspired by his playful experimentation with all materials, particularly ferrocement," says Kundoo.

Roger Anger: *Last School*, Auroville, 1971
Photo: Dominique Darr

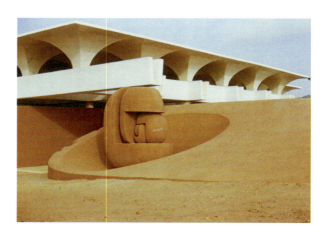

As a tribute to Roger Anger, Kundoo's buildings for the *Town Hall Complex* in Auroville echo Anger's architecture but forego grand spectacle.

Anupama Kundoo: *Town Hall Complex*, Auroville, 2005
Photo: Javier Callejas

Local Spirits

A wealth of ornamentation, craftsmanship, local and imported materials makes historical architecture in South India manifold: From traditional Tamil houses to opulent Chettinad villas to the granite structures of the temple complexes in Hampi. Anupama Kundoo integrates found objects into her architecture, reuses them, renders their beauty visible, and always treats them with the same respect that previous generations had shown when working with the valuable materials.

Wooden swings are a traditional piece of furniture in many Indian regions that offer relaxation and a pleasant breeze—provided there are ample living and reception spaces. Kundoo's swing comes from an old Tamil house. The brass suspension was replaced by steel cables due to the ceiling height in the *Wall House*.

Wall House, Auroville, 2000
Photo: Elke Krasny

Many merchant families from the Chettinad region in southern Tamil Nadu achieved considerable wealth during the colonial period in the nineteenth century. Imported materials such as teak from Burma or marble from Italy were used in their luxurious houses. Kundoo turns ceiling beams from a demolished Chettinad house 180 degrees into lavish handrails. The rosettes that formerly decorated the soffit are now also a tactile experience. Conical columns made of rosewood are split lengthways to form a table.

Wall House (top and middle);
Historic Chettinad House (bottom)
Photos: Javier Callejas (top); Elke Krasny (middle); Yashima, https://de.wikipedia.org/wiki/Chettinad#/media/ Datei:Chettinad_house_courtyard.jpg (18.10.2024), CC BY-SA 2.0 (bottom)

Kundoo names the architect George Nakashima as an important reference point. He designed all the wooden fittings and furniture in the *Golconde* building and later founded a wood workshop in the USA that now produces minimalist furniture in its third generation. When working with wood, it is important to give the tree a second life, says Nakashima in his book *The Soul of a Tree*.

George Nakashima at his Woodworkers Studio in New Hope, Pennsylvania
Photo: Nakashima Foundation for Peace, www.nakashimafoundation.org

The ruins of the temple complex in Hampi, which seem to grow out of the granite landscape, have been a UNESCO World Heritage Site since 1986 and a popular tourist destination in South India. For Kundoo, besides their beauty, they are also a built testimony to forgotten construction methods.

Photos: Adam Jones, Global Photo Archive / Flickr (left); Mithun Kundu (right)

Rocks from nearby Auroville appear not only in the garden of the *Wall House* as seating, but also on the verandah. She has space for many people and when she is alone, there is never an empty sofa, but the presence of the stones, says Kundoo.

Wall House, Auroville, 2000
Photo: Javier Callejas

Maintenance and Care:
The Abundance of Generosity

When walking on the streets of Puducherry, where one of Anupama Kundoo's studio offices is located, one cannot fail to notice the geometrical patterns drawn on the streets in front of the entrances to houses. Every morning, at the break of dawn, women draw these beautiful patterns of continuous lines. They are called *kolams*, which means form and beauty in Tamil. Typically made of rice flour, they disappear over the course of the day as motorbikes go over them, people step on them, ants and birds feed on them, and the rain washes them away. They articulate the aesthetics, ecology, and spirituality of care. With care and maintenance commonly seen as invisible labor that fulfills basic human needs, the kolam changes this understanding. It is at once communal aesthetics, human and non-human coexistence, with birds and ants literally eating what the drawing is made out of, and an offering to Lakshmi, the goddess of prosperity. The continuous lines of the drawings materialize the continuity of care. And the work of drawing, its renewal, is continued every morning. Anupama Kundoo understands "maintenance as part of the ritual of life." She regards the kolam as a part of what she calls "abundance strategies." Notions of abundance and generosity have not entered the critical feminist Marxist analysis of the labors of care and maintenance, which are one of the continuously exploited and expropriated hidden abodes of capital. While fighting this violence of capital remains key, a more nuanced appreciation of how care practices exceed the measures of capitalism is most relevant. Here we introduce the thought that maintenance and care can create an abundance of generosity, and we argue that this is particularly relevant to architecture. As architecture needs to be understood as the provision of essential care in spatial terms, introducing abundance and generosity into spatial care will, in effect, change the meaning and matter of spaces themselves. Listening to Anupama Kundoo, who speaks of the care of the kolam as "a daily reminder that the world is generous," we come to see that care provided through architecture can, in fact, materially support such generosity.

Kolam drawing, Puducherry, 2022
Photo: Anupama Kundoo

Caring for Continuity

Care is commonly understood as all the activities necessary for providing everything that is essential to the continuation of life. Such continuity of care includes what is conventionally understood as basic needs such as the preparation of food, personal hygiene, places to work and rest. At the same time, care cares for aesthetic, ecological, social, spiritual, and joyful dimensions of life, which are, as we have learned from the kolam, just as essential as so-called basic needs. Caring for continuity through the means of architecture brings these dimensions together and makes them spatial and material. This, of course, also requires the continuous renewing and remaking of the spatial and material dimensions of architecture through everyday maintenance and care.

This series of photographs, which we took during our curatorial research in 2024, show how Ambika, who goes by her first name, like everyone else in Auroville, provides care and maintenance to the materials and spaces of the *Wall House*. This is essential to the caring continuity that architecture can provide through its maintenance. It includes a deep knowledge of different materials and developing an understanding of how they weather and age.

Wall House, Auroville, 2000
Photos: Elke Krasny, Angelika Fitz (bottom right)

Ambika, the *Wall House*'s housekeeper, often brings flowers and places them in the house. Anupama Kundoo explains that the wearing and offering of flowers and flower garlands are typical of the local Tamil culture. Across India, including Bengal, where she is from, flowers are an integral part of daily life but have different expressions; specific flowers are offered to specific deities.
Photo: Elke Krasny

The acronym *S.A.W.C.H.U.* stands for Sri Aurobindo World Centre for Human Unity. The pavilion was built to mark the 125th anniversary of Sri Aurobindo's birth. The activities of maintenance and care are visible in the space. Drawings and flower garlands laid out on the ground at the entrance to the pavilion are manifestations of care, communal aesthetics, and spiritual offerings. Anupama Kundoo sees flower garlands as "genuine offerings," as "a thing you do for others. Even when you wear them in your hair you spread fragrance in the air."
Multipurpose Hall S.A.W.C.H.U., Auroville, 2000
Photos: Elke Krasny

Maintaining Liveliness

Maintenance and care have not only been described as invisible labor and a costless resource, but also as dull, repetitive, and necessary to satisfy basic needs rather than practices that are rich in knowledge, skills, and meanings. Under the regime of capital, the form and materiality of spaces often articulate the social, cultural, and economic values that the activities taking place in them hold. Maintaining the liveliness of spaces and materials in architecture is critical for an ethics of generosity that bestows liveliness on all spaces regardless of their function.

The two bathrooms in the *Wall House* are lively spaces. They connect human bodies that take care of their personal hygiene needs directly with the influences of the outdoors and the weather. Far from sterile, the liveliness of materials is experienced through their weathering and their change through use. Maintaining liveliness in architecture is thus not at all about the daily reproduction of sameness, but about owning up to the fact that material can age and change as it lives with the effects of human use and the impact of the weather.

Wall House, Auroville, 2000
Photos: Angelika Fitz (left); Javier Callejas (right)

Minimizing the labor required for maintenance is sometimes part of how liveliness is being created. The *Sharana Daycare Facility* has porous walls. They consist of terracotta screen modules that not only do away with the cleaning of windows but also allow for natural ventilation, which is key in the climatic conditions of Puducherry. Furthermore, the experience of liveliness comes from the sense of being spatially connected, yet visually shielded. The client of the daycare center is Sharana, a social and development organization. Their social and educational workers work closely with families in Puducherry and surrounding villages to make the spaces, infrastructures, and technologies Sharana provides for education, play, and learning available to underprivileged children.

Sharana Daycare Facility, Puducherry, 2019
Photo: Javier Callejas

The two kitchens, one at the *Sharana Daycare Facility* in Puducherry and the other one in *Creativity*, a low-density co-housing complex in Auroville, exemplify that maintaining the liveliness of a space by architectural means is not tied to the dimensions of a space alone, but rather to how the materiality offers possibilities of feeling free to breathe and to move while one is at work.

Sharana Daycare Facility, Puducherry, 2019;
Creativity Co-Housing, Auroville, 2003
Photos: Elke Krasny (left); Javier Callejas (right)

Focusing on Indigenous livelihoods, the Keystone Foundation has been a client of Anupama Kundoo since 2000. Working with the landscape of the Nilgiri Hills, the traditional homes of the Kota, the Indigenous, Dravidian-speaking people of Kotagiri, maintaining liveliness relies on creating conditions for livelihoods. Working for better conditions together with tribal communities operates across the interlinked scales of landscape, infrastructure, and buildings.

Keystone Foundation, Kotagiri, Tamil Nadu, 2000–ongoing
Photo: Javier Callejas

The three buildings of the *Town Hall Complex* are the Auroville Centre for Urban Research, a multimedia center, and a cafeteria. A large cantilever and the central space overlooking the cafeteria, as well as shaded walkways, bridges, and ramps, offer generous public spaces for daily use beyond the functions of services and governance. The *Town Hall Complex* was specifically planned for Auroville's governance model with its Working Groups, which are appointed by the Residents' Assembly, in which all residents of Auroville aged eighteen and above can participate. The Residents' Assembly is also concerned with Auroville's urban plan and the city's future development. Financial support for the construction of the *Town Hall Complex* came from the Asia Urbs Programme, a humanitarian development program funded by the EuropeAid Co-operation Office of the European Commission, as well as by the Dutch De Zaaier Foundation founded by Dieuwke Honig-Prager in 1985 to support sustainable development.

Town Hall Complex, Auroville, 2005
Photo: Javier Callejas

Generative Generosity

With "generating" and "generosity" sharing the same Latin root, *gener*, which translates into giving birth, generative spaces are not reduced to function alone. Generative spaces much rather bring forth more meaning, that is, they enable spatial meaning-making for those who work, live, play, or rest in these spaces. Generative spaces make possible, in Anupama Kundoo's words, "a generosity that you feel that the world is." Building an ethics of generosity counteracts spatial poverty in all its dimensions.

The low-cost housing project *Sangamam* is located on the outskirts of Auroville and challenged by conditions of water scarcity and soil erosion. Architectural care includes the infrastructure for collecting rainwater and for treating wastewater, as well as the use of soil from the site for the actual construction. The architecture also cares for spatial generosity for the spaces dedicated to social reproduction, in particular, the double-height ceilings in the kitchen show that the poverty of space can be overcome despite economic constraints.

Sangamam, Auroville, 2003
Photo: Javier Callejas

Founded in 1983, the Village Action Group forms part of the web of relationships Auroville has with the surrounding villages. Several families from the village originally sold or gave their land for the establishment of the city of Auroville. One focus of the Auroville Village Action Group is working with women: supporting the self-organization of women, setting up psychological and physical health infrastructures, contributing to financial literacy, working against violence towards women, and building resistance to the abortion of female fetuses, as we saw on the posters displayed on the wall. The *Village Action Center* provides spaces without declared functions. Seamlessly blending indoor and outdoor spaces, they can be used for working, talking, self-organizing, offering shade, and enjoying each other in conversation, creating generative conditions that clearly avoid the poverty of NGO aesthetics.

Village Action Center, Auroville, 2000
Photos: Elke Krasny (top left);
Angelika Fitz (top right)

Posters at the *Village Action Center* admonishing violence towards women and abortions of female fetuses, 2024
Photo: Angelika Fitz

The photo was taken at the *Wall House* during the curatorial research in 2024. The flower fills the space with its scent. The table, as Anupama Kundoo points out, is made of wood cut from an obsolete conical column of an old Tamil house. Now living on as a table, its previous function is transformed into new meaning, which is materially maintained through daily care. The table holds the food, with Ambika, the housekeeper, focusing on its potency when she prepares it. The table also supports the unbroken flow of conversation, as Anupama Kundoo, together with her team, think out loud about some of the material and structural solutions for a project they are working on.

Wall House, Auroville, 2000
Photo: Angelika Fitz

At the *Sharana Daycare Facility*, children who come from disadvantaged backgrounds and are faced with the effects of spatial poverty on play and learning find themselves in an enabling space: playing, resting, dreaming, and, above all, feeling that there is space to breathe, to move, and to just be.

Sharana Daycare Facility, Puducherry, 2019
Photo: Javier Callejas

In the building process of the homes for homeless children, the structures became a kiln that produced its elements including bricks, tiles, lavatories, and washbasins. This materializes architecture as generative practice. Knowing that a building has generated the energy for its own making inspires new imaginations of how architecture can care for generosity. The client, Volontariat India, was initiated by the Belgian social worker Madeleine Herman, who came to Puducherry in 1962. Dedicated to serving the poorest of the poor, Volontariat India is a non-profit, non-political, and secular organization. Core activities comprise the provision of housing, medical care, and education.

Volontariat Homes for Homeless Children, Puducherry, 2008
Photo: Javier Callejas

Climate Healing:
The Abundance of Nature

At the time of writing, temperatures were soaring worldwide. Two days in a row the Earth's heat record was broken. July 21 and July 22, 2024 were the hottest days in recorded history according to the climate data collected by the European Union's Copernicus Climate Change Service. Faced with this extremely hot weather and heat waves, the Government of Puducherry took measures such as advising employers to keep their workers hydrated and providing temporary shelters for those working outdoors. All this shows how urgent it actually is to find different ways of practicing architecture that contribute to healing the climate crisis.

For the longest time, the climate and the long-term changes in the weather and the temperature have been understood as part of the natural history of Planet Earth. In his 2021 book, *The Climate of History in a Planetary Age*, historian Dipesh Chakrabarty observes that the history of nature and the history of humans were told as separate from each other. The first was told by natural scientists who explored the laws of nature, the latter was studied by historians who, for the longest time, focused not on subaltern histories, but on those in power. Architecture is firmly inscribed into the history of humans. Here we introduce architecture as the built expression of how humans relate to nature. Architecture, therefore, can help us see how the history of nature and of humans is not separate, which also leads us to the understanding that today's climate was actually built. By studying the modern industrial development of architecture and construction, we can gain critical knowledge of how this exclusion of nature from Man-made history led to silencing modernity's colonial capitalist relation to nature. We are following anthropologist Anna Tsing's capitalization of Man to express that the Enlightenment bestowed the right to dominate nature upon this figure of Man. Capitalism used this idea of the domination of nature to transform nature into "a free gift [...] to capital" to use the words of Karl Marx.[1] Connecting Marx's diagnosis to Peggy Deamer's insight that "the history of architecture is the history of capital," we come to understand that

all House, Auroville, 2000
Photo: Javier Callejas

Karl Marx and Frederick Engels, *Collected Works*, vol. 4 (New York: International Publishers, 1975), 32–33.

architecture builds capital's relations to nature and is therefore implicated in what philosopher Nancy Fraser describes as "capitalism's cannibalization of nature."[2]

Practicing architecture as climate healing means having to build the relation to nature otherwise. This requires learning that nature is not for free, not a cheap resource to maximize profit, but that nature needs healing to recover from capitalism and to restore the very abundance of nature.

Healthy Relations

Climate healing requires architecture to build "healthy relations." For Kundoo, this means building "healthy relations with the given temperature, with the climate, with the territorial materials that Mother Nature has offered in different places." Kundoo states that "we are always having to coexist with others. I think that my architecture is definitely about that."

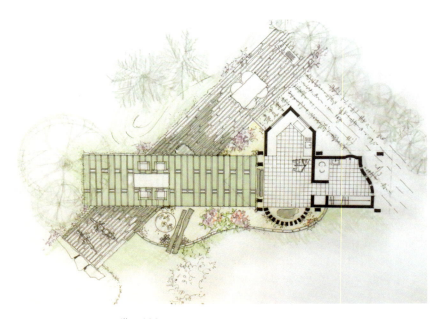

Hut Petite Ferme, Auroville, 1990
Plan: Anupama Kundoo

2   Nancy Fraser, *Cannibal Capitalism. How Our System Is Devouring Democracy, Care and the Planet – and What We Can Do About It* (London: Verso, 2022), 12.

The hut has been central to colonial narratives of development in architecture, as exemplified in the permanent exhibition of the German Architecture Museum in Frankfurt, which is titled *From Primitive Hut to Skyscraper*. If the history of architecture teaches us anything, then it is how the logic of skyscrapers resulted in the annihilation of coexistence. Kundoo's very first building, *Hut Petite Ferme*, instead, is a simple home inspired by locally prevailing construction methods. It materializes an understanding of relations to the environment as coexistence. Tying untreated casuarina trees together with coconut rope, placing them on granite, and using palm stems and woven coconut for a roof, the *Hut Petite Ferme*'s complex geometry created a lively materiality that provided shelter.

Hut Petite Ferme, Auroville, 1990
Photo: Andreas Deffner

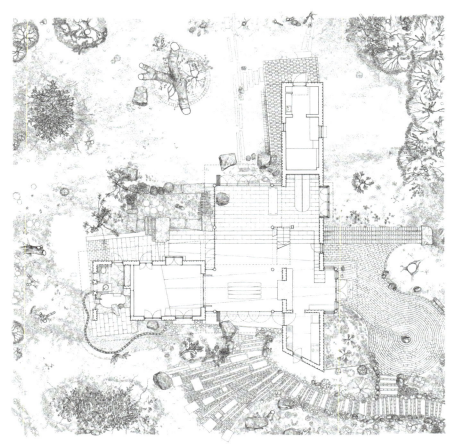

Wall House, Auroville, 2000
Plan: Anupama Kundoo Architects,
drafted by Alejandro M.
Photo: Elke Krasny

The *Wall House* continues the knowledge gained through building and living in the hut. It can be understood as a durational experimentation of carefully finding out how architecture can embody healthy relations with nature. Modern architecture made nature at once invisible and hypervisible by following the capitalist logic of cheap nature and providing the visual pleasure of looking at nature, which reduces the human body to the sense of sight. "Embodied and experiential learning" are essential for Anupama Kundoo. *The Wall House* offers spaces for the daily learning of how to be in coexistence with nature using all senses. Listening to the trees move is as much part of inhabiting the *Wall House* as is touching materials. Coexistence requires that the whole body with all its senses learns how to feel that "we are part of nature, that we are all living with all the other species, in coexistence with other species."

Wall House, Auroville, 2000
Photo: Javier Callejas

The walls of the *Sharana Daycare Facility* are made of porous terracotta. Comparing the *Sharana Daycare Facility* building to other structures in the neighborhood, one can feel how porous walls create a different feeling of how the outside connects to the inside. Bringing together material aesthetics and climatic pragmatics, the screen-like walls allow for airflow, which helps create some comfort in the hot and humid climate.

Sharana Daycare Facility, Puducherry, 2019
Photo: Javier Callejas

How we treat each other is as much a social question as it is an ecological one. The *Village Action Center* builds healing climates that bring the care for air and ventilation to spaces of working and self-organizing as villagers aim to overcome oppressions of gender and caste. The central courtyard with its soil bed materializes healthy relations of coexisting with nature, as rainwater is harvested from the rooftop and replenishes the groundwater table.

Village Action Center, Auroville, 2000
Photo: Elke Krasny

Porous Connections

We argue here that porosity offers a way for understanding and practicing architecture as climate healing. Starting from the understanding that human beings are porous is helpful to center an embodied approach in architecture that begins from our porous connections with others. This introduces the notion that inter-dependency and inter-vulnerability are central to climate healing, which includes offering healing climates for human beings. Openness and permeability, the characteristics of porosity, make us understand that human bodies are deeply permeated by the catastrophic climate conditions to which architecture contributed. If architecture contributes to climate healing in material, spatial, and climatic terms, these conditions will not only support the abundance of nature, but also permeate human bodies.

all House, Auroville, 2000
oto: Javier Callejas

Wall House, Auroville, 2000
Photos: Javier Callejas (top); Elke Krasny (bottom)

114   Angelika Fitz and Elke Krasny

Anupama Kundoo describes how the *Wall House* is based on making the air flow, yet keeping the mosquitoes out of the sleeping area, or about access to the moonlight when sitting on the stairs or being on the bathroom terrace. Porosity acknowledges the deep bodily connections between human beings, nature, and the climate. This is relevant to building climate healing, which materializes an antidote to the climate crisis as a crisis of imagination as diagnosed by writer and anthropologist Amitav Ghosh.

Wall House, Auroville, 2000
Photos: Elke Krasny

Soothing Architecture: The Abundance of Regeneration

During our visit to Anupama Kundoo's *Wall House*, as well as to the other examples of her built work in Auroville and in Puducherry, Angelika Fitz and myself had long conversations about our search for the right words to describe how we experienced her architecture and what kind of effects the spaces created by her had on us. The longer we thought about this and discussed it with each other, the clearer it became that there is not a very nuanced language in architecture to describe spaces that are peaceful, calming, or restorative. This absence is in and of itself quite telling. While we are inclined to think that this marked absence of a rich architectural vocabulary to describe subtle effects of architecture does not mean that these effects do not exist, we do feel quite strongly that this absence means that other effects, that is, other values generated by architecture, have been privileged both by the conventions of writing architecture history, as well as by the interests of capital. Thinking of terms like "modern architecture," "functional," "internationalist," "iconic architecture," "spectacular," or "global" makes it quite clear that architecture stands for the notions of modernity, internationalism, functionalism, iconicity, or spectacle. These terms proclaim the power of architecture to reign over entire periods, i.e., they claim that a specific style of architecture has come to define a certain time in history, globally.

Soothing, the word we have chosen to describe Anupama Kundoo's architecture, does not make any such claim of wanting to dominate a certain epoch or to set an international or global standard. Much rather, soothing architecture seeks to express the bodily, affective, emotional, intellectual, and, perhaps, even spiritual experiences that the architecture created by Anupama Kundoo makes space for. While we chose soothing architecture to describe our own experience, in particular, the experience of spending many hours in the *Wall House*, we encourage readers to think of their own experiences of soothing architecture and how they felt in spaces that generously and generatively allowed for regeneration, for a process of feeling restored and at peace. The following three sections invite readers to relate to the spaces captured in the images and to feel how they create regenerative possibilities for taking time, for recharging, and for resting.

nupama Kundoo on a rock in
ont of the *Wall House*, 2024
hoto: Elke Krasny

Taking Time

Spaces need time to happen just as much as bodies need time to happen in space. Creating conditions for taking time in architecture aims to overcome the fast experience of architecture and the conspicuous consumption of space.

Hut Petite Ferme, Auroville, 1990
Photos: Andreas Deffner

Angelika Fitz visiting the *Wall House*, Auroville, 2024
Photo: Elke Krasny

Anupama Kundoo sitting on one of the stones in front of the *Wall House*. The stones and the space around them are as much part of the *Wall House* as the building itself.
Photo: Angelika Fitz

The Power of Recharging

Spaces can give people power. While the power of architecture has been analyzed in Foucauldian terms to examine how architecture disciplines and controls, in political theory, more broadly, to understand how architecture represents regimes of power, and in Marxist terms to understand how architecture builds the power of capital, we are also interested in understanding how spaces can support bodies and minds so they feel recharged and gently empowered.

Library Nandalal Sewa Samithi, Puducherry, 2018
Photo: Javier Callejas

Town Hall Complex, 2005 (top); *Creativity Co-Housing*, 2003 (bottom), both Auroville
Photos: Elke Krasny (top); Javier Callejas (bottom)

Resting

Resting means that one's body is supported to remain in a specific position. It also means that one can find one's strength again, and, as we want to add here, one's power of imagination. Recovering one's strength to be with and in the world is among the most powerful, most needed, and most gentle things spaces can provide for. Understanding how to create spaces for resting, including resting together with others, in the midst of many other functions that the very same spaces fulfill, is central to how Anupama Kundoo's soothing architecture creates conditions for regeneration.

Sangamam, Auroville, 2003
Photo: Javier Callejas

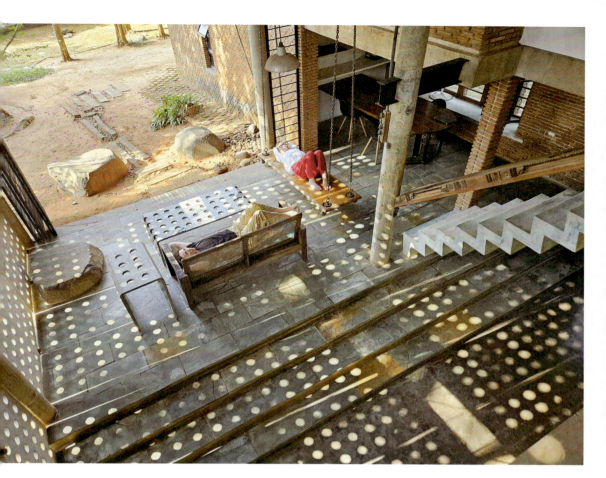

Angelika Fitz and Elke Krasny visiting the *Wall House*, 2024 (top)

Photo: Anupama Kundoo

Anupama Kundoo, Elke Krasny, and Angelika Fitz discussing the meaning of soothing spaces while resting together, *Wall House*, 2024 (bottom)

Photo: Gobinath Dinakaran

List of Selected Projects

Anupama Kundoo
List of Selected Projects

Hut Petite Ferme
1990

Location: Auroville, India
Size: 45 m²
Type: Residence
Client: Anupama Kundoo
Photo: Andreas Deffner

Wall House
2000

Location: Auroville, India
Size: 226 m²
Type: Residence
Client: Anupama Kundoo
Photo: Javier Callejas

Multipurpose Hall
S.A.W.C.H.U.
2000

Location: Auroville, India
Size: 307 m²
Type: Public Building
Client: Auroville Foundation
Photo: Javier Callejas

Village Action Center
2000

Location: Auroville, India
Size: 420 m² (building area),
190 m² (semi-covered area),
610 m² (total plinth area)
Type: Public Building,
Education, Community
Client: Auroville Village
Action Group
Photo: Elke Krasny

Keystone Foundation
2000—ongoing

Location: Kotagiri, India
Size: 14,165 m² (total land area),
1,692 m² (built-up areas for buildings)
Type: Community and
Research Campus
Client: Keystone Foundation
Photo: Javier Callejas

Auroville Institute of
Applied Technology
2001

Location: Auroville, India
Size: 259m² (building area),
66m² (semi-covered area),
325 m² (total plinth area)
Type: Education
Client: Auroville Village Action Trust
Photo: Angelika Fitz

Residence Spirit Sense
2001

Location: Auroville, India
Size: 130 m²
Type: Residence and Workshop
Client: Auroville Foundation,
in collaboration with Ray Meeker
Photo: Andreas Deffner

Abri Transport Service
2003

Location: Auroville, India
Type: Public Infrastructure
Client: Auroville Foundation
Photo: Deepshikha Jain

Sangamam
2003

Location: Auroville, India
Size: 474 m² (Sangamam Phase 1)
Type: Social Housing
Client: Auroville Foundation
Photo: Javier Callejas

Creativity Co-Housing
2003

Location: Auroville, India
Size: 3,252 m²
Type: Collective Housing
Client: Auroville Housing Service
Photo: Javier Callejas

Town Hall Complex
2005

Location: Auroville, India
Size: 1,703 m²
Type: Public Building
Client: Auroville Foundation
Photo: Javier Callejas

Mitra Youth Hostel
2005

Location: Auroville, India
Size: 1,114 m²
Type: Collective Housing
Client: Auroville Foundation
Photo: Javier Callejas

Volontariat Homes
for Homeless Children
2008

Location: Puducherry, India
Size: 512 m²
Type: Collective Housing
Client: Volontariat
Photo: Javier Callejas

Light Housing Prototype
2013

Location: Auroville, India
Size: 30 m²
Type: Housing
Client: Anupama Kundoo Architects
Photo: Marta San Vincente

Full Fill Homes
2015

Location: Auroville, India
Size: 30 m²
Type: Housing
Client: Anupama Kundoo Architects In collaboration with National Association of Schools of Architecture (NASA, India) and MARG Institute of Design and Architecture Swarnabhoomi (MIDAS)
Photo: Javier Callejas

Easy-WC
2015

Location: Auroville, India
Size: 5 m²
Type: Sanitary Facilities
Client: Anupama Kundoo Architects
Photo: Javier Callejas

Shah Houses
2016

Location: Brahmangarh, India
Size: 253 m²
Type: Residence
Client: Atul Shah and Ketan Shah
Photo: Javier Callejas

Library Nandalal
Sewa Samithi
2018

Location: Puducherry, India
Size: 268 m²
Type: Public Building, Education, Community
Client: Nandalal Sewa Samithi
Photo: Javier Callejas

Sharana Daycare Facility
2019

Location: Puducherry, India
Size: 766 m²
Type: Public Building, Education, Community
Client: Sharana
Photo: Javier Callejas

Modernities, Colonialities, Frictions
Essays

Unreal City:
Utopia and Its Afterlives

Ranjit Hoskote

Wolken kann man nicht *bauen*. Und darum
wird die *erträumte* Zukunft nie wahr.
— Ludwig Wittgenstein, 1942[1]

1.

I write this essay seated on a terrace in the Himalayan foothills, facing the panorama of the snowclad Dhauladhar range, watching the clouds as they drift across its peaks. Wittgenstein's wry remark finds graphic resonance at these heights: "You can't *build* clouds." No, indeed: clouds must form by themselves, in response to cycles of evaporation and condensation, shifts of physical state and transitions between strata of temperature. The conclusion that Wittgenstein draws from his nephological observation, switching gear without warning from the natural to the human realm, is more enigmatic: "And that's why the *dreamt-of* future never happens."

To build is to give concrete form to a dream, to translate an inchoate desire for transformation into actuality through the patterns and templates of a coherent vision. And when such a vision focuses on a city as its material and symbolic articulation, what is at stake is nothing less than a radical wager on architectural and human perfectibility. Such a striving to attain excellence in urban planning reflects the hope that the form of collective life that the new city will serve as habitation and stage will, likewise, be motivated by the ameliorative values of freedom, equity, opportunity, and justice. The belief that guides such a project—whether it is implicitly conveyed as design or explicitly stated as manifesto—is that an architecture premised on a better future will produce the society of the future, unencumbered by the psychic and social impedimenta of the past. In brief, such a visionary city connotes nothing less ambitious than the achievement of the ideal of Utopia, which would serve the great human adventure as a landmark.

1 Ludwig Wittgenstein, *Culture and Value*, ed. G. H. von Wright with Heikki Nyman, trans. Peter Winch (Chicago: University of Chicago Press, 1980), 41.

And yet, almost invariably, this ideal becomes its own worst enemy. The mandate to enforce perfection can play out in oppressive and sinister ways, committing itself to perfecting the instruments of enforcement rather than to deepening the quest for perfection. So that the dreamt-of future almost always departs from the script and falls short. Utopia does not last. It becomes a caricature of itself, or degenerates into a prison society, or collapses under the weight of its discontents. It persists in visceral experience and popular imagination as a ruin, or the hollowed-out shell of the dream it had briefly incarnated, or as a cautionary tale—because Utopia must always contend, in Kant's vivid and memorable phrase, with the "*krummem Holze, als woraus der Mensch gemacht ist*," the crooked timber of which humankind is made, and which refuses intransigently to be straightened out into furniture.[2]

2.

Perhaps owing to the vexed yet critically productive proximity of Modernism to our own time—as a historical horizon of cultural experience and production—we tend to identify the Utopian impulse as a leitmotif of the Modernist reenvisioning of the world. This sweeping process got underway in the early decades of the twentieth century and achieved its peak in the three decades immediately following World War II. During this time, it imposed its ascendancy, especially in architecture, by legislating a rupture with tradition and announcing its universal applicability as a talisman of progress.

Mies van der Rohe, Walter Gropius, and Le Corbusier—three magisterial practitioners who would go on to define what would come to be known as the International Style—had all been fellow apprentices together, between 1908 and 1911, at the Berlin office of the architect and industrial designer Peter Behrens—who would later work with Albert Speer on Hitler's megalomanic plans for "Germania," a Berlin Haussmanified into an architectural apotheosis of Nazi mythology. Even as young men, Mies, Gropius, and Le Corbusier believed that architecture could express the will of its time, before the notion of such a collective or preordained will became discredited on its adoption by Nazi ideologues. Their austere elegance and their invocation of aerodynamics, scale, and speed helped navigate the public imagination towards an appreciation of the forms of the Machine Age. Through their work, pedagogy, and writing, Modernism manifested itself as a confident and relentless neo-classicism. Insisting on a purity of structure and a mini-

Immanuel Kant, *Idee zu einer allgemeinen Geschichte in weltbürgerlicher Absicht*, 1784 (Berlin: Berlin-Brandenburgische Akademie-Ausgabe Vol. 8), 23.

malism of effect, it enacted an erasure of all prior forms of architectural expression between classical antiquity and itself, dismissing these as decorative, decadent, or redundant.[3]

From the 1970s onward, however, and at an uneven pace across the globe, Modernism lost its authority. Its neo-classical linearity and its ultimately colonial and patriarchal certitudes became overwhelmed by the messiness of a world rendered turbulent by crises of location and identity, the politics of anti-colonial struggle, the civil rights movement, the feminist upsurge, and the vigorous assertion of suppressed sensibilities. Looking back at such Modernist projects as Le Corbusier's never-realized *Villa Contemporaine* (1922) and his 1929 book, *The City of To-morrow and Its Planning*, we see how diverse strands in human aspiration were brought together under the sign of Utopia. On the one hand, such projects embody a genuinely humane and liberal commitment to political equity, the reduction of economic asymmetry, the possibility of a community based on empathetic interrelationships, and the large-scale provision of social housing. On the other hand, they reveal an authoritarian obsession with a grandeur of the individual structure and a monumentalism of urban scale.[4]

As well, we find here a fascination with technologies of self-containment that would render the building sufficient unto itself—linked to the neighborhood only by minimal and instrumental connections—and an enthusiasm for technologies of mobility that would, in Le Corbusier's chilling phrase, "abolish the pedestrian." Effectively, such strategies advocated the alienation of humankind from its natural environment, and its cocooning within a technological membrane. As we see from our contemporary predicament, this advocacy has had catastrophic consequences.

Above all, such Utopian projects were driven by a compelling devotion to the future, conceived almost in theological terms as a soteriology in which the architect-planner would act as the savior of suffering humankind. Utopia, in this paradigm, signified a means of transcending the limitations and deficits of the present. It would offer (to liberals) an opportunity to correct a past flawed by inequity and injustice or (to conservatives) an occasion to reinstate a supposedly golden age eroded by debate and reform.

3.

The saliency of Utopia as a key feature in Modernist architectural thought—which still forms the dominant framework for our habitations and settlements, and for our ideas about built form—can sometimes occlude from view the

3 See Henry-Russell Hitchcock Jr and Philip Johnson, *The International Style: Architecture since 1922* (New York: W. W. Norton, 1932).

4 See Le Corbusier, *The City of To-morrow and Its Planning* (New York: Dover, rpt. 1987, orig. pbl. 1929).

fact that Utopia has been available to the political imagination (at first in the West and later more globally) as a vital trope since 1516, when the Renaissance humanist Thomas More published his book about an imaginary island-society, governed on near-ideal lines, under that title. At once an allegorical critique of the social and political forms prevailing in his embattled historical moment and a constructive counterpoint to these, More's *Utopia* takes conversation as its discursive format, allowing for an interplay of perspectives. In this masterwork of political theory, the reasonably disposed community, bound by mutuality, is privileged over a surveillant state; the public assembly, and not a legal apparatus, arrives at social arrangements; property is held in common trust rather than privately owned.

More did not develop his account in a literary or philosophical vacuum. Both in terms of its subject and its format, *Utopia* is the outcome of its author's critical engagement with the ideal of Kallipolis (literally, "beautiful city"), a city-state efficiently if also repressively administered by a class of philosopher-kings presiding over a rigid class order, delineated by Plato in his influential dialogue *Politeia* ("The Republic," c. 375 BCE). Fully aware of the perils of such a system as Plato prescribed, More punned elegantly on the Greek-derived words *Ou-topia* ("No Place") and *Eu-topia* ("Good Place") in his celebrated neologism, characterizing the alternative afterlives awaiting his ideal of social and political organization for the future: the impossibility of actualization or a benign approximation.[5]

4.

After India won its independence from the British Empire in 1947, the Utopian project became integral to the trajectory of this newly liberated country. Resurrected after several centuries of colonial exploitation, India was set on the path to economic recovery and cultural self-assertion by the *dirigiste* government of Prime Minister Jawaharlal Nehru (1889–1964) and his constellation of humanist thinkers, policy makers, administrators, and cultural activists. Crucial to the Nehruvian vision was the gesture of modernization. By this, Nehru meant an emancipation both from the oppressive structures and reflexes internalized during colonial subjection, and from the regressive constraints of traditions that had become ossified and incapable of responding to the challenges of a fast-changing global environment.

In recent decades, Nehru has been pilloried by his detractors on the Right as having been alienated from the essence of Indian culture. Needless to say, such essentialism has no great understanding of the palimpsestic

Thomas More, *Utopia*, trans. Dominic Baker-Smith (London: Penguin Classics, 2004).

complexity of the culture it claims to defend. Meanwhile, Nehru's critics on the Left, especially the environmental Left, deplore the ecological devastation wrought by his policy of rapid and heavy industrialization. While this is evident in hindsight, it is unclear how else a newly postcolonial nation-state, devastated by systematic extractivism and the exactions of World War II, could have reorganized itself to ensure self-sufficiency during the 1950s and 1960s. Some measure of the empirical, open-ended pragmatism that underwrote Nehru's commitment to a Utopian vision may be gleaned from this passage in his beautiful meditation, *The Discovery of India*, published two years before India's independence:

> "The adventurous and yet critical temper of science, the search for truth and knowledge, the refusal to accept anything without testing and trial, the capacity to change previous conclusions in the face of new evidence, the reliance on observed fact and not on pre-conceived theory, the hard discipline of the mind — all this is necessary, not merely for the application of science but for life itself and the solution of its many problems."[6]

Arguably the most visible manifestation of Nehruvian India's impulse towards Utopia was the creation of a number of cities in every cardinal direction across the country during the vibrant, two-decade period between 1948 and 1968. These included New Bhubaneswar in Orissa (as it then was; now Odisha) in the east (1948–1960), Chandigarh in the newly partitioned Punjab to the north (1950–1953), Gandhinagar in the freshly created state of Gujarat (early 1960s) and New Bombay (now Navi Mumbai) in Maharashtra to the west (1965–1971), as well as Auroville, which is situated partly in Tamil Nadu and partly in Pondicherry, in the south (1968–1980).

This process took place under three related yet distinctive wagers on the modern as the promise of the "yet-to-be." Each of these wagers emanated from a different locus of influence in postcolonial India and required the architect to play a distinctive, context-specific role. First: Bhubaneswar, Chandigarh, and Gandhinagar were sponsored by the State as all-new provincial capitals intended to symbolize a trajectory of renewal for the provinces that they would oversee; here, the architect functioned as a participant in the grand adventure of nation-building. Second: New Bombay was proposed by a coalition of citizens, an architect among them, as an alternative to the over-extended urban center of Bombay, a colonial port city and industrial hub, and executed by the State; here, the architect acted as an intellectual gadfly and provocateur. And third: Auroville was a city

---

6   Jawaharlal Nehru, *The Discovery of India* (Calcutta: The Signet Press, 1946), 453.

Le Corbusier, Open Hand – a monumental sculpture in the Chandigarh Capitol Complex
Photo: Rahul Mehrotra

imagined into being by a spiritually oriented, transnational organization essaying an experimental and cosmopolitan form of community; here, the architect served in the office of a pilgrim carrying forward the wishes of a guide and teacher.

5.

The British colonial administration had carved the state of Orissa out of Bengal, Bihar, and the Madras Presidency in 1936, with the ancient city of Cuttack as its capital. In 1948, after the claims of several towns had been considered, the Nehruvian State settled on the temple town of Bhubaneswar as Orissa's new capital. The architect and planner Otto Königsberger (1908–1999)—a stateless Jewish refugee from Nazi Germany who had lived and worked in India since 1939 and was given Indian citizenship by Nehru in 1950—was entrusted with drawing up the master plan. Königsberger devised a fan-shaped layout, with neighborhood units arranged along a single arterial transport axis yet threaded through with a variety of walkways and subsidiary routes. It allowed for the protocols and official requirements of an administrative center while emphasizing the value of the self-sufficient and nurturing neighborhood. He had requested that his plan be opened to public discussion by its potential residents, but this progressive suggestion was overruled by the State.

Unfortunately, New Bhubaneswar has been eclipsed in the public imagination as well as the annals of global architecture history by Chandigarh. Few in present-day India have heard of Königsberger, and his work is of niche interest to scholars beyond its borders. The Nehru government offered Chandigarh to East Punjab as a capital in the early 1950s, to compensate for the emotional and material loss of Lahore, the state's historic capital, which had become part of Pakistan after the Partition.

The Chandigarh plan had been initiated by the American architect Albert Mayer in collaboration with the Polish architect Maciej Nowicki, but Mayer gave up the project after Nowicki's tragic death in an accident. The project was then handed over to Le Corbusier, who incorporated elements of the Mayer-Nowicki plan but placed his own signature impress on the city, both through monumental structures like the Capitol Complex and artistic flourishes such as the public sculpture of the Open Hand.[7]

Gandhinagar was established during the early 1960s as the capital of the new state of Gujarat, which had been formed after the dissolution of the old Bombay Presidency. Named in honor of the Mahatma—Gujarat's most legendary scion—it was also meant to act as a counterpoint to Ahmedabad, which had been the traditional Gujarati mercantile and cultural hub, and whose elite patronage had already been hospitable to international architects such as Le Corbusier and Louis Kahn. Unlike New Bhubaneswar and Chandigarh, the Gandhinagar plan was assigned to two Indian architects and planners of the younger generation, H. K. Mewada and P. M. Apte, who had apprenticed with Le Corbusier.

While Gandhinagar was taking shape on the drawing board, the MIT-trained architect Charles Correa (1930–2015), who had studied with Buckminster Fuller in Michigan, joined forces with the civil engineer Shirish Patel and the architect-scholar Pravina Mehta to conceive a twin city to

---

7 What is truly startling—although this is rarely mentioned in Indian architectural discussions where Le Corbusier continues to enjoy semi-divine cult status—is that the liberal and democratic Nehru was persuaded to bring in Le Corbusier, whose instincts were profoundly authoritarian, and who had had no qualms in offering his services to the collaborationist Vichy regime during 1940–1941 (Marshal Pétain dismissed his ideas as too avant-garde). Le Corbusier never deviated from his convictions, formed early on, that a modern city is defined by the clarity of straight lines and axial grids, and to whom the curve was anathema. "The winding road is the result of happy-go-lucky heedlessness, of looseness, lack of concentration and animality. The straight road is a reaction, an action, a positive deed, the result of self-mastery. It is sane and noble," he wrote in the late 1920s. This obsession continued in a paean to the new, reconstructed Paris of his dreams, and by extension, his conception of Everycity: "Paris is a dangerous magma of human beings gathered from every quarter by conquest, growth and immigration; she is the eternal gipsy encampment from all the world's great roads; Paris is the seat of a power and the home of a spirit which could enlighten the world; she digs and hacks through her undergrowth, and out of these evils she is tending towards an ordered system of straight lines and right angles; this reorganisation is necessary to her vitality, health and permanence; this clearing process is indispensable to the expression of her spirit, which is fundamentally limpid and beautiful." See Le Corbusier. *The City of To-morrow and Its Planning*, pp. 10 and 25.

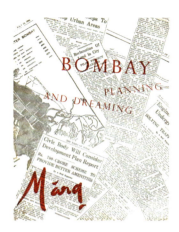 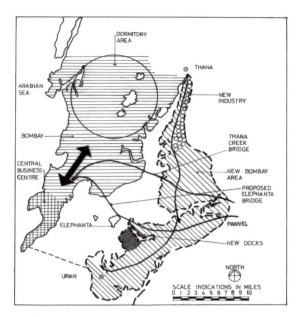

Cover of *Marg* 18, no. 3 (June 1965), the *Bombay: Planning and Dreaming* issue
Credit: Marg Foundation

Charles Correa's initial sketch, explaining the logic of developing a New Bombay across the East Bay.
Credit: Charles Correa Associates/ Charles Correa Foundation

Bombay. Even as early as the 1960s, India's prominent west-facing island-city was unable—or, more accurately, its administration was unwilling—to cope with a constant influx of immigrants from the rural hinterland seeking their fortunes in its factories and textile mills. Bombay's infrastructure and services were under severe strain, and yet, no official effort had been made to reimagine its megalopolitan future.

Correa, Patel, and Mehta responded to this problem with a radical proposal—published in a 1965 issue of the remarkable arts and culture journal, *Marg*, then edited by the novelist-critic Mulk Raj Anand—for a New Bombay, to be built on the mainland, across the East Bay from Bombay, and for a new land and water transport system to bridge the two. It was not until 1971 that the New Bombay Plan was formally drawn up, and the city and its civic administration assumed gradual form over the 1970s.[8]

Even as intellectual and bureaucratic circles in Bombay were engaged in a process of dialogue—with its periodic advances and retreats, its promises and betrayals—to actualize New Bombay, a very different conception of the Utopian urban future was floated in the south by an extraordinary figure, known to her votaries simply as The Mother. Born Mirra Alfassa (1878–1973) to a Francophone Ottoman Jewish family, she had come, early in life,

For the plan for a New Bombay originally proposed by Charles Correa, Shirish Patel, and Pravina Mehta, see *Marg* 18, no. 3, *Bombay: Planning and Dreaming*, 1965.

into the ambit of the poet and mystic Sri Aurobindo (1872–1950), a fervent Indian nationalist who had given up the path of violent revolution and become transformed into a spiritual teacher, taking up residence in the then French-ruled enclave of Pondicherry near Madras. Sri Aurobindo anointed The Mother as his successor. She became the custodian of his legacy, nurturing his ideal of a future community that would be dedicated to spiritual transfiguration. Transnational in its scope, this community would welcome all adherents irrespective of race, nationality, gender, and creed.

To this end, in 1968, The Mother announced that a new experimental city would be established in a semi-arid zone near Pondicherry, largely scrubland and wetland. She named it Auroville. This designation was both an act of homage to Sri Aurobindo and a reference to *aurore*, "the dawn" in The Mother's native French. The architect she chose to give shape to this futuristic settlement was the French Roger Anger (1923–2008); his master plan for Auroville has never been fully realized, although several major elements of it have been translated into platforms, pavilions, emergent neighborhoods, and the geodesic dome, covered with golden discs, known as the Matri Mandir ("The Mother's Temple").

6.

The afterlives of these Utopian wagers on the future have not lived up to the visionary ambitions that drove them into existence. New Bhubaneswar, to quote the architect and civil rights activist P. K. Das, who grew up there, no longer reflects Königsberger's emphasis on an array of neighborhood units in which people could form connections across sectarian and ethnic lines. "Even his ideas of open spaces, market location and the provision of other social amenities were not followed. Land use and building activity in these areas has meant high-cost and unaffordable mega housing complexes, corporate-run hospitals and schools, even universities, but very little public open spaces and accessible amenities for the less privileged who are a substantial section of the city's population. ... The city's planning narrative – a master plan by a well-known planner, implemented by politicians, bureaucrats and engineers, and little to nothing of people's participation – is now familiar across India. Even when people's participation is sought, it is perfunctory. However, this is possible if the concept of the neighbourhood unit – the basic brick in Königsberger's master plan – was embraced and people allowed to shape spaces within their neighbourhoods. The concept of the Königsberger neighbourhood unit expanded to neighbourhood-based city planning is possible – even necessary today."[9]

As for New Bombay, it was never allowed to fulfil its promise. The Maharashtra government reneged on its commitment to shifting the main ministries and the central business district, situated in Bombay, to the city across the water. For several decades, New Bombay became a "dormitory town," its residents commuting to work in Bombay and back. Expressing his sorrow at such a situation in a 2008 interview, Correa deplored the manner in which all efforts to sustain viable metropolitan systems and ensure civic reform in India were consistently thwarted by a political-bureaucratic complex that treats major cities as "profit centers," perpetuating a system of favors and kickbacks. Addressing the problem of how urban development schemes were ratified without adequate scrutiny, he said, "No planning body is consulted in the process. In fact, because such bodies might embarrass the authorities by asking intelligent questions, any planning capability that existed in the city has been systematically destroyed."[10]

Meanwhile, Auroville has come to be wracked, in recent years, by rancorous disputes over the proper path forward. Visiting there and speaking with a broad range of contributors to the debate, I came away wondering whether the realization of Roger Anger's master plan was still relevant, if it came at the cost of deforestation. Is a large-scale, high-rise urban center the optimal form of settlement in a semi-arid zone deficient in water sources? As runaway urbanization has become the default setting for collective life in South Asia, might a truly radical solution not lie in turning away from the big city, to explore other schemes of disaggregated yet linked habitation?

Moved, yet left unsettled by the experience of meditating in the inner chamber of the Matri Mandir—an interior that has justifiably been compared to a *Star Trek* set—I found solace in *Golconde* in Pondicherry, which was India's first reinforced-concrete Modernist building. A dormitory for the Aurobindo Ashram, *Golconde* was designed by a troika of architects: the Czechs Antonin Raymond and François (František) Sammer, and the Japanese-American George Nakashima. Its construction, between 1935 and 1945, was slowed down by the war-time interruptions of material supply lines and by Nakashima's cruel internment by the US authorities, with other *Nissei*, as a person of Japanese origin. Reminiscent of a cave monastery, *Golconde*'s beton brut edifice and elegantly spartan interiors induce a serenity of spirit notably absent in the highly ritualized collective scenarios of circulation and reflection enjoined on the visitor in Auroville.[11]

Ultimately, rather than settling organically into the landscapes on which they were imposed, it would seem that postcolonial India's Utopian cities

See P. K. Das, "How Bhubaneswar's master plan was overtaken by unsustainable development," Question of Cities, January 27, 2023, https://questionofcities.org/how-bhubaneswars-master-plan-was-overtaken-by-unsustainable-development/ (accessed March 2, 2025).

10   Charles Correa, *A Place in the Shade: The New Landscape & Other Essays* (Panaji: Charles Correa Foundation, 2018), 129.

11   See Smita Dalvi, "Golconde: India's First Modern Building," *Tekton* 3, no. 1 (March 2016): 46–63.

Golconde, Pondicherry (1935–1945): The austere elegance of its cave-monastery-like corridors
Photo: Smita Dalvi

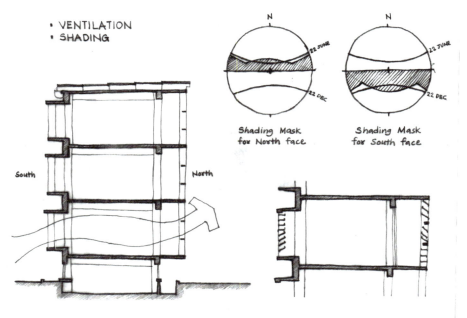

Golconde, Pondicherry (1935–1945): Orientation towards the sun, shading and ventilation
Drawing: Smita Dalvi

have come to resemble unwelcome UFOs—shaped more by an outmoded ideology than by a response to the needs and urgencies of their inhabitants. At such a dystopian historical moment as ours, can the classical Modernist conception of Utopia—identified with expert culture, unwelcoming of the participation of the multitudes, indissolubly linked to class privilege even while projecting an ideal of the greater common good—hold any meaning for us? In the midst of the ongoing ecological meltdown of the planet, is the megalopolis—with its propensity for exponential consumption—to be regarded as the best possible guarantee of freedoms and opportunities? Looking upon the afterlives of Utopia, I am reminded of Eliot's melancholic evocation of the urbanscape in "The Waste Land," from a century ago:

"… Unreal City,
Under the brown fog of a winter dawn
A crowd flowed over London Bridge, so many,
I had not thought death had undone so many."[12]

7.

If the lineage of Utopian Modernism has let us down, could we look elsewhere in South Asia's recent history for other genealogies of architecture and urban planning that might provide us with future cities that are habitable, sustainable, nurturing, and capable of supporting our collective hopes and dreams? In this quest, perhaps we could turn to a figure whose work was seminal and remains urgently relevant to the present—yet who has been tragically neglected, his contributions ignored. I speak, here, of the Scottish scholar and activist Patrick Geddes (1854–1932), who worked in India from 1915 to 1924 and was passionately committed to the reanimation of its cities. In striking contrast to the grandiose Utopian schemes that we have considered so far, Geddes championed a more modest and artisanal approach, focused on the granularity of the social and natural spheres.

Geddes was an accomplished botanist and a freelance town planner; during his time in India, he also became the founding professor of sociology and civics at the University of Bombay, and the first head of its Sociology Department. Travelling the length and breadth of the subcontinent, he prepared nearly fifty town plans for Indian cities—from Ahmedabad, Surat, and Lahore in the west to Indore in central India, Dacca (now Dhaka) in the east, and Tanjore (now Thanjavur) and Madurai in the south. Some of these plans were commissioned by native princely rulers; others were requested

12 T. S. Eliot, "The Waste Land,"
Selected Poems (London: Faber, 1956), 53.

by colonial administrators. An environmentalist *avant la lettre*, Geddes' work was richly informed by his belief that social life was inseparable from its deep sources in, and its strong responsibilities towards, the natural lifeworld.

As the historian Ramachandra Guha writes in his scintillating account of the Indian phase of this polymath's life and work: "Geddes's methodological contributions to the art of town planning were his concepts of 'diagnostic survey' — an intensive walking tour to acquaint oneself with the growth, development and existing status of the city being planned for — and 'conservative surgery', the practice of gentle improvements with minimal disruption of people and their habitat. These ground rules were meticulously observed in his Indian town plans. However, his town plans are far from being dry-as-dust technocratic reports. Wonderfully idiosyncratic, they are shot through with throwaway lines and bon mots, while his philosophy emerges in the most unexpected places."[13]

At the heart of Geddes' plans lay his insistence on linking spaces of residence, spaces of livelihood, and spaces of recreation; the processes of urban restoration and expansion that he laid out for colonial India's rulers pivoted around gardens and water bodies. In city after city, he called for the clearing, de-silting, and rescue of wells, tank systems, lakes, and riverine passages that had been allowed to fall into disrepair, choked with garbage or poisoned with effluents. "It cannot be too often and clearly affirmed," wrote Geddes (the emphatic capitalization appears in the original passage), "that the old Tank Parks of so many Indian Cities are not only the glory of India, but are without rival in Europe, often surpassing in their beauty of mingled land and waterscapes, the glories of Versailles and Potsdam…"[14]

Taking the opposite stance to that espoused by the dogmatists of Modernism, Geddes was inspired by the resources of lived experience, as enshrined in custom and practice. Writing in the context of Indore, which he had wished to transform into a city luxuriant with gardens of every description, he declared: "Civilisation, alike in its higher movements and achievements and on its comparatively permanent levels, has flourished best in smaller aggregates; and — despite the megalomania of every Megalopolis, and the deep and manifold depression of every minor city accordingly — it tends to do so still; and may do again, more fully."[15]

And yet again, articulating fervently the trinity of core values that Guha describes as his respect for Nature, Democracy, and Tradition, Geddes wrote (or rather, declaimed—for this is an evangelist's voice) in his report

---

13 Ramachandra Guha, *Speaking of Nature: The Origins of Indian Environmentalism* (New Delhi: HarperCollins/Fourth Estate, 2024), 121.

14 Patrick Geddes, *Town Planning in Balrampur: A Report to the Honourable the Maharaj Bahadur* (Lucknow: Murray's London Printing Press, 1917), 44–45.

15 Patrick Geddes, *Town Planning Towards City Development*, Part II (New Delhi: Vitasta, rpt. 2016, orig. pbl. 1918), 233.

on the small and usually under-regarded Gujarat town of Nadiad: "So here – nowhere better than in Nadiad – may be created the very type of that decentralised and semi-rural garden city which is the best hope of the future; best for the health of individuals and of the race, and even best for quality of civilisation also. For history abundantly shows that in arts and crafts, in thought and in religion, in character and personality, in initiative and action... the small cities are surpassing the great."[16]

Unfortunately, Geddes' unorthodox methods of inquiry and advocacy did not endear him to the officials of the colonial administration. Doubtless they also looked with suspicion upon his gift for befriending and making common cause with Indians, and on his ability to immerse himself in the country's everyday life. In the princely states, Geddes seems to have been regarded as an eccentric. He neither conformed to the British code of conduct in India, nor did he answer to the stereotypes that Indians had cultivated about the British. His proposals were either ignored by the maharajas whose attention he sought or rejected by their ministers on specious grounds of cost and difficulty of execution. His heroic efforts at the documentation of India's architectural heritage went unappreciated; his wise counsel was disregarded by those he sought to advise. Growing increasingly frustrated and disillusioned, he left India's shores in 1924, never to return. His work remains to us as a legacy, however, if only we could retrieve it from the archive and reactivate it in our built and lived environments.

8.

Despite the many ambient reasons for bleakness, I would like to conclude this essay on a note of qualified optimism. In this spirit, I turn to Charles Correa's 1999 essay, "The Ideal City," in which this heir to the tradition of global Modernism wrote in an unconsciously Geddesian spirit: "For the city that we each experience is, of course, much more than just a physical plant – it is also a set of powerful mythic images and values that give sustenance and enrichment to our lives. This, in the final analysis, is what cities are about. What culture is about. And what, hopefully, our towns and cities could once again become."[17]

Following in the direction towards which Geddes pointed us, a century of lost opportunities and wrong turnings ago, we must confront the fact that architectural practice in South Asia must be radically reinvented. While it

Patrick Geddes, *Reports on Replanning of Six Towns in Bombay Presidency* (Bombay: Government Central Press, rpt. 1965, orig. pbl. 1915), 15.

17 Charles Correa, *A Place in the Shade*, 133.

has emancipated itself from the residual pieties of Modernism to a considerable extent—especially in the work of younger practitioners—architecture in South Asia has yet to free itself from an architectural pedagogy that continues to be effectively colonial in its emphasis on a consumerist-extractivist mentality and a vassalage to a powerful clientele. Above all, architecture in South Asia has suffered because of its reluctance to break down the hierarchy between the academy-trained, officially licensed architect and the artisanal practitioner of what is both descriptively yet also pejoratively described as "vernacular architecture."

Collaborations across that hierarchy are not uncommon. And yet, do they achieve parity and solidarity between practitioners operating from sharply different levels of cultural and economic capital? Acts of translation and adaptation across that hierarchy will become necessary, as well as a redistribution of acknowledgement and reward, if architecture is truly to thrive in South Asia. Architects cannot simply stand back as suppliers of a service, as they too often do. They must conduct themselves as contributors to ways of living together, actively engaged in questions of just livelihood, replenishing community, and appropriate technology.

It is time, not to embrace vernacular architecture uncritically, but to reimagine the vernacular in architecture.

The Legacy of Women in Modern Architecture of India

Madhavi Desai

This article attempts to frame the historic backdrop and genealogy for the works of Anupama Kundoo, whose transnational achievements are uniquely placed among contemporary women architects of India. It counteracts the canonical and hegemonic master narratives as the mainstream architectural histories. Modernism and its legacy are important in reference to women architects, but it has been consistently overlooked. I bring to the fore the marginalized yet immense contributions and heritage of women modernists of the twentieth century. The write-up draws on the career trajectories of some of the significant first-generation women architects in India: Perin Mistri, Eulie Chowdhury, Gira Sarabhai, Pravina Mehta, etc., who began their practice in the colonial era and continued after political Independence in 1947. It locates them within the socio-political context of modern India—a milieu that shaped the gender roles and was also transformed by them. Through micro-histories, it lists the professional challenges they faced, framed within the intersectionality of their socio-cultural and class backgrounds. It also analyzes their design attitudes in the period when architects were striving to go "modern" in terms of aesthetics, building materials, and techniques.

Modernism came to India as a dominant paradigm that was intrinsically connected to colonial rule, especially the British Raj. Its authoritarian imperialism transplanted and imposed new institutions, technology, concepts, and forms based on its notions of modernity. It affected not only architecture and urbanism but also the professions connected with the built environment. From the 1920s onwards, foreign and Indian architects often borrowed European (state-of-the-art) Modernist and Art Deco styles to be up-to-date. India gained independence from colonial rule in 1947 when the main architectural challenge became the articulation of the national identity as well as adopting a progressive ideology as an anti-colonial stance. For a brief period, there was a search for a balance between preserving traditional elements and embracing the imperatives of modernity[1] while simultaneously

Rahul Mehrotra, Devashree Shah, and Pranav Thole, *Architecture of Transition:* *Emerging Practices in South Asia* (Barcelona: Altrim Publishers, 2024), 11.

Institute of Indology designed by Balkrishna Doshi,
Ahmedabad, 1962
Photo: Miki Desai

resisting and accepting Western ideologies. It was a time of political and social change, as India stood on the threshold of industrialization. Gradually, however, revivalism gave way to full-fledged international modernism. From the 1950s to the 1970s, a new generation of Indian architects came to prominence, bringing distinctive modernist styles to the region with new ways of production and aesthetics. Their projects reflected the geo-cultural complexity of the country through various approaches towards architecture.[2]

As European architects/partners of Indian firms increasingly withdrew from active practice, Indian architects began to get substantial and varied design commissions. In the 1950s, India's first Prime Minister Pandit Jawaharlal Nehru invited the famous architect Le Corbusier to design the new capital of Chandigarh. Later, in the 1960s, another well-known international architect from the USA, Louis Kahn, came to the city of Ahmedabad to design the Indian Institute of Management Campus. These designers'

[2] Kazi Ashraf and James Belluardo, *An Architecture of Independence: The Making of South Asia* (New York: The Architectural League of New York, 1998), 19.

formal structuralist approach brought in the most profound modernist influence on Indian architects' search for a new, appropriate expression of the built environment.[3] In the early years, Habib Rahman to Achyut Kanvinde, Charles Correa to Balkrishna Doshi, and Laurie Baker to Raj Rawal, among many others, helped establish a design culture in the postcolonial period with plural forms of modernities and its interpretations.[4] However, throughout the past seventy-seven years after political Independence, the role and contribution of Indian women architects have been largely missing from innumerous national and international conferences, exhibitions, and publications.

The narrative of women in the discipline almost parallels the development of modern architecture in the sub-continent. As a few women took hesitant steps to join the field in the 1940s, they were influenced by ideals of nationalism due to the freedom struggle led by Gandhi being at its peak then. At the same time, their design attitudes were impacted by global intellectual currents such as Art Deco, International Style, Brutalism, and the Garden City movement. Mostly educated in the West, they were shaped by the aesthetics and utopian aspirations of early modernism. Though limited in numbers, this first generation of women architects quietly broke the male bastions and paved a way for the next generations to follow in their footsteps. However, their stories and pioneering contributions, like elsewhere in the world, have remained rather invisible in the canonical historiography of modern architecture, where the knowledge space has been dominated by the male (star) architects mentioned above as erasure has been built into the conventional frameworks within the academic and professional practice of architecture.

Facing this scholarly challenge, I undertook the task of researching and writing the first narration of seven pioneering women architects' trajectories, as well as twenty-eight contemporary practices in mainstream architectural history, in a book titled *Women Architects and Modernism in India: Narratives and Contemporary Practices* (New York and Oxon: Routledge, 2017).[5] Despite the almost non-existent archives, the book sheds light on their unusual achievements and trials. It also traces the post-Independence generation that struggled hard to develop an identity and successful professional achieve-

Jon Lang, Madhavi Desai, and Miki Desai, *Architecture and Independence: The Search for Identity, India 1880 to 1980* (Oxford and New Delhi: Oxford University Press, 1997), 191.
Jyoti Hosagrahar, *Indigenous Modernities: Negotiating Architecture and Urbanism* (New York and Oxon: Routledge, 2005), 2.

5   In the twenty-first century, there has been a growing scholarly and social media interest in the ongoing struggles against historic erasures based on gender, race, and class within the profession of architecture, including prevalent gendered spatial inequities in the built environment. In Europe, the USA, and parts of Asia, there is an increasing presence of research, writing, and activism with complex gendered layers. I have been passionately involved in this area for the past thirty-plus years, and I have networked with many organizations involved in this subject. This article is my work in progress.

ments within a masculine culture of the profession and the society. The book redefines and pluralizes the concept of professional work, encompassing a greater range of activities beyond successful practice, to include pedagogy, mentoring, or even activism. I developed a format that weaves together social, professional, and biographical factors into an intricate and productive feminist history. This locally grounded account not only demonstrates the diversity of modern architectural practices but uncovers the ways in which architectural modernism in India was shaped by the energies of women.

Women and the Indian Society

At the turn of the twentieth century, Indian society was beginning to come out of its rather medieval/feudal mentality with its moorings in tradition, religious dogma, and many social ills. At that time, the social structure was largely community-/caste-based, with adherence to traditional roles and customs as prescribed by the community. Within this, the individual self was rather insignificant. Typically, a woman was married after puberty and spent her life bringing up numerous children, looking after the house and the members of a joint family. However, there began to be a gradual change in this situation due to new political, economic, and educational institutions and processes, including the effect of forces of modernization during the colonial rule, especially in the first half of the twentieth century.

Further structural changes took place in the social setup from 1950 to 1970. The role of a woman underwent a slow but definite transformation. Girls' education, social awareness against child marriages and widow remar-

A joint family in India, circa 1912
Photo: Archicrafts archives

riages, the beginning of participation in economic activities like the service sector and the professions brought about a gradual transformation.[6] The turning point came through the freedom struggle against British rule led by Gandhi in which women began to boldly join public life in a major way in the mass movement, giving them new self-worth and dignity, as well as political and social freedom. In other words, it brought them out of their kitchens and homes into the public streets and political life. By 1960, education for women became an accepted norm in urban areas. As the century progressed, many women's institutions and organizations came up. There were also other changes like women gradually gaining economic independence through not only traditional occupations like cooking, sewing, and teaching but also becoming qualified in various professions such as law, medicine, engineering, architecture, and others.

With the above background, this locally-grounded chronicle of the early modernist era in India celebrates the women architects as part of a feminist historical narrative. These women paved the difficult way for the subsequent generations of designers to follow, making it much easier for them to walk on the path to a profession that existed (and still does) within a dominant masculine culture. Belonging to well-connected and liberal elite families in a patriarchal society, these women were exceptional; not only in their choice of the profession but also in their personal lives as they worked towards careers that made them transgress established internal and external, spatial, and social boundaries of home.

Family Backgrounds

Perin Jamsetjee Mistri (1913–1989), the first woman architect of India, was born in Mumbai (then Bombay) into a progressive, upper-middle-class Parsi family. Her father, Jamsetjee Mistri, was a civil engineer by education but an architect by temperament, who set up the firm J P Mistri in the 1880s. He designed buildings not only in Mumbai but also in Karachi (where the firm had opened a branch in 1916) and several other places in India.[7] Mistri was married to Ardeshir Bhiwandiwala, a founder-partner of the Great Eastern Shipping Company, and had one son. Pravina Mehta (1923–1992), from a wealthy middle-class family in Mumbai, was another influential architect. She was the daughter of a prominent Mumbai solicitor, who grew up in a household where important nationalist leaders met with her father

Madhavi Desai, "The Bungalow in the Colonial and Post-colonial Twentieth Century: Modernity, Dwelling and Gender in the Cultural Landscape of India," in The Routledge Companion to

Modernity, Space and Gender, ed. Alexandra Staub (New York and Oxon: Routledge, 2018), 353.

7   Reema Gehi, "Building Upon a Legacy," Sunday Mumbai Mirror, November 2, 2019, https://

mumbaimirror.indiatimes.com/others/sunday-read/building-upon-a-legacy/articleshow/71872536.cms.

during the struggle for Independence against British colonial rule. She was herself impacted by Gandhi's leadership, participating in the movement, and even going to jail in 1942. She was married twice but did not have any children. Hema Sankalia (1934–2015), though born in Sialkot in undivided India, now in Pakistan, also grew up in Mumbai after her father passed away when she was only one year old. Her mother moved to Mumbai with her sister to live in their paternal uncle's household. Hers was a socially and economically privileged and well-connected Maharashtrian Brahmin family. Hema married Shirish Sankalia, a man of ideas, in 1956. He had graduated with a degree in history but he started a furniture-making company and took on interior projects. Sankalia brought up three children while being in active architectural practice. The only architect belonging to an elite, very wealthy, industrialist family was Gira Sarabhai (1923–2021) of Ahmedabad. Her ancestor, Sheth Karamchand Premchand, established the Calico Mills in 1880, one of Ahmedabad's earliest and most prominent textile mills. Under the stewardship of her father, Ambalal Sarabhai, it became a modern, path-breaking production unit, manufacturing cotton textiles during the first half of the twentieth century. Her family also became a long-time supporter of Gandhi and his struggle for Independence. Sarabhai remained unmarried until the end of her life. Last but not the least, Urmila Eulie Chowdhury (1923–1995) was born in Shahjahanpur, in the north Indian state of Uttar Pradesh. She grew up and travelled in several countries as her father was a diplomat. Chowdhury was married to an engineer called Jugal Kishore but later divorced him. They had no children. She not only worked closely with Le Corbusier in Chandigarh but also had a long career after 1947.

Perin Mistri family
Photo: Mistri family archives

Education

Chowdhury, Sankalia, and Mistri had only a bachelor's degree in architecture, Chowdhury from Sydney, Australia, and the other two from Sir J. J. School of Art in Mumbai. Sankalia joined Sir J. J. in 1951 when there were only three female students in her class of sixty. Pravina Mehta had also enrolled in Sir J. J. but she had to discontinue her education when she went to jail during the nationalist fight in the 1940s. But she later attended the School of Design in Chicago (now the IIT Institute of Design), studying under Chermayeff and others, imbibing the Bauhaus philosophy. She also went on learning under the legendary Rexford Tugwell while pursuing a master's degree in planning from the University of Chicago, before returning to India. Gira Sarabhai, on the other hand, was a homeschooled and totally self-taught designer, never having opted for formal learning. As a young girl in her late teens, Sarabhai lived in New York City with family members. She also trained with Frank Lloyd Wright at his Taliesin West studio in Arizona from 1947 to 1951. It should be noted that the elite upbringings of these women took them far beyond their actual education due to their exposure to travelling, cultural practices, arts, and crafts.

Personality and Other Achievements

All the women architects profiled here were very intelligent, determined, and rebellious by nature. They had multiple skills, talents, and interest in arts and culture. A woman of principles, Hema Sankalia had a formidable personality, and always smoked a *bidi* in an age when smoking by women was looked down upon. At the same time, she was a humanist who insisted on paying for the education of her servants' children. She had a tough yet warm persona. The Sankalias were instrumental in establishing the Contemporary Arts and Crafts store (1962), India's first and very successful contemporary lifestyle store, in Mumbai in partnership with Wayna Mody. Sankalia was a hard-core teacher and taught in many colleges of architecture, first in Mumbai and then in Pune, almost until the very end of her life. Eulie Chowdhury had a bohemian and unconventional personality, living life on her own terms. She smoked, drank, and had a daring lifestyle. Though dominating by nature, she was a person of integrity and honesty. She insisted on strict discipline at the workplace but was also a fun-loving person who founded the first theater group in Chandigarh for which she wrote and acted in plays. Besides teaching at the Chandigarh College of Architecture, she was the director of the prestigious School of Planning and Architecture in Delhi for a brief period. Sumit Kaur, who had a close friendship with Chowdhury, says, "This multifaceted, highly talented architect, painter, teacher, sculptor was the author of excellent architectural drawings, sketches,

Gira Sarabhai
Photo: Archicrafts archives

photographs, and writings, including furniture design. Through perseverance, time management, clarity of purpose, and a keen eye for detail, the bold and daring Eulie Chowdhury achieved great heights in the then male-dominated profession of architecture."

Pravina Mehta was bold and outspoken. Deeply humane, she loved beauty in all forms and had an infectious sense of humor. She was an innovative and visionary thinker. Committed to egalitarian values and social justice, she headed a research unit to deal with these issues. Gira Sarabhai was an exceptional woman with a wide and deep understanding of design. An unassuming person, she had refined taste and a sophisticated understanding of aesthetics. Archana Shah, a textile designer who knew her well, says, "Sarabhai paid attention to details, every aspect in the design process, whether it was building her mud house, or the display of art objects at her museum, spending hours to get the perfect lighting or alignment. She appreciated good craftsmanship and enjoyed spending hours with skilled masons, carpenters, or gardeners as much as interacting with the most famous, internationally known designers." Besides starting India's first textile design studio and the first advertising agency, she played a major role in setting up the National Institute of Design, as well as the renowned Calico Textile Museum in Ahmedabad. Perin Mistri had a charismatic and a larger-than-life persona. Her niece Tina Sutaria says, "She was a formidable woman, with multi-dimensional strengths and capabilities. She was strong, capable and had the ability to finish whatever she began." She was much ahead of her time and truly prepared a historic path for other women to tread. "Perin effortlessly donned numerous skins as the first Indian woman architect,

Hostel block, Government Home Science College designed by Eulie Chowdhury in Chandigarh, 1961
Photo: Archicraft archives

head of a prestigious firm, founder president of the Soroptimist Club, a passionate advocate for environmental issues, a music aficionado, a dedicated family person and many more…[8]

Architectural Practice and Design Approach

Gira Sarabhai was a most unconventional practitioner who refused to identify herself as an architect but preferred to be called a designer. Her work evolved from "Wrightian" modernism to craft-oriented mud houses and dismantling and reconstructing traditional buildings in new forms, as she got interested in experimenting with an Indianized expression in her contemporary projects in Ahmedabad. Through collaborations with her brother Gautam Sarabhai, she contributed immensely to the modernist architecture of India, including institution building. Eulie Chowdhury, who worked closely with

Theertha Gangadharan, "India's First Woman Architect – A Tribute to Perin J. Mistri," Art Deco Mumbai, May 24, 2021, https://www.artdecomumbai.com/research/perin-j-mistri/.

Le Corbusier and his team of international architects in Chandigarh, developed her distinct modernist style during the post-Independence era as she designed a wide variety of buildings for the government as well as commercial and private clients in Chandigarh and Punjab, including housing, townships, schools, industrial buildings, and others. Perin Mistri, on the other hand, was involved with her father's large firm in Mumbai as a partner. She began her work in the 1930s with the state-of-the-art Art Deco style on projects mainly in Mumbai but also in several other Indian cities. Her designs evolved with time and became more functional in the modernist vocabulary. Pravina Mehta and Hema Sankalia had a partnership for seven years in Mumbai, Mehta being older and more accomplished. Sankalia always considered her a guru. Both were ardent teachers. Mehta was an innovative and visionary thinker with a clear-headed grasp of complexity. She linked form, structure, and systems in an integrated design approach that was advanced for its time. Mehta's design ideology was to juxtapose the past and present. She subtly brought together the complex geometries and proportions in classical Indian design and city planning canons into contemporary expressions. Her major contribution was the concept of New Bombay (a twin city of Mumbai) in 1965 along with Charles Correa and Shirish Patel.

A house designed by Hema Sankalia
with Pravina Mehta in Pune, 1966
Photo: Archicraft archives

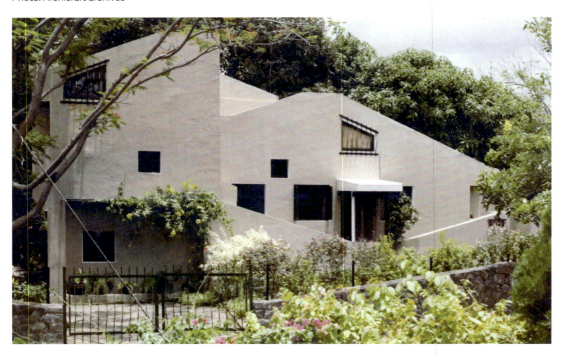

Sankalia has at least fifty buildings to her credit as per recent research, ranging from extensive housing projects to office complexes and hostels. Her mainstream work expressed modernist functionality with an inert sensitivity.

Historical Legacy

These few examples of the first generation of women architects show us the firm basis of their architectural achievements. When their careers progressed in the 1950s and the 1960s, architecture was in its nascent stage in a newly independent country. They belonged to upper-middle-class families and were socially well-connected. They joined the professional course due to their families' liberal views and unconditional encouragement. These women were rebellious, headstrong, and visionary. They led unconventional personal lives in a society where women were traditionally defined by family, marriage, and children. They had sophisticated taste and were cultured in arts such as literature, painting, dance, and music. Their privileged socio-economic background and exposure gave them the arrogance of class and perhaps helped them develop a career whereas other contemporaries of theirs failed to make a professional dent. Their inner spirit, multiple talents, and fierce independence made them challenge the existing male bastions and transgress established feminine boundaries set by society. Their projects and life stories exist within the limitations of fractured documentation and minimal archival materials. Well-travelled, they were familiar with the art and architecture of the world. With their relative obscurement and neglect in the dominant cannon in the public realm, their work is largely overshadowed by more well-known Indian male (star) architects who are celebrated nationally and internationally.

The Following Generations

Within this context, we need to locate the works of the younger generations that followed. For such a large country like India, with its heterogenous women that have the intersectionality of caste, class, religion, ethnicity, and community, one must resort to generalization. Contemporary women are products of a postcolonial, modernizing society that has retained its traditional and patriarchal roots. It underwent major socio-cultural shifts during the last seventy-five years which have affected the role of women inside and outside their homes. Since the mid-twentieth century, the economic, political, social, and professional changes have profoundly altered the lives, education, and practices of especially the emerging generations of women architects, including the culture of architectural production. The next generation that followed the first women in architecture in the post-

An apartment building designed by Vandana Ranjitsinh in Waked, Pune, 2005
Photo: Vandana Ranjitsinh

Independence period did not have it easy either, despite the examples above. These women took hesitant steps in the profession without mentors and network support, while dealing with severe social restrictions. They mostly belonged to the upper middle class but had to negotiate several forces of resistance while venturing into the public realm, sometimes with non-conventional approaches and attitudes to reach a level of professional excellence. They studied architecture in the 1960s and the 1970s, during the heady days of Nehru's vision for a modern, scientific, and industrializing India, when they were all exposed to modernist theories and praxis which formed an underlying layer to their design approach as they searched for a postcolonial identity.

Since the 1970s, and especially after the 1990s, more and more women have been joining the Colleges of Architecture in India, and yet this is not being reflected in the real world of professional practice, as elsewhere in the world. Many models of practice have also developed over the years: husband-wife teams, male and female/female-female partnerships, group practices, etc. As women architects matured and gained confidence over the decades, one can perceive them taking multiple design directions as they struggle to arrive at an Indian consciousness in architecture. Modernity still exerts a profound influence on most contemporary architects, but many have challenged the universality of modernism. They have moved beyond the formal dictates of rationalism and functionalism, transcending modernist banalities while seeking freedom from the rigidity of the modernist grid.

For them, modernism is reframed as fundamentally transient, plural, and regionalized. Not being aware of the women's movement in the country and belonging to the postfeminist generation, most women architects prefer to call themselves "architects" and perceive no discrimination in the professions.

Anupama Kundoo

A young and rebellious woman architect, Anupama Kundoo, emerged within this scenario in the early 1990s and began a risky, experimental practice in Auroville, a town in the south of India. Auroville arose from an innovative idea of a collective living community where people from different cultures could exist in peace and harmony, regardless of nationality, religion, caste, or politics. Kundoo's main breakthrough came through the design of her own house (*Wall House*) there, as she simultaneously worked with and was mentored by Roger Anger of France, the visionary chief architect of this idealistic settlement project. In the last three decades, Kundoo, who is equally involved in research, education, and practice, has become a global citizen teaching at prestigious universities in various countries of the world, while her projects are largely located in India.

Embedded in the local, Kundoo works with and learns from the craftspeople during the collaborative design and construction process. Her imagination draws from principles of the vernacular but gives it a contemporary, modern form. Involved in exploring innovative technology, alternative building materials, and placed-based context, she is responsive to issues of climate change, sustainability, and community engagement. The integration and synthesis of traditional Indian building customs, crafts, and materials in design are important to her. She lets the process evolve the building aesthetics, with an emphasis on the play of textured surfaces and light, the human scale, and human skills, using "time" as an undervalued resource. Though influenced by the works of Charles Correa and Laurie Baker, she strives for sensual modernism and a search for beauty in her architectural designs.

Being a mother of two children, her achievements take on another level. Though initially in denial about gender disinclination in the profession of architecture, Kundoo is part of the growing awareness in architectural pedagogies that there are injustices, including gender, ethnicity, race, etc. As she continues to teach in many schools of architecture across the globe, Kundoo aims to be a role model to all her students, not only women, on how to become practitioners of architecture who work for justice. Thus, Anupama Kundoo represents a tremendous breadth of accomplishments as well as a heterogeneity of design approaches. The meaning of professional work in her career is plural, as she moves with fluidity within her multiple pursuits. Though Kundoo is embedded in the twenty-first century, her multi-talented personality, high self-esteem, and non-traditional modes of practice link her to the legacy of the first generation of women architects in India. She indeed enjoys a unique place in the contemporary scenario with her transnational achievements and rather earthy Indian ethos.

It is time to decolonize and "depatriarchalize" the discourse in architectural history. This article counteracts canonical and hegemonic master narratives and mainstream histories that are centered both on Western and male canons. It also breaks the myth of the "lone genius" in architecture, either male or female, often linked with success by emphasizing the collaborative model with a bottom-up, inclusive approach. By bringing the pioneering architects' trajectories to the fore, a female genealogy of modernist architecture emerges, which is a relevant context to understand Anupama's contribution to the modern and contemporary architecture of India. The work of contemporary architects stands on the strong shoulders of the generations before her, which is a powerful, existential fact completely missed by today's women. This is an enduring legacy that needs to be built upon for the sake of correcting feminist history.

Anupama Kundoo and a Post-capitalist Future

Peggy Deamer

"Engaging human resources could reduce expenditure of natural resources."[1]

The three main themes of Anupama Kundoo's work—material, human resources, and time—each bring to mind other architects who in different times and different settings have carried the torch of production/social emancipation as they generate architecture. Like hers, all their architectural acts are motivated by theories contesting the dehumanization of both workers and environments that attend industrialization; they all call for replacing capitalism's call for efficiency with that of reinspiring human agency and intelligence. Placing Kundoo's work alongside three others is justified, I feel, not just because they provide resonating analogies but because their a-synchronicity itself provides examples of a theory of time implicit in Kundoo's work. Enter the thoughts of the neo-Marxist, Ernst Bloch, whose theories of history and time can be seen, I'm suggesting, as a stand-in for Kundoo's and for putting her thoughts into a more complete philosophy.[2] At the same time, this theory of a-synchronicity justifies the seemingly random pairings. For materiality, Kundoo is paired with Karl Friedrich Schinkel; for human resources, she is paired with Sérgio Ferro; and for utopianism, she is paired with Tommaso Campanella.

Ernst Bloch (1885–1977) was a German Marxist philosopher who, in his optimism about the future transcending his era's horrific present, was an outlier in Marxist circles. He believed in the "incompleteness" of a world that was "pregnant with unrealized possibilities."[3] In his utopian hermeneutics, he emphasized the immediacy of human experience that itself was character-ized by non-identity and fragility but also the "not yet" of future possibility. His view of history was based on the idea of non-contemporaneity that,

Daylight and Architecture, "Rethinking Materiality: Human Resources and Natural Resources' by Anupama Kundoo." Daylight Talk #16, YouTube video, 1:33:26, https://www.youtube.com/watch?v=Krkn4PgYyoU (accessed September 9, 2024).

2 Thanks must go to Prue Chiles of Newcastle University whose presentation entitled "Talking Time on Site" at the 2024 Production Studies Conference alerted me to the value of Bloch's thinking in organizing an optimistic approach to post-capitalism production.

3 For this summation of Bloch's thinking, I rely on *The Stanford Encyclopedia of Philosophy*, "Ernst Bloch," first published January 25, 2023, https://plato.stanford.edu/entries/bloch/#CoreIdeaUtopPhil.

unlike Marx's teleology, saw change as the result of small acts performed not by the central figures of politics but rather by seemingly peripheral figures who can form "a sudden convergence of every road on an overgrown, insignificant side road that becomes the main road to human progress."[4] This non-identity of historical time gives voice to multiple temporalities—non-Western and Western, quotidian and hegemonic, rational and irrational—and thereby links to efforts at emancipation in one time and place with others spatially and temporally distant. In this way, Bloch saw in history not the failure of the realization of the socialist revolution but rather its potential success in the future.

The connection of this thinking to Kundoo's is certainly based on its optimism. But again, I hope it justifies these non-contemporaneous pairings, each linking her work to other specific eruptions of resistance to the status quo.

Material and Schinkel

While Kundoo is clear that her ultimate interest in material is its connection to human ingenuity (which is the topic of the next section), her attention to and love of materials themselves makes her work unique.[5] Her experiments with bricks, terracotta, and ferrocement demonstrate a tactile, almost essentialist connection to a material's physical properties. She loves the funky nature of a non-standardized brick with its two distinct sides that reveal its making—the rough one that lies on the ground while drying and the smooth one that faces the sky. She loves the "scoop of the volume of earth that could be held within the hands of the craftsman."[6] She loves the firing kiln that itself is made up of the same bricks it will fire. She loves the particular thinned branches of the trees that will make the fire in the kiln. She loves the "bad" brick that in its weakness requires a structural wall to be thicker than the norm and therefore offers better insulation. She loves that the small brick can be deployed for large expanses of walls, floors, and roofs, and these in endless possibilities from smooth/plain to patterned and deco-

4 Ernst Bloch, *Geist der Utopia*, (The Spirit of Utopia), trans. Anthony A. Nassar (Stanford, CA: Stanford University Press, 2000), 15. This is a translation of the Second Edition of this work, published as *Geist der Utopie: Bearbeitete Neuauflage der Fassung von 1923*, Frankfurt am Main, this version Suhrkamp, 1964, https://www.monash.edu/arts/philosophical-historical-indigenous-studies/eras/past-

editions/edition-five-2003-november/ernst-bloch-and-the-utopian-imagination.
5 This summation is gathered from various online sources, the majority of them interviews: "'Rethinking Materiality: Human Resources and Natural Resources' by Anupama Kundoo," Daylight Talk #16; Anupama Kundoo, "Life with Objects," *Achkal*, https://lifewithobjects.org/Anupama-Kundoo.html; "Rethinking

Materiality: Building voids with less resources - Excerpts from a lecture by Anupama Kundoo," transcribed and edited by Cecília Obiol, *Docencia*, https://upcommons.upc.edu/bitstream/handle/2099/15814/3754-864-1-SM.pdf? sequence=1&is Allowed=y.
6 Anupama Kundoo, "Life with Objects." *Achkal*.

rative. She loves the terracotta coming from the same earth that allows for variety of form and structure.

She rejects the tools and materials of modern construction and the protocols that distance the hand from the material and replace care with efficiency. She rejects a system of production that doesn't respect the particular skills of the Indian worker. She embraces instead the brick's embodiment of India's cultural value.

Karl Friedrich Schinkel's interest in brick, unlike Kundoo's, was standardization. But he, like Kundoo, appreciated the essential nature of brick within human production: its connection to locale, its registration of the community of workers, its role in culture-building.[7] Schinkel's Berlin Bauakademie (Academy of Architecture)—constructed between 1832 and 1836—was a freestanding cubic building made entirely of brick: the structure, infill, and terracotta decoration. Institutionally significant and set in a prominent location, the building programmatically brought together all the local institutions training Prussian architects and engineers. Schinkel, as both academy educator and architect, wanted the students to appreciate the need to master local materials and not fall back on the pervasive use of stucco favored for Berlin institutional architecture. In allowing the too-easy application of historical styles and bypassing the supposedly unseemly display of small units that too directly express human labor, stucco would not be right for the academy. The all-brick Bauakademie stimulated the site inspector, Emil Flaminius, to write, "it is easy to overlook the fact that the…entire architecture…strives to embody the indigenous fired clay in all parts of the building and, through this, to show [the brick's] suitability for the various aspects of construction and form and, in its perfection of technical workmanship, to stimulate new advances in the manufacturing process itself."[8] Schinkel also wanted the public to understand that Berlin's essential nature was not bourgeoise haute culture (stucco historicism) but, rather, its humble and severe Prussian character.

The story of Schinkel's Bauakademie is completely taken from Laila Seewang's "Landscapes of Clay," *Curatorial Design: A Place Between*, eds. Dubravka Sekulić, Anousheh Kehar, and Julia Wagner. was introduced to this work through my participation with the editors of *Curatorial Design* on a piece for this same issue entitled Construction as Plan: A Conversation on Design Materiality," a conversation between myself and Albert Refiti, https://www.curatorialdesign.org/landscapes-of-clay/ (accessed September 9, 2024).

8   Emil Flaminius, "Ueber den Bau des Hauses für die allgemeine Bauschule in Berlin," *Allgemeine Bauzeitung* 1, no. 3 (1836): 4.

The reinstatement of a craft-based material into Berlin architecture required standardization, not seen by Schinkel as challenging the value of the hand-made but as its refinement. Until the Bauakademie, the projects requiring large quantities of brick were resourced from various local brickyards, the mixture of brick quality and appearance presenting no problem since they were largely used for non-aesthetically-driven infrastructural projects. But for his building, Schinkel needed to go outside Berlin to find a factory that could experiment with new techniques of production. At the Wentzel's brickworks in Brandenburg, the mixing of water and clay, traditionally done by feet, was augmented by machine, although the feet were the final arbiter of smoothness. Drying, usually done outside, was moved indoors where hot air could be piped in. The wood firing the kiln was aged so moisture would not degrade the strength of the brick. And a newly invented kiln that, with a second interior shell that prevented ash from falling on bricks and causing discoloration, needed to be purchased. Meanwhile, the terracotta necessary for the finishing work—which could not be done by the Wentzel workers—required Schinkel to seek out local sculptors with no previous construction knowledge but now became tradesmen on site.

The result was a building that not only showed off its earthy production but also symbolized what I would call a Blochian understanding of history. As Friedrich Adler, the Austrian socialist politician declared at the time, the Bauakademie "belongs neither to antiquity, nor even less to the Middle Ages or to the Renaissance. It reveals the transcendence of any narrow historical attachment; it is like a grain of seed, which promises further organic unfolding."[9]

Again, Schinkel's goal of brick standardization is the opposite of Kundoo's praise of non-standardization. But the similarity of their shared respect for innate materiality, for the workers who engaged with it, and for the cultural meaning embedded in its use is evident, as is their shared commitment to swerve architectural production away from their era's idea of "modern" construction, where "modern" implies both bourgeoise taste and economic efficiency. They form a Blochian super-contemporaneity that reveals an ongoing plea to redirect architectural "progress" toward a simpler, more sustainable logic.

9   Friedrich Adler, "Schinkelfestrede," *Zeitschrift für Bauwesen* 19 (1869): 473, in Laila Seewang's "Landscapes of Clay," *Curatorial Design: A Place Between.*

Human Knowledge/Resource and Sérgio Ferro

Kundoo writes, "Often [the] hand-crafted…holds the life of the maker within it," and she wonders "if the human is in control or if the tool has started controlling the human."[10] In this, she follows in the tradition of John Ruskin who believed, in his support of Gothic architecture, that the stone carvers of past centuries should see their familiarity with stone as an opportunity to explore self-expression and creative fulfillment. Like Ruskin, Kundoo insists that human knowledge is best released via material engagement; books, they both insist, mean nothing if they remain outside the human body. And she, like Ruskin, believes that this tactile intelligence builds social and historical intelligence. In this, Kundoo is also a follower of Mahatma Gandhi, who was influenced by Ruskin. Gandhi, who famously wrote that "The progress of a country depends not on mass production, but on the production of the masses," honored work that united heart, hand, and mind.[11]

Kundoo's dislike for India's pervasive use of reinforced concrete was similar to Schinkel's of stucco: it does not use or empower local knowledge. But her critique goes beyond the specifics of concrete; it is directed at the mechanization of labor in modern construction in general. Sérgio Ferro, (1938–present), the Brazilian Marxist architect now exiled in France, is not as devoted to the science of materials as Kundoo but he nevertheless is dismissive of all materials that mask construction labor—cladding, for example, exists only to hide the work on the structural shell—and he decries the wasted labor deployed in producing the non-essential materials invented only for bourgeoise aesthetic pleasure. But his particular disgust, as it was for Kundoo, is saved for reinforced concrete, which he says replaced the on-site carpenters and masons with the unskilled labor of mixing and casting concrete and moved skilled labor to the engineer's office.[12] The result was not only the evisceration of local production knowledge but the disarming of construction unions.

Ferro came to his Marxist theory of construction labor abuse via his observations of construction practices during the building of Brasília. There he came to see the dangerous on-site working conditions as the systemic exploitation of construction labor. He writes: "I lived with workers who participated in that construction. They told me of a suffering that we

---

"Rethinking Materiality: Building voids with less resources – Excerpts from a lecture by Anupama Kundoo," transcribed and edited by Cecília Obiol, *Docencia*.

11 I thank Mary Woods for pointing this connection to Gandhi out.

12 See Paula Koury's chapter entitled "Unionization as a Political Issue: The Debate in the Architects' Union of São Paulo

(1972–1981)" in the forthcoming *Building Sites: Architecture, Labour, and the Field of Production Studies* (London: Routledge, 2025), chap. 6.

understood poorly then: numerous suicides, workers throwing themselves under trucks, dysentery almost every day, surrounded, without being able to leave."[13] In this, Ferro saw that the architecture profession was particularly complicit in capitalism's alienation of labor. Through drawings that presented an exclusive language foreign to constructors, through an assumption of an ignorant and resistant workforce, and through an unquestioned acceptance of the division of trades labor, architects, Ferro believed, performed capitalism's dirty work.

Ferro developed a sweeping theory of architecture history that rested on three main ideas. The first is his foregrounding the construction site as the arena of study. In bypassing design as the essence of architecture history, he moved the subject of architecture away from the white-collar office to the location of construction work. He viewed the history of architecture as the sequence of the design profession's adaptation to the different stages of labor's exploitation.[14] The second was his identification of architecture as "manufacture," a state of arrested development in industrialization that still relies on the vast array of workers providing surplus labor and surplus value. As Ferro writes, "[Manufacture] is a discontinuous, heterogeneous and heteronomous process in which the totalisation of the collective worker at its root inevitably comes from the outside, i.e. from the side of the owner of the means of production. Without this totalisation, and under the crumbling and prevailing acephalic conditions imposed on production, there cannot be a product — nor, therefore, a commodity."[15] The third was his realization, à la Bloch, that most Marxist teleology missed the real sites worthy of analysis. As the historians Pedro Arantes and Mariana Fix write:

> For Sérgio, the principal field of experimentation is not within capitalist or so-called conventional production but in "socially liberated" territories by popular organisations (such as agrarian reform settlements, urban occupations, and social housing zones in major centres). These areas possess malleability because capital shows little interest in them; they are "pockets" socially liberated

13 Sérgio Ferro quoted in Richard J. Williams, "Brasília after Brasília," *Progress in Planning* 67, no. 4 (May 2007): 301–66. And found in Spatial Agency: Se Ferro, https://www.spatialagency.net/database/Sérgio.ferro.

14 At the start of "Concrete as Weapon," Ferro cites Karl Marx in *Capital*, "It would be possible to write quite a history of the inventions made since 1830, for the sole purpose of supplying

capital with weapons against working class revolt." See "Concrete as Weapon," in *Sérgio Ferro: Architecture from Below* (London: Mack, 2024), 177, although manufacture is discussed on pages 25–28 in that book. See also *Karl Marx, Capital: A Critique of Political Economy*, Volume 1 (London: Penguin: *New Left Review*, [1867] 1976), 563. Also in *Harvard Design Magazine* no. 46, 2018, 8.

15 This quote is from "The building site and the design; The form of commodity form," a piece read in the Ferro reading group that I was a part of; it is not published in the book of his translations, *Sérgio Ferro: Architecture from Below* (London: Mack, 2024), although manufacture is discussed on pages 25–28 in that book.

that globalisation itself leads to form. The indispensable conditions are: the suppression of capitalist relations of production, total autonomy of production, recognition of the workers' know-how, including the recovery of knowledge and constructive cultures that have been lost or erased/decimated by capital.[16]

Kundoo does not explicitly write about India's analogous huge nation-building projects that exploited labor at least at the scale of Brazil. Nehru's ambitious program of modernization—think Chandigarh and the hydro-electric dams—which were deemed "temples of India," were not just dismissals of local building trades but full-scale disruptions to local communities.[17] Kundoo's and Ferro's critique of industrialization must be then viewed as not just a plea for better construction conditions in general, but as preservation of their countries' ability to integrate labor knowledge and community building. As both countries entered capitalism's world stage through the BRICS (Brazil, Russia, India, China, and South Africa) economic "revolution," they imitated Western expansionist exploitation even as they struggle to get away from the domination of the US dollar. In our Blochian narrative, we can say that Ferro and Kundoo present, in different countries and slightly different eras, an alternative vision of growth based on local construction knowledge.

Time/Utopia and Tomasso Campanella

It might be unfair to link Kundoo's notion of time to utopianism. She dislikes the term and when it comes up in the context of her work, wants to replace it with other aspirational terms. She would "rather use the word idealistic than utopian."[18] She would rather think of her place of retreat, Auroville, as a lab or an experiment. But she protesteth too much. Her optimism about time as it stretches toward the future—one similar to Bloch's and his direct linking of time's reach toward utopianism—is, on the one hand, non-linear and individually activated and, on the other, motivated by possibilities for the future. Kundoo, like Bloch, wants to find the ways the future can be

---

6   Pedro Fiori Arantes and Mariana Fix, "The Building Site and the City: Radical Criticism and Emancipation in Sérgio Ferro and David Harvey," in the forthcoming *Building Sites: Architecture, Labour, and the Field of Production Studies* (London: Routledge, 2025), chap. 4.

7   Kundoo did not witness these construction projects as did Ferro in Brazil, but she was part of a generation of architects who rebelled against Indira Gandhi's "Emergency" policies that, in continuing a push for growth, suspended civil liberties and imprisoned political opponents. Thank you to Mary Woods for drawing my attention to this observation.

18   Zohra Khan, "Anupama Kundoo on furthering the urban vision of Auroville as the 'City of Dawn,'" *Stir World*, February 24, 2023, https://www.stirworld.com/inspire-people-anupama-kundoo-on-furthering-the-urban-vision-of-auroville-as-the-city-of-dawn.

discovered, recognized, and explored in the present. She says, "Time is the most essential resource that we have access to as living beings, and it points to a future of continued knowledge collection."[19] Likewise, Auroville, where she lived from 1989 to 2005 and where she was Head of Urban Design until 2024,[20] is based on the typical utopian goals of idealism, self-fulfillment, social harmony, spiritual awakening, communal ownership, lack of competition, a classless society, and the denial of material goods.

Conceived in 1965 and inaugurated in 1968, the City of Dawn, as Auroville was named, was designed as a place for like-minded people who, liberated from daily chores and investing their time in the nourishment of higher consciousness, live harmoniously with each other and the cosmos. The community was conceived of by Blanche Rachel Mirra Alfassa (The Mother; 1878–1973) in spiritual collaboration with Sri Aurobindo (1872–1950), the Indian philosopher, yogi, maharishi, poet, and Indian nationalist. The Mother wanted the City of Dawn to be, in the words of Kundoo, "a site of physical, material and spiritual research, and a laboratory for human society."[21] The charter for Auroville is:

> Auroville belongs to nobody in particular. Auroville belongs to humanity as a whole. But to live in Auroville, one must be a willing servitor of the Divine Consciousness.

> Auroville will be the place of an unending education, of constant progress, and a youth that never ages.

> Auroville wants to be the bridge between the past and the future. Taking advantage of all discoveries from without and from within, Auroville will boldly spring towards future realizations.

> Auroville will be a site of material and spiritual researches for a living embodiment of an actual Human Unity.[22]

The Mother's vision was made concrete and complete by the French architect Roger Anger. Anger's city, or what he called the "Galaxy Plan," is 3.2 miles in diameter, organized around a central golden spherical meditation center, the Matrimandir. Two design strategies radiate out from this center. One is a series of six concentric rings that separate quiet green spaces from contemplative, active, and solitary spaces. The other organizational feature is a series of twisting sweeps of different functional zones—residential, cultural, industrial, and international—that spiral out of the center. The

---

19 Ibid.
20 Ibid.
21 Ibid.

22 Maddy Crowell, "Trouble in Utopia," *Slate*, July 24, 2015, https://www.slate.com/articles/news_and_politics/roads/2015/07/ auroville_india_s_famed_utopian_community_struggles_with_crime_and_corruption.html.

design as a whole symbolizes the interconnectedness of the city with the energy of the cosmos, on the one hand, and the energy of the interior life of the individual, on the other. Everything is collectively owned, competition for material accumulation and social status is shunned, and self-sufficiency, curiosity, and the pursuit of future knowledge tie the community together.

Tommaso Campanella's *City of the Sun* (1602) was a text written by the Italian Dominican friar, philosopher, theologian, astrologer, and poet while in prison for conspiring against the Spanish rulers of Calabria. The book is constructed as a dialogue between a Genovese sea captain and an interrogator in which the sea captain describes in detail an ideal city he found in Taprobane (an actual island in what is now Sri Lanka).

The *City of the Sun* is a text, but Campanella describes his ideal city in such detail that its plan and architecture can be easily drawn; it feels physical. The town is two miles in diameter and organized around seven concentric rings/walls. These rings are named for and based on the patterns of the sun and the (at that time) six known planets of the solar system. In addition to their cosmic reference, the seven rings serve multiple purposes: dwelling, fortification, education, and work. The central temple houses the Meta-physician, who is wise to all things and controls the three equal powers: Wisdom (arts, mechanics, and science), Love (partnering and breeding), and Power (war and peace). But the Metaphysician's role was not to control as much as to offer a religion of nature that establishes a sort of osmosis between the city and the cosmos. As a structure, the temple is open to the stars and directs attention to the mystery of the physical universe.

Knowledge was central to Solarian citizenship and the city is essentially a didactic information machine using painted murals on the ring walls that depict images from the arts and sciences. Because Campanella believed that knowledge was a physical sensation and not enclosed in books — indeed, he believed that non-human objects had sensations — the visual lessons of the murals, Campanella believed, promoted a quicker and more efficient form of learning. As a believer in the idea that non-human objects had sensations, the physical design of the palaces that made up the rings (and housed the community) themselves were manifestations and conveyors of knowledge. Obsessed with various inventions — Campanella explored vessels capable of sailing without wind, carts with sails, and stirrups that permit one to guide horses using only one's feet — he saw the City of the Sun as a center of innovation, a lab of experimentation.

Work was also guided by the enclosing walls with different jobs being located in the spaces between rings walls, each trade harmoniously aligned with the planets linked to the rings' identities. Citizens are not identified with a "family" but rather with their trade; Solarians each experience all lines of work, then chose the one for which they are most suited. No job was considered vile or inferior to another; where Plato had excluded artisans, peasants, and those involved in manual labor from the category of full citizenship and from the highest levels of virtue, Campanella prioritized their physical, tactile work. The only forbidden thing was idleness, an attribute linked to nobility. In this redeemed world, with no slaves or servants, property was held in common and citizens were spared competing for goods, prestige, or power and, as a result, no one experienced injustice.

The City of the Sun is similar to Auroville/City of Dawn not just for its central organization, various concentric rings, cosmological references, and metaphysical spirituality, but also for many of the attributes Kundoo has supported in her work having nothing in particular to do with Auroville. The emphasis on knowledge as a human resource to be developed through physical, tactile engagement; the idea that productive and self-fulfilling work links one to communal citizenship; the belief in sensation as a source for experimentation; the belief in material as a living presence—all of this links Kundoo to Campanella. And given that Auroville/City of Dawn exists in 2024 and City of the Sun was proposed in 1602, one has to think that the more things change, the more they stay the same. This sameness can be a reason for criticizing utopianism: it keeps popping up and never fulfilling a revolutionary promise; after all, Marx and Lenin were critical of utopias for this failure, noting that utopias lacked a dialectical, teleological framing of their role in history. But as Frederic Jameson (a follower of Bloch) has written about utopian thinking, "The Utopian idea, on the contrary, keeps alive the possibility of a world qualitatively distinct from this one and takes the form of a stubborn negation of all that is."[23] It is, for him, a form of praxis. Schinkel, Ferro, Campanella, and Kundoo: they form a constellation of architects pushing for architectural and social reform.

Summary

Kundoo's reticence to identify as Marxist, socialist, or anti-capitalist might be strategic for either ideological (she recognizes the problems of identifying as a utopian optimist) or political reason (it prevents her from getting work in India). Or she just may not believe. Nevertheless, one wants to see her

---

23 Frederic Jameson, *Marxism and Form: Twentieth Century Dialectical Theories of Literature*, (Princeton: Princeton University Press, 1971), 110–111, https://www-jstor-org.yale.idm.oclc.org/stable/pdf/20719758.pdf?refreqid =fastly-default%3Aa7f6de1c2f1 130b2f624bfcb5b8a82eb&ab_ segments=&origin=&initiator= &acceptTC=1; see also Frederic Jameson, "The Politics of Utopia," *New Left Review*, https:// newleftreview.org/issues/ii25/ articles/fredric-jameson-the-politics-of-utopia (accessed September 9, 2024).

position on architectural production as a fight against architecture's role in capitalism. Her work is merely brave and well-intentioned as a one-off but as proof of an ongoing and lively praxis striving for a post-capitalist future, it might have historical value.

Indeed, without her placement in a lineage of like-minded architectural thinkers, the "success" of her work would look frustratingly compromised.[24] At the local level, Auroville must be contextualized by the lack of harmony amongst its residents, as there are unspoken but real hierarchies regarding who is an authentic Aurovilian and who is not, as well as a community divided by disagreements over the need to complete Anger's "Galaxy Plan."[25] At the regional level, Auroville's role as a sanctuary sequestered off from worldly problems is compromised by the fact that the Indian government supports Auroville with annual payments of $200,000 and expects political allegiance in exchange.[26] At the national level, India's ambitious goal to become a developed nation by 2047 relies heavily on promoting a dynamic real estate sector that contributes 7.3% to GDP[27] but ignores the environmental damage "growth" policies bring—India is a major participant to the built environment's 42% global contribution to annual global CO_2 emissions—and the fact that growth favors the Indian elites. During the last five years, the income of the top 1% grew from 10% to 22% while that of the bottom 50% has been matched by a corresponding decline.[28] Likewise, despite (or because of) her hope for the City of Dawn, her practice has been disconnected from that of other (largely women) Indian architects working for building

24 Being unfamiliar with Kundoo's work prior to the invitation to write this piece, I must thank my colleague Mary Woods, whose familiarity with the women architects in India and the context in which Kundoo works has been both indispensable and enlightening.

25 See Emily Schmall, "Build a New City or New Humans? A Utopia in India Fights Over Future," *New York Times*, March 5, 2022, https://www.nytimes.com/2022/03/05/world/asia/auroville-india.html, and Hannah Ellis-Petersen "Bulldozers, violence and politics crack an Indian dream of utopia," *The Guardian*, January 16, 2022, https://www.theguardian.com/world/2022/jan/16/bulldozers-violence-and-politics-crack-an-indian-dream-of-utopia.

26 The government-appointed secretary of the Auroville Foundation, Jayanti Ravi (a civil servant), a primary advocate for Auroville's continued development, has a high-profile position in Prime Minister Narendra Modi's home state.

27 Anshuman Magazine, "How Modi government can turn India into a real estate powerhouse in Union Budget, brick by brick," *The Economic Times*, July 16, 2024, https://economictimes.indiatimes.com/industry/services/property-/-cstruction/how-modi-govt-can-turn-india-into-a-real-estate-powerhouse-in-union-budget-brick-by-brick/articleshow/111781479.cms?from=mdr.

28 Architecture 2030, Why the Built Environment?, https:// www.architecture2030.org/why-the-built-environment/ (accessed September 9, 2024).

policy changes in India. One wishes there were a more overt political or organizational agenda beyond her idealist praxis.[29]

Despite this, one should resist agreeing with what hard-core Marxists might say about Kundoo's work on materials, human resources, and utopian time: that it constitutes at best a tiny, small island in an ocean of capitalism. A Blochian interpretation counters this crude Marxism by positing a different view on how the "revolution" will occur. The architectural acts that build up to a post-capitalist world, in his framing, are never isolated and never linearly rolled out. Rather, they add up over time, become constituent parts of our knowledge, and take up space in our being. This paper is an effort to persuade us architects of the importance of giving this space light and air.

29   It should be noted that all the other architects identified here were engaged in politics. Campanella's involvement in a conspiracy to overthrow Spanish rule in Calabria in the hope of replacing it with a new society led to his arrest in 1599 by the Spanish authorities; after he was released, he was arrested a second time and subsequently tortured. Ferro was exiled to France due to his involvement in left-wing political activities during Brazil's military dictatorship (1964–1985). Schinkel was not a radical nor did he hold official Prussian governmental positions, but he was variously Chief Architect for the Prussian Court, a member of the Prussian Building Commission, and Director of the Prussian Office of Public Works.

Capital, Extraction, Labor
Essays

Constructing Carbon Colonialism: The Body, The Built Environment, and the Global Politics of Extraction

Laurie Parsons

Drip, drip, drip, tamp, scribble, rip, turn over, f-, sorry...
but on again, the drip, drip, drip. I'm sorry, please wait a moment,
I'm sorry, oh for f-...

So transpired one of my first, truly physical confrontations with the built environment in the global South. It was the late noughties and I had come to interview a community of construction workers on the outskirts of Phnom Penh, Cambodia, to learn about their livelihoods at the coalface of the rapidly expanding urban sprawl. At this time, in this expanding urban periphery, the interlinking lakes and marshes that once defined the Cambodian capital were still a feature of the landscape. Former irrigation canals filled with rubbish connected pools of water, stagnant yet fecund with sprouting morning glory. Blocks of rented rooms punctuated this limbo landscape: an interstitial, transient stage between the rural and the urban, a place hurrying both to appear and disappear and fully aware of its impermanence.

Having arrived in this dusty, humid land of change and seeking an appropriately ethical privacy for my interviews, I accepted an invitation into one of those workers' rented rooms: an 8×8-foot square box amongst a single story, single skin, brick block of a dozen or so similar apartments. And learn I did, but just not in the way I had anticipated as I arrived, armed with a list of questions and pen. I learned with my body, my pores, my frustration and embarrassment. I learned by my ostentatious failure to do the normal tasks that constitute my working life. I learned that competence is contextual; that the nuts and bolts of expertise rest on architectural privilege; that the built environment doesn't just support livelihoods, it molds them, by cutting off certain avenues and leaving others open.

It didn't, however, feel like learning at the time, as I tried and failed, over and over again, to note down what the construction worker I was speaking with was saying. Yet time and again, the drips from my forehead kept coming, smudging, wetting, spoiling. Until finally I admitted defeat. This time, this place, this activity, were not compatible. You cannot sit and write and speak in privacy in a Cambodian late afternoon. Or more specifically, you cannot do it here, in this room, or one of the hundreds of thousands just like it that house Cambodia's huge internal migrant worker population. You cannot write in peace, read or speak alone, if you are a construction worker, a garment worker, or a garbage worker. These are activities for other places and other people.

This should not have surprised me. After all, it is a rather similar point to the one made by Virginia Woolf[1] almost a century ago. Her famous contention, then, in a very different climate and a very different context that "a woman must have money and a room of her own if she is to write fiction" helped to elucidate the relation between the built environment and the reproduction of unequal privilege in society. Yet its wider implications tend not to be examined in much depth. If unequal privilege in the built environment structures the capacity for creative thought, how might it structure other forms of work? How, indeed, do the objects we spend our lives within structure our embodiment of the climate?

This was not a question I was expecting to be asking at this point. After all, I was no stranger to this country or its climate—or at least I thought I wasn't. Yet there is a difference between passive knowledge of our environment and what Bharat Venkat[2] calls "positive knowledge": Knowledge acquired through "the body as a kind of sensing technology" which not only absorbs the heat it perceives but is transformed by it. This is a very different way of knowing the climate to that which can be acquired through thermometer data or newspaper weather forecasts. And it is precisely this kind of knowledge that is needed to interpret the construction of carbon colonialism.

As a foreigner blessed with all the privileges and exceptions that brings, I had never previously struggled to write, to think, even to *be* in the built environment I inhabited. And this, at last, was the point. I had lived for years mere minutes from this place, yet as I had not until that soggy moment realized, I did not share the city with those who built it. Instead, I lived within an invisibly stratified grid within that city: one in which the sharpest corners of the environment had been sanded off.

And this was no unique feature of my own privilege. The man who owned the block of rented rooms did not have to suffer their rigors. Nor did the shopkeepers nearby, although as roadside dwellers they faced their own problems with the endless exhaust fumes of their passing trade. No, as I

Virginia Woolf, "A Room of One's vn," (London: The Hogarth Press, 29), 5.

2   Bharat Jayram Venkat, "Through a glass darkly: race, thermal sensation and the nervous body in late colonial India," *BJHS Themes* 7 (2022): 124.

would later come to realize, neither I nor the construction worker I had been sweated so profusely at is an exception. Everybody inhabits their own grid, often without realizing it. Everybody's positive knowledge of the environment is shaped by its built components and, by extension, the social inequalities baked into them.

This is a principle that transcends scales: as true in the sweat of a rented room as it is on a global scale. It is also as true of the present as it was of the colonial era, when heat began to be configured as both biological variation and a pathology: a "specific configuration of human–environment relations, one in which various kinds of bodies were understood to be differentially affected" by it.[3] We live, as we did then, within worlds built on these embodied prejudices: a scientific, ethical, and architectural normalization of thermal inequality.

So in this chapter, my aim is to elucidate and connect some of these relations, to link the embodied physicality of a hot and humid room both to the politics of extraction that saw it thus constructed, and the economics of inequality that keeps its inhabitants bound to structures like these. In this regard, a key goal is to extend the genealogy of tropical architecture into the wider context of the global economy and its dynamic yet durable inequities. Much as Ching has done for its architectural dimensions,[4] this chapter will emphasize the material and human underwiring of everyday architecture in the tropics. Focusing on the hot, humid, low-income country of Cambodia as its key exemplar, it will thus contribute to wider debates around environmental imperialism[5] by highlighting the less visible impacts of the built environment on laboring populations within and outside the global supply chains that drive and shape urban development.

Carbon Colonialism and the Built Environment

Though all of us live within the built environment, those of us who do not study or make a living from it tend to give it little thought until it goes wrong. Only when the temperature drops to the point that we have to reach for another jumper, or rises so high that we need to wipe our brow, do we start thinking about matters like insulation and ventilation. If discomfort like this keeps happening, then we might arrive at the conclusion that our environment is badly made. We might even diagnose the cause—whether poor insulation, or a lack of ventilation—but this reflection rarely extends beyond

3 Ibid.: 119.
4 Francis D. K. Ching, *Architecture: Form, Space, and Order*, 4th ed. (Hoboken, NJ: John Wiley & Sons, 2016).

5 See, for instance, Alfred W. Crosby, *Ecological Imperialism: The Biological Expansion of Europe, 900–1900* (Cambridge, UK: Cambridge University Press, 1986).

the circumstantial. The question almost never asked is what the underlying factors were that led to the construction of an uncomfortable home.

Yet this is a question that, once unpacked, opens up a great many more. After all, whenever your house, apartment, or office was constructed, it is unlikely to have been thrown up in ignorance. Buildings are designed and constructed for a reason. If they are poorly made, this suggests not a disinterest in doing better, but either a lack of money to achieve a better outcome, or a building meeting an environment distinct from the one in which it was designed.

With this in mind, one of the things that has most often struck me about my encounter with construction workers in the global South is the contrast between the buildings on which they work, and those in which they live. In Cambodia, the bulk of construction workers spend their working life moving between mid- to large-scale, prestige projects that they will never be able to own, rent, or even visit once they are complete. This is a huge and dynamic industry, by national standards. In 2023 alone, for example, the Ministry of Land Management approved 3,207 projects, the majority in the capital Phnom Penh.[6] The average cost of an apartment in the dominant "high end" condo sector was a staggering 2,200 USD per square meter at the last count.[7] Yet a construction worker earns on average 5-10 USD per day, or about 150-300 USD per month. Even if he or she saved their entire salary, it would take forty years for a construction worker to earn enough money to purchase a fifty square meter, one-bedroom flat that they had built.

So they do not, of course, purchase one. Instead, construction workers have one of two choices. They can either live with other construction workers for free in the skeleton of the building they are constructing—with only a mosquito net, a mattress, and a few cooking pots to call home—or they attempt to put down roots in the city they are building, in one of the blocks of airless rented rooms we encountered at the start of this chapter. It is a decision that rests often simply on lifecycle. A young, single construction worker of twenty may be content to enjoy the freedom and spare cash of life in a building skeleton, but an older one with a family may not wish to spend their life in the company of their workmates. And so, the choice presents itself: to remain a homeless laborer or live in a home of restriction and discomfort. Choose as you wish, but sweat is the cost of any roots you may wish to put down.

Chea Vanyuth, "Construction investments rise to $5.4 billion," *Khmer Times*, April 9, 2024, https://www.khmertimeskh.com/501469670/construction-investments-rise-to-5-4-billion/.

7   CBRE (Cambodia Business and Real Estate), *Phnom Penh Mid-Year Review 2024* (Phnom Penh: CBRE, 2024).

This juxtaposition between the labor that sends the soaring skyscrapers of the global South's capitals skyward and the reward it brings, between the builders and the owners of the urban landscape, is a discomfiting reality. Yet a closer look brings deeper disjunctures still. If the labor that organizes the materiality of the built environment brings little reward, that which crafts those materials is worth next to nothing. Around the world, the brick industry, the hidden engine room of a global urbanization acceleration that has seen almost two billion urban dwellers born or arrived since the turn of the millennium,[8] is a hotbed of modern slavery and child labor.[9] In many cases, brick workers are only paid in the sense that they are kept alive, for a time.

Unable to leave, unable to repay the debts that bond them, unable even in some cases to imagine a better life for their children—who in some cases must take on their debts when they are too old to service them[10]—life in the brick sector is for many, a "burning prison."[11] Exposed not only to the ferocity of the sun, but also the fierce heat of brick kilns which reach up to 1500°C at their peak, brick workers are amongst the most environmentally vulnerable populations in the world. In Cambodia, even the corrugated zinc houses in which they sleep—set mere meters from the kiln—are little respite.[12]

So, it is little surprise that, as emerging data suggest, brick workers' bodies are living in a different environment entirely to most of those who live amongst the bricks they mold. A recent study I conducted of thirty Cambodian brick workers[13] indicated that every one of them experienced core temperatures over 38°C—the generally agreed occupational safe working limit[14]—during the seven working days they were surveyed. Within this, brick workers spent on average 8.7% of their working time with a core temperature over 38°C: equivalent to over six hours of an average seventy-hour working week. In one brick kiln, workers spent 15.23% of working minutes above this threshold, equivalent to more than an hour a day every

---

8   World Bank Group, "Urban Development," April 3, 2023, https://www.worldbank.org/en/topic/urbandevelopment/overview.

9   See Katherine Brickell, Laurie Parsons, Nithya Natarajan, and Sopheak Chann, *Blood Bricks: Untold Stories of Modern Slavery and Climate Change from Cambodia* (Egham: Royal Holloway University of London, 2018), as well as Doreen S. Boyd, Bethany Jackson, Jessica Wardlaw, Giles M. Foody, Stuart Marsh, and Kevin Bales, "Slavery from Space: Demonstrating the role for

satellite remote sensing to inform evidence-based action related to UN SDG number 8," *ISPRS Journal of Photogrammetry and Remote Sensing* no. 142 (2018): 380–88.

10   Brickell et al., *Blood Bricks*.

11   BBC News, *Working conditions in Cambodia like 'a burning prison,'* February 1, 2024, multi-format television, radio, print, and online exposé, in collaboration with Laura Bicker, https://www.bbc.com/news/world-asia-68102771.

12   Brickell et al.

13   Laurie Parsons and Ly Vouch Long, *Heat Stress in the Cambodian Brick Sector. Thermal*

Working Paper #1 (Egham: Royal Holloway University of London, 2023).

14   Dallon T. Lamarche, Robert D. Meade, Andrew W. D'Souza, Andreas D. Flouris, Stephen G. Hardcastle, Ronald J. Sigal, Pierre Boulay, and Glen P. Kenny, "The recommended Threshold Limit Values for heat exposure fail to maintain body core temperature within safe limits in older working adults," *Journal of Occupational and Environmental Hygiene* 14, no. 9 (2017): 703–11.

day: an intolerable physiological risk in any other context and one whose impacts brick workers themselves are well aware of. As one worker stated:

> "They don't let us to take a rest till break time. Then, I feel close to dying. If the time is not up, then we have to continue working although we are extremely exhausted... They don't allow us to take a break because they are afraid of slowing down the production. If [somebody] reports [an unauthorized break] to the boss, they will blame us badly... [It is normally hottest in] March and April. However, [this year] it is still hot till May. Now many workers and their children are sick. They are being injected [with glucose in order to work]." (Sarath, brick worker, May 2023)

As Sarath continued:

> "If it is so hot like this, we cannot survive as the owner does not allow us to take a short break during working time... It has been so hot since Khmer New Year [April 15, 2023]. The owner does not come and they don't lend money. We don't have money to buy food. It is very miserable. Some workers... have to find clams and snails at the back of the kiln for food. Even then, though, we get blamed by the kiln manager by not working at the brick but going to find the snails and clams." (Sarath, brick worker, May 2023)[15]

Before long, all of this adds up to a single downwards pathway in health, livelihood, and well-being. There is a bleakness and resignation to kiln work that is unusual in other sectors; an awareness of the end to which all these unendurable labors are pointing. As one brick worker had previously outlined to me in gruesome detail:

> "Kiln work has harmed my health, and I nearly died. I suffered from bleeding because the place was extremely hot... Most workers have health problems like me, like problems with their lungs. Most of them became thinner and thinner, and whilst some workers were allowed to go home, some died, and the owner's only assistance to them was in giving them a coffin to be buried in."[16]

There are innumerable similar examples, from concrete makers to welders, from those who dredge the sand to make windows, to those who cut the trees to make doors, tables, and chairs—but the crux is the same: there is one environment for the builders and one for the buyers. One economy, two environments. Or more accurately, one economy, two directions: an economy in which the fruits of environmental exploitation move inexorably

---

5 Parsons and Long, *Heat Stress.*

16 Brick worker Tola, cited in Brickell et al.

in one direction, whilst the risk and waste associated with exploiting those environments moves in the other.[17]

What, though, does this have to do with colonialism? As it turns out, everything. Economic trajectories like this do not simply happen by accident. They have to be envisioned, implemented, nurtured, and sustained. And this is exactly what has happened in Cambodia, over its ninety years of colonial rule and the subsequent seventy years of postcolonial emplacement within the global economy. Like many of its global Southern peers, Cambodia's economy is built for extraction, both in the form of labor and resources. The result is a system in which the environmental cost of wealth generation is paid in places far from where that wealth is accumulated.[18]

And so it manifests in the Kingdom's proliferating urban landscape. In one direction flows the value generated by Cambodia's property boom, absorbed by foreign buyers, investors, and companies.[19] In the other flows— or, better put, stagnates—the degradation that accompanies that value, absorbed by Cambodian bodies, sweltering in environments built from a tiny proportion of the value they create, and Cambodian lands, denuded of their forests and baked into the proliferating urban skyline. This is the engine of the climate crisis.

Constructing Climate Change

The construction sector is responsible for almost two fifths of global energy-related emissions,[20] a staggering statistic in one sense, but also one with an inherent ring of truth. In perception and discourse, the expansion of the built environment has always been closely connected to environmental breakdown, whether the "dark satanic mills" of William Blake,[21] or in a more recently positive sense, as the "sustainable cities"[22] that will deliver us from the crisis we have created. So, whether for good or for bad, the building, the urban, the materiality of construction is always there, always

17 Laurie Parsons, *Carbon colonialism: How rich countries export climate breakdown* (Manchester, UK: Manchester University Press, 2023).

18 See Parsons, *Carbon colonialism*; Farhana Sultana, "The unbearable heaviness of climate coloniality," *Political Geography* 99 (2022): 102638; Jason Hickel, Christian Dorninger, Hanspeter Wieland, and Intan Suwandi, "Imperialist appropriation in the world economy: Drain from the global South through unequal

exchange, 1990–2015," *Global Environmental Change* 73 (2022): 102467.

19 Gabriel Fauveaud, "The new frontiers of housing financialization in Phnom Penh, Cambodia: The condominium boom and the foreignization of housing markets in the Global South," *Housing Policy Debate* 30, no. 4 (2020): 661–79.

20 UNEP (United Nations Environment Programme), *Beyond foundations: Mainstreaming sustainable solutions to cut*

emissions from the buildings sector, Global Status Report for Buildings and Construction (Nairobi: UNEP, 2024).

21 William Blake, "And did those feet in ancient time," in *William Blake, Milton: A Poem in Two Books* (London: Associated University Presses, 1808).

22 Graham Haughton and Colin Hunter, *Sustainable Cities* (London: Routledge, 2004).

changing, but always growing too. We can change how we build, but build we must. It is how we bend the world around us to our will. It is what we do.

After all, building is as fundamental a human activity as they come. Digging matter from the ground and using it to recraft the overground landscape: on beaches around the world this kind of activity is literally child's play. We flatter ourselves, amidst the complex dynamism of globalized production, to believe that we've moved beyond the simplicity of buckets and spades; to believe that our relationship to wealth has transcended the mundanity of matter. Yet the numbers tell a different story. Amalgamate all the matter that comes out of the ground or chopped down on its surface and you have an almost perfect temporal proxy for global GDP growth. When growth slows, the digging and the cutting slows. When growth takes off, the rate of extraction steepens.[23] Despite all the sophistication we attribute to our global economy, we have not, in fact, transcended the little boy on a beach, digging out material for his sandcastle. We have simply scaled up his play.

And the scaling up continues. In 1970, the world extracted approximately 30 billion tons of matter globally, comprising 12.7 billion tons of biomass, 9.5 billion tons of non-metallic minerals, 6.1 billion tons of fossil fuels, and 2.6 billion tons of metallic ores.[24] By 2020, half a century later, this figure had tripled to 90 billion tons. The United Nations Environmental Program (UNEP) estimates that by 2060, it will have increased by a further 60%, reaching over 160 billion tons. Far from being mediated amidst growing awareness of environmental breakdown, our use of the Earth's resources is spiraling exponentially upwards in the pursuit of growth.[25]

Yet the conceptual narratives that underpin sustainable construction, like those underpinning sustainable production more generally, do not see it this way. Paradigmatic theories of sustainability, from the Kuznets Environmental Curve—which argues that all societies pass through an inverse U of rising and then falling environmental impact[26] —and the green growth theory associated with William Nordhaus[27] amongst others—which argues in a more general sense that the separation of emissions and growth is possible—underpin the viewpoint that building can and will be separated from waste. Yet even after decades of focus, less than 9% of all global materials consumed are circular.[28]

23 Jason Hickel and Giorgios Kallis, "Is green growth possible? *New Political Economics* 25, no. 4 (2020): 469–86.

24 Material Flows, *Matflow 2.0.*, https://materialflows.net (accessed October 1, 2024).

25 UNEP, *Beyond foundations*.

26 Susmita Dasgupta, Benoit Laplante, Hua Wang, and David Wheeler, "Confronting the Environmental Kuznets Curve," *Journal of Economic Perspectives* 16, no. 1 (2022): 147–68.

27 See, for example, William D. Nordhaus, "The 'Dice' Model: Background and Structure of a Dynamic Integrated Climate-Economy Model of the Economics of Global Warming," *Cowles Foundation Discussion Papers* 1252 (New Haven, CT: Cowles Foundation for Research at Yale University, 1992).

28 Circle Economy, *The Circularity Gap Report 2022* (Amsterdam: Circle Economy, 2022), 8.

And this is only part of the story. Besides its responsibility for 37% of global energy-related carbon dioxide emissions,[29] there are huge hidden costs also. Added to its carbon impact, for example, is that of black carbon, or soot. Some 20% of global black carbon is attributable specifically to brick kilns, 90% of which are in central Asia.[30] This is not only a dangerous local pollutant, responsible in large part for the South Asian brown cloud which shapes weather patterns on the subcontinent,[31] but also global warming more generally.[32]

Local environmental impacts like this intensify the impacts of climate change, magnifying climate-linked pressures on crops, livestock, and the humans who depend on them. In highly climate-vulnerable contexts like Bangladesh and India, this combination of local pollutants with climate pressures creates a vicious cycle of agricultural abandonment, urbanization, and a displaced workforce who both need new homes and participate in building them. As one farmer near Dhaka complained:

> "Smoke from brick production is affecting the health of local people. Local people's shortness of breath is increasing, especially when they leave the house in the morning. Then I see everything [looks] dark because of the smoke. There is a strong stench. Our body is always covered with the dust and sand particles. The skin of the people here becomes completely black. Children, the old and people of all classes in the area are being affected by this trend. Not only people but also animals, birds and cattle are being affected by this." (Alamgir Bhuiyan, farmer and petty trader, February 2021)[33]

Viewed this way, construction creates many of the problems that it solves. Material production at the urban periphery sets in motion a vicious cycle of demand for those materials, even as the language of sustainability circulates at the upper echelons of architectural planning. Yet even this complex knot is ultimately only one hemisphere of the problem: in climate parlance, the mitigation of our emissions. Equally important is the adaptation dimension:

---

29 UNEP, *Beyond foundations.*

30 World Green Building Council (WGBC), *Bringing Embodied Carbon Upfront: Coordinated Action for the Building and Construction Sector to Tackle Embodied Carbon* (London: WGBC, 2019).

31 Mark G. Lawrence, "Asia under a high-level brown cloud," *Nature Geoscience* 4, no. 6 (2011): 352–53.

32 Climate and Clean Air Coalition, *Bricks: Mitigating Black Carbon and Other Pollutants from Brick Production*, 2020, https://www.ccacoalition.org/ (accessed July 5, 2021).

33 Laurie Parsons, Ricardo Safra de Campos, Alice Moncaster, Tasneem Siddiqui, Ian Cook, Chethika Abenayake, Amila Jayasinghe, Pratik Mishra, Tamim Bilah, and Luis Scungio, *Disaster Trade: The Hidden Footprint of UK Production Overseas* (Egham: Royal Holloway University of London, 2021), 66.

the ways in which the built environment can ameliorate the worst impacts of climate change, to sand off, as we saw above, the rough edges of an increasingly capricious environment.

Social Cyborgs in a World System

That humans are adaptable is a truism. Our presence amidst all of the world's diverse and often dangerous environments is a testament to human capacity to adjust to the world around them. Yet the word humans here is doing some heavy lifting. Humans in society are hardy, adaptive, and resilient, but stripped of their social carapace, the human body itself is far more fragile. All things being equal, it can tolerate a slightly elevated core temperature of $38.2°C$, only $0.7°C$ above the norm, for only around eighty minutes, or $39°C$—$1.5°C$ above normal—for around forty-five minutes before it begins to shut down. And the external temperature needed to raise the core temperature to this dangerous level is only around $35°C$ in a very humid environment,[34] leaving many areas of the world uninhabitable to the de-socialized human.

In fact, only a narrow tropical band, where the air temperature averages $27°C$, feels comfortable to the naked human body, so in order to feel comfortable in an environment different to this, we have to recreate it. The warm air trapped next to our skin by a t-shirt or jumper, the insulation provided by an enclosed room, central heating, or air conditioning: all create the illusion of our body's adaptability as we transition between seasons and geographies in environments far beyond our inherent tolerance.

Viewed in this way—and paraphrasing the terminology developed by Erik Swyngedouw[35] and Matthew Gandy[36]—humans confront their thermal environment effectively as social cyborgs. Wholly dependent on the built environment for even short-term survival, they expend their energies in reproducing that environment—and their position within it. In temperate and colder regions, workers exchange their labor for a sheltered environment and the means to heat it. In warmer climes, it is cooling that is purchased, whether in the form of an electric fan or more recently air conditioning.

For many people, this is an arrangement that functions fairly effectively. Yet look beyond the upper stratum of society in both cases and the relationship between income and thermal comfort becomes rather more direct. Even in a wealthy country like the UK, fuel poverty is a major issue, affecting a

34 Georg Mathisen, "Humans Are Tropical Animals," *Science Norway*, February 26, 2014, https://www.sciencenorway.no/ adaptation-body-temperature-forskningno/humans-are-tropical-animals/1397429.

35 Erik Swyngedouw, "The city as a hybrid: On nature, society and cyborg urbanization," *Capitalism, Nature, Socialism* 7, no. 2 (1996): 65–80.

36 Matthew Gandy, "Cyborg Urbanization: Complexity and Monstrosity in the Contemporary City," *International Journal of Urban and Regional Research* 29, no. 1 (2005): 26–49.

substantial proportion of the population: 13% in England, 12% in Wales, 18% in Northern Ireland, and 25% in Scotland.[37] For those who fall into this category, the thermal landscape is an economic landscape. The loss of a part-time job, or an unexpected expense, is felt not only in a depleted bank balance, but in long, cold, sleepless nights until the next paycheck provides relief.

In the global South, this relationship is similarly direct. Better-off workers use a floor fan to diffuse the heat where necessary, whilst those whose incomes are lower, or economic responsibilities greater, simply bear the heat through the long, sticky nights. In both cases, wakefulness—the inability to escape the material realities of the body or the circumstances it meets—is a foremost symptom of this economic-environmental dialectic. Social privilege in the built environment manifests as the luxury of forgetting one's environment. The price of a less favorable positionality is a constant, inescapable awareness of it; environmental intrusion into every aspect of life and work.

Building Colonialism

Interpreting the colonial character of the built environment is in one sense impossibly complex: an analysis that crosses scales, eras, and disciplines. Yet it takes only a simple directive to begin this unpicking: the imperative to take the environment not simply as is, but as constantly, repeatedly, and purposively created in circumstances of unequal privilege. In many cases, you may think you have done this. It doesn't take much insight to notice the ways in which housing inequality structures health and livelihoods in a given urban environment. This is the bread and butter of urban studies[38] and critical architecture.[39] But recognizing the coloniality of the built environment means extending this analysis beyond its conventional limits. The whys cannot stop at the border. Nor can they blinker themselves to the present alone.

On a practical level, confronting these politics means, above all, linking the too-often bifurcated hemispheres of adaptation and mitigation. The construction sector has engaged with mitigation for a number of years now, with varying success.[40] More recently, this interest in the carbon cost of

---

37 Suzanna Hinson and Paul Bolton, *Fuel Poverty, House of Commons Library Research Briefing*, July 8, 2021, https://commonslibrary.parliament.uk/.

38 See, for example, Thomas D. Matte and David E. Jacobs, "Housing and health—current issues and implications for research and programs," *Journal of Urban Health* 77 (2000): 7–25.

39 See, for example, Yael Padan, "Researching Architecture and Urban Inequality: Toward Engaged Ethics," *Architecture and Culture* 8, nos. 3–4 (2020): 484–97, and Susan Bickford, "Constructing Inequality: City Spaces and the Architecture of Citizenship," *Political Theory* 28, no. 3 (2020): 355–76.

40 World Green Building Council, *Bringing Embodied Carbon Upfront*.

building has extended to materials.[41] Yet this is only the beginning of a wider reckoning with the environmental impact of the built environment. Construction workers are amongst the most climate-vulnerable in the world, with intensive labor and outdoor work compounding the physical strain of rising temperatures.[42]

And this, again, is only the beginning. People, after all, have not only to put these materials together, but to make them in the first place. The conditions in which this putting-together takes place are a crucial but all too often neglected dimension of the climate-construction nexus. Cambodia is only one case, but it is a microcosm of a far wider global phenomenon. In India, for example, between 10 and 23 million people work in the brick industry alone,[43] to say nothing of the cement makers, the sand dredgers, or the woodworkers. Here and elsewhere in the rapidly urbanizing South, laboring communities are at the frontline of the climate crisis and as material mobility rapidly increases globally,[44] their physical travails are increasingly baked into the urban environment.

But our net must be cast wider than this still. All of those materials, molded, transported, and erected amidst the travails of climate breakdown, have to come from somewhere. In many cases this means deforestation for timber, illegal sand dredging of the kind that is rife in many low-income countries, or the vast environmental impacts of brick production, where former fields are choked by fumes for much of the year, intensifying the impacts of climate change for those who neighbor them. Long, complex material supply chains and a lack of legal accountability mean that, from the perspective of end users, these processes of extraction are either a black box, an irrelevance, or both.[45]

This black box is highly profitable. The diffusion of responsibility along long, complex supply chains facilitates a hugely effective system of buck passing that leaves lead firms in the construction sector and beyond lucratively free from liability. When environments and working populations are abused, it is invariably partner firms—legally distinct entities from the multinational conglomerate that commissions them—that bear responsibility. With international supply chain law sparse and largely ineffective at addressing the

---

1 For an overview, see Rahman Azari and Alice Moncaster (eds.), *The Routledge Handbook of Embodied Carbon in the Built Environment* (London: Routledge, 2023).

2 International Labour Office, *Working on a warmer planet: the impact of heat stress on labor productivity and decent work* (Geneva: ILO, 2019).

43 Andrew Eil, Jie Li, Prajwal Baral, and Eri Saikawa, *Dirty Stacks, High Stakes: An Overview of Brick Sector in South Asia* (Washington, DC: The International Bank for Reconstruction and Development/ World Bank, 2020).

44 UNEP, *Beyond foundations*.

45 See Miriam Posner, "Breakpoints and Black Boxes: Information in Global Supply Chains," *Postmodern Culture* 31, no. 3, (2021), https://dx.doi.org/ 10.1353/pmc.2021.0002, and Parsons et al., *Disaster Trade*.

problems it addresses,[46] builders and investors alike are effectively able to make any environmental claim they wish without the threat of repercussions if demonstrated to be untrue.

This fundamental inequality of voice is the foundation on which carbon colonialism in the built environment rests. Yet it is rarely recognized as such. By foregrounding the rigors of the natural environment—particularly ecology and climate—as "the prime determinants of architectural form and space,"[47] this discursive inequity is downplayed, naturalized, and elided. To think differently, the falsity of this position must be recognized. The purportedly timeless, unchanging essence of tropical design[48] is in reality a continual, systematic process of division: of value from waste, labor from profit, comfort from discomfort; and minds from a room of their own.

46   Genevieve LeBaron and Jane Lister, "The hidden costs of global supply chain solutions," *Review of International Political Economy* 29, no. 3 (2021): 669–95, https://doi.org/10.1080/09692290.2021.1956993.

47   Ching, *Architecture: Form, Space, and Order*, 18.

48   Ibid.

Architectural Extractivism in Times of Post-accountability: A Restorative Approach

Charlotte Malterre-Barthes

"Good morning, and thank you, Tom (…). I acknowledge the Gadigal people of the Eora Nation on whose traditional lands we are gathered today. And I pay my respects to elders, past and present. I extend that respect to all indigenous people across the globe. I acknowledge the important role that continues to play within communities and our business." This heartfelt land acknowledgment was pronounced in Sydney, Australia, by Jakob Stausholm, Chief Executive Officer of Rio Tinto Group, on the occasion of the company's second quintile call of 2024 (Q2 2024 Earnings Call, on July 31, 2024, at 9:30 p.m. ET).[1] Stausholm was appointed CEO of the large mining conglomerate after its predecessor left, following a vote of 61% of shareholders rejecting the firm's executive remuneration package. This was in retaliation for Rio Tinto's decision in 2020 to—legally—destroy one of Australia's most significant archaeological research sites belonging to the Puutu Kunti Kurrama and Pinikura people, ancestral guardians of the land, to expand the Brockman 4 mine located in the Pilbara region, Western Australia. Searches conducted in the rubble after the blasting revealed a 28,000-year-old animal bone tool and a 4,000-year-old belt made of plaited human hair—but they sat above some eight million tons of high-grade iron ore, with an estimated value of $104m.[2] "We have changed" Stausholm has since then been touting. As a sign of the attempt to clean up its image, the company's website is ripe with contrite statements and promises of better practices: "Since the tragic destruction of the rock shelters at Juukan Gorge, (…), we have been changing the way we work in every part of our business. While we have made progress, we know it will take time to transform our culture and regain trust. But, together with the Indigenous peoples of the

---

Motley Fool Transcribing, "Rio Tinto Group (RIO) Q2 2024 Earnings Call Transcript," The Motley Fool, August 1, 2024, https://www.fool.com/earnings/call-transcripts/2024/08/01/rio-tinto-group-rio-q2-2024-

earnings-call-transcri/.

2   Staff, "Juukan Gorge: Rio Tinto Investors in Pay Revolt over Sacred Cave Blast," *BBC News*, May 7, 2021, https://www.bbc.com/news/business-57018473.

lands on which we operate, we are committed to ensuring cultural heritage is respected, valued, and conserved for future generations."[3] How effective are such performative acknowledgments in addressing the inherently extractive nature of architecture and construction today? How can they serve as an entry point, on the one hand, for addressing the complicity of space production's actors and, on the other, toward a restorative approach for the construction sector? What can the tension between mining industry practices, their mock-progressive politics, cultural greenwashing, and extractive worlding teach us about architecture? Furthermore, how might the planning sector move from performing social and ecological responsibility gestures toward real change?

An epistemological rebuttal must be articulated regarding the differentiation between architecture, the construction sector, and the industries that power and constitute the matter it consists of. Many theorists and practitioners have taken great pains to support such an imaginary division.[4] First, through intellectual gymnastics, these have sought to dissociate the disciplinary aspect of building from any economic and political realms and, secondly, to discount construction's material weight and accountability. However, scholars such as Reinhold Martin and Keller Easterling have debunked this detachment, arguing that financial, corporate, and infrastructural sectors exert enormous influence over the built environment and that architecture is inextricably linked to these global forces.[5] It is mainly through the works of geographers that the political economy of space has been unpacked, particularly in terms of its grounding in capital accumulation, but scholars in planning and architecture too are increasingly contributing to this discourse, emphasizing the extractive nature of both urban development and construction. Authors such as Fanny Lopez, Jane Hutton, Martin Arboleda, and Catalina Mejía Moreno highlight how construction industries are not only extractive regarding resources but also operate through financial mechanisms deeply rooted in speculative real estate markets. Lopez's work explores the material footprints of architecture and how energy infrastructures shape urban environments, while Hutton's research delves into the ecological histories of construction materials.[6] Arboleda, on the other hand, focuses on the broader political economy of construction, connecting urbanization processes to

3 Rio Tinto Group, "Juukan Gorge," Trending Topics, 2024, https://www.riotinto.com/en/news/trending-topics/juukan-gorge (accessed October 10, 2024).

4 As Sara Ahmed articulated, citation politics matter, and it is intentional that "important" names are omitted here. See Sara Ahmed, *Living a Feminist Life* (Durham, NC: Duke University Press, 2017).

5 Reinhold Martin, Jacob Moore, and Susanne Schindler, *The Art of Inequality Architecture, Housing, and Real Estate: A Provisional Report* (New York: The Temple Hoyne Buell Center for the Study of American Architecture, 2015); Keller Easterling, *Organization*

Space: Landscapes, Highways, and Houses in America (Cambridge, MA: The MIT Press, 1999).

6 See Fanny Lopez, *A Bout De Flux* (Paris: Editions Divergences, 2022); Jane Mah Hutton, *Reciprocal Landscapes: Stories of Material Movements* (London: Routledge, 2020).

global supply chains and resource extraction, while Mejía Moreno examines the geopolitical and social consequences of mining and architecture's reliance on it.[7]

Both extraction and real estate can be viewed as two intertwined arms of the construction sector. One provides the material basis—oil, iron, steel, glass, aluminum, concrete—while the other acts as the financial engine, driving speculative development that demands ever-increasing amounts of these materials. This mutually reinforcing relationship is often obscured, yet it is critical in shaping much of the infrastructure and buildings humans produce—and, at times, inhabit. These relationships are economic and political, rooted in unequal power dynamics that disproportionately affect marginalized communities and ecosystems, as unpacked by geographers and planners David Harvey, Neil Smith, and Ananya Roy.[8] Extractive economies of mining and real estate work in tandem, propelling and propelled by architecture while perpetuating cycles of environmental degradation and social inequality.

Before discussing how the extractive nature of construction and architecture plays out, the following key and adjacent terms can be defined: extraction, extractive industries, and extractivism. "Extraction" removes natural resources from the Earth for industrial use, such as minerals, oil, gas, or timber, through mining, drilling, or logging. This physical labor involves a global workforce made up of miners and mining engineers (on underground and surface mines), oil and gas workers (rig operators, drillers, geologists, and engineers on onshore fields and offshore rigs), loggers and forestry workers harvesting timber—felling trees, cutting them into logs, and transporting the wood to mills for processing, plus all the manutentions operators across these industries maneuvering heavy machinery (i.e., bulldozers, excavators, and trucks), and as a large population of workers at processing facilities that handle the refining, processing, and transportation of raw materials, turning them into usable products for industry. By extension, "extractive industries" are those active in the removal/displacement of non-renewable natural resources from the Earth for economic purposes. While the *Merriam-Webster.com Dictionary* defines extractive as an activity "tending toward or resulting in withdrawal of natural resources by extraction with

Catalina Mejía Moreno, "'Nos Están Matando': (We Are Being Killed)," *Journal of Architectural Education* 74, no. 2 (2020); Martin Arboleda, *Planetary Mine: Territories of Extraction under Late Capitalism* (Brooklyn, NY: Verso Books, 2020).

See David Harvey, *The Urbanization of Capital* (Oxford: Blackwell, 1985); Neil Smith, *Uneven Development: Nature, Capital, and the Production of Space* (New York: Blackwell, 1984); Ananya Roy and Nezar AlSayyad, *Urban Informality: Transnational Perspectives from the Middle East, Latin America, and South Asia* (Lanham, MD: Lexington Books, 2004).

no provision for replenishment," signaling the destructive and careless aspect of what it is attached to, it does not know the term "extractivism."[9] Yet extractivism has been coined and defined as a development model or economic system that prioritizes large-scale extraction of natural resources, typically for export, with minimal value-added, with environmental degradation, socio-economic inequalities, destabilizing political consequences, and exploitation of local communities, especially in resource-rich developing countries.[10] Scholars outside spatial disciplines have extensively debated these terms, and not all agree on what they stand for. Additionally, "extractive" and "extractivism" have come to be used interchangeably in academic literature. In *The Extractive Zone: Social Ecologies and Decolonial Perspectives*, decolonial scholar Macarena Gómez-Barris discusses the intersection of extractivism, environmental degradation, and colonialism, focusing on how Indigenous communities resist these forces.[11] Anthropologist Paula Serafini understands "extractivism" as the term used to "describe the logic behind economic and social dynamics in the current stage of neoliberal capitalism, following a displacement of the frontiers of extraction toward other economic fields and spheres of the social."[12] Serafini points that "the framework of extractivism (…) is used for describing and critiquing the economic model of several Latin American and other Global South countries which base their economies on the intensive extraction of natural resources for export. Extractivism is thus characterized by the primacy of activities such as open-pit mining, oil extraction, and agribusiness monocultures."[13] Yet this is an understanding that has been challenged, as outlined by Arboleda in his article "From Spaces to Circuits of Extraction: Value in Process and the Mine/City Nexus," as he lays out how the term extractivism was redefined by many Marxist and value scholars to challenge what they perceive as too close a definition of an exploitative system relying on the extraction of raw materials.[14] Arboleda offers a broader understanding of extractivism, grounded in the real-world dynamics of raw material production and circulation, stressing how extractive industries are reshaping urban, financial, and logistical landscapes to reflect their operational models. But out of many scholarly efforts that work on unpacking these, it is the definition of political scientist Thea Riofrancos that is most valuable here to articulate what a possible definition of "architectural extractivism" could be:

9   *Merriam-Webster.com Dictionary*, s.v. "extractive," https://www.merriam-webster.com/dictionary/extractive (accessed November 11, 2024).

10   See James Ferguson, *Global Shadows: Africa in the Neoliberal World Order* (Durham, NC: Duke University Press, 2007).

11   See Macarena Gómez-Barris, *The Extractive Zone: Social Ecologies and Decolonial Perspectives* (Durham, NC: Duke University Press, 2017).

12   Paula Serafini, *Creating Worlds Otherwise: Art, Collective Action, and (Post)Extractivism* (Nashville, TN: Vanderbilt University Press, 2022), 4.

13   Ibid., 4.

14   Martín Arboleda, "From Spaces to Circuits of Extraction: Value in Process and the Mine/City Nexus," *Capitalism Nature Socialism* 31, no. 3 (2020) : 1.

"Extractivism is a capacious concept. (…) It admits of granular, internal differentiations such as 'neoliberal' extractivism versus 'neo-' or 'progressive' extractivism (Burchardt and Dietz 2014; Gudynas 2009). It travels across spheres of capitalist life. The concept has migrated from its origins in diagnosing the natural resource sectors often located in rural peripheries to the densely spatialized inequalities of cities, themselves key hubs of transnational commodity flows ('urban extractivism'). It also encompasses the operations of digital platforms ('data extractivism') and stock markets ('financial extractivism') and the governing logic of the global transition to renewable energy ('green' or 'aeolian' extractivism). Nearly anything, then, can be extracted: 'mineral resources, labor, data, and cultures.'"[15]

Besides, Serafini defined the "concept of cultural extractivism as a way of understanding the ways that the logic of extraction is manifested in the cultural and creative industries, and how these, as a result, reproduce extractive dynamics as part of a wider program of development and modernization."[16] Architecture, as a cultural industry, certainly fits the bill. But much like with Dante Alighieri's *Inferno*, there are circles beyond Arboleda's value extractivism, Riofrancos' list of mineral, neoliberal, urban, data, and financial extractivism, and Serafini's cultural extractivism.

It is argued here that architecture operates in intrinsically extractive ways. The discipline's foundations rest on referential historical examples and systems that continually exhaust the past for inspiration and validation, rendering it extractive of cultural wealth and past narratives—depending on which ones are used. While acknowledging the importance of building upon existing knowledge, questioning novelty, and rejecting non-referential design principles, this constant "mining" and appropriation of existing works also turns historical and cultural resources into commodities for aesthetic and academic capital, depleting these sources of their original context—without compensation. As a case in point, entire careers have been built on Indigenous architectural references, from the Indonesian longhouse to the growing bridges of India. While one cannot point to a specific Indigenous architectural source for Le Corbusier's brise-soleil or pilotis, it is evident that he-who-never-quotes drew from examples in vernacular architecture. As another example, Team X's Candilis-Josic-Woods' designs for "Les Muriers," the villas in the new modernist town of Le Mirail, bear a

Thea Riofrancos, "Extractivism and Extractivismo," *Global South Studies: A Collective Publication with The Global South*, November 11, 2020, https://globalsouthstudies.as. virginia.edu/key-concepts/ extractivism-and-extractivismo.

16 Serafini, 6.

striking resemblance to Moroccan traditional residential typologies, where the architects had previously conducted "experiments."

Financially, architecture is tethered to exploitative funding structures driven by pension and hedge funds, debt and mortgage, and all the predatory mechanisms of real estate capitalism. By siphoning value from individuals, communities, or entire sectors and leveraging financial mechanisms such as high-interest loans imposed on vulnerable borrowers or serving real estate speculation with properties built, bought, sold, or flipped for profit without regard to communities' well-being, ecological conditions, or actual housing needs, architecture is both fueled by and serves these exploitative mechanisms, commodifying space and housing.

Regarding operation, the creative tools that define the practice—CAD, BIM, and the data infrastructure that supports design processes—rely on minerals feeding into a global web of material extraction. Computers require a range of mined resources, particularly rare earth elements (REEs), tantalum, lithium, indium, and others. While digital tools are prevalent across all sectors, overreliance on these masks the environmental toll embedded in seemingly immaterial protocols.

Extractive pedagogies also shape architecture education. Depending on where they study, students may be burdened with exorbitant tuition fees and indebted, trained to become obedient office workers within exploitative practices, sustaining an economy of unpaid labor. At the same time, adjunct faculty endure precarious, short-term contracts, perpetuating cycles of undervaluation and labor extraction within academia: "Our working conditions are your learning conditions," read posters during the Royal College of Art staff strike in 2023.[17] The devaluation of academic work mirrors the industry's undervaluation of the labor force, highlighting how architectural education is built on exploitation.[18] Under pressure by other forces, the profession also extracts value through the underpaid labor of interns and junior or foreign architects.

Construction is "naturally" extractive at the material level because it is nourished through the mined resources, the violence exerted on land and communities, and the intensive labor required to produce, transport, and assemble construction materials and fuel on-site operations. This reinforces global inequalities by extracting cheap labor from vulnerable populations while depleting natural resources on an industrial scale, leaving a trail of destruction. The physical act of building is a direct practice of extraction, with the literal excavation of sites displacing communities and degrading

17 Tobi Thomas, "Royal Society of Arts Staff Vote to Strike for First Time in Its History," *The Guardian*. September 5, 2023, https://www.theguardian.com/uk-news/ 2023/sep/05/royal-society-arts-staff-vote-strike-first-time-history). Thank you to Dubravka Sekulić for this reference.

18 For further investigations on this topic, see Charlotte Malterre-Barthes and Dubravka Sekulić, "Curriculum Repair," *ARCH+ The Great Repair*, no. 250 (2023).

environments and, in most places, exploiting a racialized, often undocumented workforce.[19] Building operations are extractive, from land removal to labor exploitation. A similarly exploited workforce made of gendered and racialized bodies undertakes the maintenance of spaces once in use. These workers, often invisible, bear the physical burden of maintaining the spaces that others profit from, continuing the cycle of extraction long after construction is finished.

Finally, demolition embodies extractivism, disregarding the ecological and social impacts of constant resource consumption while perpetuating land value recapitalization—freeing the land to be built again. This relentless cycle of demolition and rebuilding generates waste and pollution, health hazards, and saturated landfills.

Overall, extraction through architecture is also a form of past and future extraction, removing both past accountability and livable time from those who come after us. Architecture—construction—thus perpetuates a legacy of irreversible harm by locking future generations into a cycle of environmental and social depletion.

A combination of financial, material, territorial, cultural, temporal, and human extraction, deeply embedded in architecture's processes and outcomes, reflects an industry tied to the destructive forces of global capital, environmental degradation, and planetary wreckage. One could argue that this is the case for any industry in our accumulative economy. But construction tops the list among destructive sectors. Not to give in to the manic obsession of limiting the assessment of damage to carbon emissions, but simply as an indicator of how much the built environment and its related industries— from mining to architecture—partake in environmental damage, the built environment has the most significant gas emission footprint globally.[20] Plus, it requires massive infrastructure: oil pipelines, rail and road networks, power grids, mining pits, and kilns. There has been a rising awareness among actors in the construction industry of its damaging impact, yet this awakening has primarily resulted in turbo-greenwashing practices—such as Rio Tinto's land acknowledgments after the destruction of the Juukan Gorge.[21] These exemplify a post-accountability tactic where not only the problems of extractivism are externalized, but these demolitions are deployed cynically to serve the blanching of the company image and deflect criticism, as well as used to redefine the company's image under the guise of a genuine reckoning. A company whose entire economic model relies on mineral

---

[19] See Namita Vijay Dharia, *The Industrial Ephemeral: Labor and Love in Indian Architecture and Construction* (Oakland, CA: University of California Press, 2022).

[20] Lizhen Huang et al., "Carbon Emission of Global Construction Sector," *Renewable and Sustainable Energy Reviews* 81 (2018).

[21] See Marc Angélil et al., *On Architecture and Greenwashing— The Political Economy of Space Vol. 01*, ed. Charlotte Malterre-Barthes (Berlin: Hatje Cantz Verlag, 2024).

extraction performing land acknowledgments is virtue-signaling—practiced by predatorial extraction structures benefiting from colonial legacies.[22] Accountability is being weaponized to a new level here. Shifting the focus from the act of destruction to performative gestures of regret, the company uses acknowledgment of harm as a shield, framing itself as conscientious and responsive while continuing to profit from the same extractive practices, just elsewhere. This marks a dangerous evolution in corporate strategies, where expressions of remorse are co-opted to sanitize ongoing exploitation, and accountability is manipulated to serve corporate interests rather than help repair the harm done to affected communities or the environment. Research conducted on the post-Juukan Gorge disaster revealed that "this type of destruction was not a rare occurrence, but rather a routine practice reflecting the prevailing dynamics of legal and structural inequality that underpins the (…) resources sector."[23] This behavior can be expected from the mining industry globally. Rio Tinto has, in fact, been embroiled in several problematic cases across the board, at all scales, for decades. As it looks to expand the exploitation of the Brockman mines in Australia, it risks decimating stygofauna.[24] The company has been accused of political collusion and confronted with strong civic opposition against a planned lithium mine in Serbia.[25] Further allegations include polluting waterways in Madagascar, failing to remediate toxic leaks that have persisted for 35 years in Papua New Guinea, and attempting to override Indigenous religious rights on Arizona's San Carlos Apache lands, among many other ongoing cases.[26]

This is when, yet again, a second epistemological step could be taken. If one agrees to conflate architecture and construction, this inseparable relationship forces us to trace the legacies between the practical realities of construction and those of mining industries. Architecture exists as a conceptual and aesthetic endeavor but relies on material choices, building techniques, and labor. Because so much mainstream construction depends on mined minerals (i.e., oil, aggregates, iron ore), architecture could be seen as the mining industry's double. 40% of CO_2 emissions attributed to

22 Ana María León and Andrew Herscher, "Land, Property, Colony," in *Architecture and the Greenfield—The Political Economy of Space Vol.02*, ed. Charlotte Malterre-Barthes (Berlin: Hatje Cantz, 2024).

23 Deanna Kemp, Kathryn Kochan, and John Burton, "Critical Reflections on the Juukan Gorge Parliamentary Inquiry and Prospects for Industry Change," *Journal of Energy & Natural Resources Law* 41, no. 4 (2023).

24 Adrian Rauso, "Stygofauna Headaches Spread to Infamous Rio Tinto Mining Hub That Employs Thousands of Australians," *The Nightly*, March 12, 2024, https://thenightly.com.au/business/mining/stygofauna-headaches-spread-to-infamous-rio-tinto-mining-hub-that-employs-thousands-of-australians-c-13917413.

25 Agence France-Presse in Belgrade, "Thousands of Serbians Protest in Belgrade against Lithium Mine," *The Guardian*, August 10, 2024, https://www.theguardian.com/world/article/2024/aug/10/thousands-of-serbians-protest-in-belgrade-against-lithium-mine.

26 Neha Wadekar, "Rio Tinto's Madagascar Mine May Face Lawsuit over Pollution Claims," *The Guardian*, April 4, 2024, https://www.theguardian.com/envi

the built environment include emissions from the energy used in the operation of buildings (heating, cooling, lighting, etc.) as well as the embodied carbon in construction materials, which include the extraction, manufacturing, transportation, and assembly of building materials.[27] However, while mining industries are recognized as destructive industries with well-known environmental damage, architecture's trail of devastation is less acknowledged. The relationship between architecture and extraction is often narrowed to one usual culprit: concrete. Because it is prevalent in global construction and has acute environmental impacts, concrete's harm tends to overshadow the many other material issues of building activities, not to mention the immaterial ones. But despite this exposure, building practitioners and developers are not even held accountable for overusing concrete, a versatile and inexpensive material with relatively short supply chains, notwithstanding some meek legal restrictions and incentives. It is thus not surprising that the many other materials used in construction that have a heavy CO_2 footprint—such as iron ore, the base raw resource for steel, prevalently used in reinforced concrete, are not even denounced for it.

Rio Tinto's cases of environmental, territorial, political, and cultural neglect are only here used as a paradigmatic example of the intersection of mining and architecture; it highlights a troubling parallel where the extraction of resources like iron ore can be parallel to its executive and materialized form, namely construction, and how these are prioritized over anything else. It is known that architectural projects, especially large-scale urban developments, rely on vast quantities of steel sourced through Rio Tinto, for example. Architecture is thus fully complicit in this extraction cycle that dismisses the past and forecloses the future for the sake of present construction needs. This is where architectural extractivism emerges as a critical framework for understanding this relationship, positioning the several layers and types of extraction as a foundational aspect of architectural practice. The hope is to encourage the discipline to pay attention to its reliance on and connivance with these ugly, destructive industries and to move toward intentionally inventing new protocols and systems for life. To rethink and challenge the

ronment/2024/apr/04/rio-tintos-madagascar-mine-may-face-lawsuit-over-pollution-claims; Marina Faa, "Landmark Report Uncovers Human Rights Abuses at Rio Tinto Gold Mine in Bougainville, 35 Years after Closure," *ABC*, October 13, 2024, https://www.abc.net.au/news/2024-10-13/human-rights-abuses-found-at-rio-tinto/104463224; Prateek Levi, "Indigenous Activists Push US Supreme Court to Intervene in Rio Tinto's Copper

Mine Dispute," *NewsX*, September 12, 2024, https://www.newsx.com/world/indigenous-activists-push-us-supreme-court-to-intervene-in-rio-tintos-copper-mine-dispute/.

27   Huang et al.

existing paradigms that dominate space production, it is necessary to fully recognize architecture's multi-strata of destructive implications so a future where architecture is no longer entangled in extractive practices can be envisioned. This movement is already ongoing, with non-extractive architecture practices paving the way toward a vision for a reparative construction industry that embraces the care of the living as its core mission through world making rather than simply building: architectural practices that not only acknowledge their historical and material contexts but also actively contribute to healing the wounds inflicted by the extraction of the past, that rethink their functioning models, their economic functioning, and so on.[28] If many aspects of the ongoing financial, material, territorial, cultural, temporal, and human extraction that exemplifies "architectural extractivism" are grounded in more prominent mechanisms, the sector must enter into such reparative effort—architecture can show the way.

Overcoming what thinkers from Arundhati Roy to Mark Fisher have identified as the crisis of imagination and the impossibility of envisioning alternative ways of living, thinking, or organizing society outside of current systems and norms, there are many ways towards a restorative approach to architecture—here, reparative is used as synonymous with non-extractive. To beat the hopeless and lethal post-accountable behaviors of entities such as Rio Tinto, Isabelle Stengers and Andrew Goffey write, "to hear this cry is to hear what makes the difference between the compassion that is possible for whoever is in a position of responsibility and feels out of their depth and the distance to be taken with regard to those whom I am characterizing as responsible for us."[29] To surmount architectural extractivism, a shift is needed toward a construction ethos that transcends mere technical achievement to embrace a deeper sense of care and accountability, restorative world making practice with diverse ways of knowing and acting collaboratively rather than relying on universal or technocratic solutions, re-engaging with local knowledge, building alliances across disciplines and communities, and emphasizing care and responsibility over exploitation, a more imaginative, experimental, and responsive approach to dealing with space production. This also aligns with a call for a disciplinary pivoting toward restoring and honoring the connections between people, places, and the materials we use for our needs—beyond land acknowledgements.[30]

28 See V-A-C Foundation Space Caviar, *Non-Extractive Architecture: On Designing without Depletion* (Moscow, Berlin: V-A-C Press; Sternberg Press, 2021).

29 Isabelle Stengers and Andrew Goffey, *In Catastrophic Times: Resisting the Coming Barbarism* (London: Open Humanities Press, 2015), 118.

30 See Charlotte Malterre-Barthes, "A Moratorium on New Construction," in *Critical Spatial Practice*, eds. Nikolaus Hirsch and Markus Miessen (Berlin: Sternberg Press, The MIT Press, 2024).

Drawing and Building: Architecture and the Global Building Industry Architectures of Care

Elke Krasny in conversation with Jordan Carver

Jordan Carver is part of Who Builds Your Architecture? (WBYA?), a coalition of architects, activists, scholars, and educators. While drawings by architects have been central, almost fetishized, in how architectural history is written, the histories of building have remained largely untold. Today's exploitative and extractivist conditions of the globalized construction sector are disconnected from architectural discourse and architecture schools. The following interview discusses architecture and design in relation to drawing and building and foregrounds the politics around the devaluation of building and how architects and educators can organize around and against this devaluation. This interview with Jordan Carver was conducted via email by Elke Krasny.

Elke Krasny Architecture depends on building, that is, on the physical construction of buildings and the human labor necessary for the act of building. Even though it is quite obvious that building is central for buildings to come into the world, the conditions of building have neither been central to the history and theory of architecture nor to teaching practices in architecture schools. We could even go so far as to claim that building is architecture's best-kept secret. Can you elaborate on how you became interested in the conditions of building and how you work on the ethics and politics of the contemporary building sector? Together with Kadambari Baxi, Laura Diamond, Tiffany Rattray, Lindsey Wikstrom, and Mabel O. Wilson, you are the team of the platform Who Builds Your Architecture? (WBYA?). Can you tell us a bit more about your own background and that of the people who are part of the WBYA? team and the most important contributions of the platform so far?

Jordan Carver The centrality of building, as a verb, is, as you note, not as obvious as perhaps it should be. I might even step back and consider that buildings, as nouns, are a less obvious part of the practice and pedagogy or architecture than they should be. In a very real sense "architecture" simply does not mean "building"—no matter what grammatical construction. Architecture is a set of protocols and procedures, a series of intellectual practices and exercises that can be described as "design" or at least the professionalization of some form of design practice. Architecture as both pedagogy and profession occur in many different spaces, predominately digital spaces. Architecture takes place in the gray matter of Rhino and rendering engines, within the black abyss of Revit and AutoCAD, in Zoom meetings and other meetings. A lot of meetings. It takes place in showrooms and material libraries. And then, at best, it takes place on a job site or a mockup location. All of this is to say that architecture is a highly abstract process, it occurs in abstract spaces, and its relation to the objects of its intended output is highly mediated. An architect's job, at least in the normative sense, is to create drawings, which are themselves abstractions of plans and future constructions. I would agree with Pier Vittorio Aureli when he says that abstraction, understood as a retreat from the world, is "dominant within the discipline of architecture."[1] But where Aureli develops his critique through architecture's relation to industrialization, modernism, and various Marxian discourses, we have tried to erase abstraction by trying to ground architecture as a material practice that is foremost a collaborative and social act. All of us that are now, and have been in the past, involved with Who Builds Your Architecture? (WBYA?) have tried to link the inherent abstractions that govern the teaching and practice of architecture with their very real consequences—whether the material production of buildings or other spaces, or linkages to other forms of abstraction like labor relations, exploitation, and transnational politics. This is not to say abstraction is not an important mode of work or representational strategy. But we aim to understand abstraction within a much broader history that links abstraction to processes of racial subjectivity (via, for instance, Ruth Wilson Gilmore) or the marking and accumulation of property relations and all the violence it entails (via, for instance, Brenna Bhandar).[2] Abstraction removes and conceals, and at its core it tends to operate through norms and narratives not empirical evidence and specific linkages. We are trying to reveal and illuminate archi-

1   Pier Vittorio Aureli, "Form and Labor: Toward a History of Abstraction in Architecture," in *The Architect as Worker: Immaterial Labor, the Creative Class, and the Politics of Design*, ed. Peggy Deamer (New York: Bloomsbury Academic, 2015), 103.
2   Ruth Wilson Gilmore describes racism as "a practice of

abstraction, a death dealing displacement of difference into hierarchies that organize relations within and between the planet's sovereign political territories." Ruth Wilson Gilmore, "Fatal Couplings of Power and Difference: Notes on Racism and Geography," *Professional Geographer* 54, no 1. (2002): 16.

Similarly, Brenna Bhandar writes, "Scientific techniques of measurement and quantification, economic visions of land and life rooted in logics of abstraction, culturally inscribed notions of white European superiority, and philosophical concepts of the proper person who possessed the capacity to appropriate (both on

tecture's various entanglements through narrowly defined research questions and precise representation.

EK In a conversation published in *Artforum*, Mabel O. Wilson puts forward the argument that "drawings" are "instruments of communication" and that "they convey precise instructions for building."[3] If architects were to always start from the understanding that drawing is directly linked to building, what does this mean to a process of communication where those who draw rarely communicate directly with those who build in the context of globalized construction sites. Can you think about the implications of this broken communication?

JC The status of the architectural drawings is always complex. The drawing is central to our thinking as students, educators, and practitioners, but also to other forms of spatial and building practices. Of the many ways to think about drawings, one is to see the drawing as a mode of practice that performs the work of abstracting the architect away from building and labor. The drawing sublimates the material process of construction for the intellectual process of design. The drawing is very much the material embodiment of the humanist turn that located architecture as a rational, intellectual pursuit distinct from the labor of construction. Drawing is what removes the architect from the site. At the same time, drawings are intended to communicate many types of information—measurements, means and methods, but also formal constructions, desires, intent, and the discursive projections of the designer. The notion that communication between designer and worker is broken, or at the least highly mediated, is true. It is also simply non-existent. In this I mean there are whole classes of workers that never even look at a drawing set, much less study them, read them, and use them for their intended purpose. The problem of communication within the drawing set is multiple. But the fact that drawings *need* to communicate, or that communication is a fundamental principle of drawing is instilled into the foundational narrative of architecture. The challenge is that what needs to be communicated within school is much different than what needs to be communicated in the field or on the site. One way of acknowledging this difference is to be very clear about what drawings can do within academia while also addressing how drawings are used beyond it. The flip side of this is to acknowledge

the level of interiority and in the external world) worked in conjunction to produce laws of property and racial subjects." Brenna Bhandar, *Colonial Lives of Property* (Durham, NC: Duke University Press, 2018), 6.

3   Mabel O. Wilson and Julian Rose, "Changing the Subject: Race and Public Space," *Artforum* 55, no. 10 (2017), https://www.artforum.com/features/changing-the-subject-race-and-public-space-234352/.

what sorts of communication drawings cannot do. Again, architecture is a collaborative practice and there are other means of exchanging knowledge beyond drawings. I note this to say that architects have a certain claim on drawings, but there are other methods of practice, other knowledge bases, and other forms of exchange that exist and might even be better than drawing.

EK While drawing is seen as central to architecture and architectural drawings are understood as cultural heritage, collected by museums around the world, celebrated for their beauty and originality, and, of course, used as a source of information by architecture scholars, as well as by those who teach in architecture schools, the same does not hold true for building. Building is absent from architecture museums and not considered a source of information by architectural historians and by educators in architecture schools. What does this cultural separation of drawing from building, which is also an economic and political separation, mean? When did this split between drawing and building begin and how did it make one of these two practices culturally as well as socially and economically valued and the other one devalued? What does the historical process of the devaluation of building mean to the understanding as well as the production of architecture?

JC This, I think, is one of the key questions that we as a group, and many of us individually have been trying to address. The split between drawing and building goes back to the beginning of when we understand architecture to be its own particular discipline. Vitruvius wrote about the distinction between *fabrica* and *ratiocinatio*—(loosely understood here as) the practice of building and the concept behind it. Whether this distinction creates a hierarchy, as some of have critiqued, or a leveling of various processes required for buildings projects (as Pavlos Lefas has recently argued) is an open debate.[4] But a distinction within the field of "architecture" in contrast to that of "building" has been present within the Western conception of architecture from its very inception. Or, to be more exact, it is very difficult to conceptualize the figure of "the architect" outside its historical claims of rational thought and the entire edifice of Western humanist individuality. The word "architecture" is of Latin origin and, of course, the history of architecture often starts with the Greek temple and its associations with civilization, democracy, and (certain) idealized bodies, so the discourse of

4 See Pavlos Lefas, "A Contemporary Reading of Vitruvius' Opening Statements and a Proposed New Partial Translation of De Architectura I.1," *Architectural Theory Review* 26, no. 2 (2022): 326–44.

architecture, architectural pedagogy, and even architectural criticism is part of the intellectual tradition of Western rationalization. This history is long, complex, and varied, but even in this very quick digression we see that building practices have been removed not only from our conception of practice but from our conception of rational thought. Museums and higher education would also fit with this tradition of rational thought and the creation of the rational subject. The exclusion of buildings—and the labor that creates them—from museums and academia fits within this larger historical/epistemological context.

EK Turning to Michael Polanyi's concept of tacit knowledge to think about the skills and knowledge required for building, could you think about how industrialization has, at the same time, eroded and captured the knowledge of building, the knowledge of crafting buildings?

JC Polanyi's concept of tacit knowledge is interesting for a few reasons. On the one hand, as you mention, there is an inherent disconnect between the forms of knowledge Polanyi theorizes—that of personal knowledge, from interaction, repetition, or more broadly, embodied experience—and the strictures of industrialization, which we could even expand into a larger critique of global capitalist exchange.[5] On the other, there is a (perhaps overly romantic) notion of knowledge as a form of embedded practices that can be passed down through exchanges of labor and expertise. Polanyi was keen to upend one form of knowledge hierarchy that preferred scientific objectivity or other knowledges that can be codified through language and/or documentation. But we should also be aware of other forms of hierarchical knowledge, such as apprenticeships, that Polanyi presented. This is particularly important for architectural practice as this master-apprentice model engrains other unequal hierarchies that the profession is starting to address. I think we should be careful not to reify any form of knowledge that has to be shared through any form of hierarchical structure. However, Polanyi, at a more abstract scale, was also a champion of knowledge systems that come into being through communication, collaboration, and working through inter-personal means and methods. Those are the forms of practice, if not explicit forms of knowledge that might be useful—are useful, and perhaps necessary— to address labor and other inequalities that are only heightened through

My experience working with Polanyi and his theory of "Tacit Knowledge" is limited. It has been helpful to revisit his ideas in Michael Polanyi, *Personal Knowledge Towards a Post-Critical Philosophy* (Chicago: University of Chicago Press, 2015) and through the "Tacit Knowledge: Making It Explicit" primer from the London School of Economics, https://www.lse.ac.uk/Economic-History/Assets/Documents/Research/FACTS/reports/tacit.pdf.

industrial production. Industrialization in and of itself may not be the enemy of collaborative knowledge practices, but the sequestration into individual silos that industrialization dictates are real barriers to alternative forms of knowledge exchange and possible forms of practice. I believe this is the sort of "capture" you are referring to. Any form of knowledge that is captured and held within the building design and construction process—or anything else, for that matter—leaves gaps. These gaps can be construction methodologies and other material concerns, but also questions of labor equity, material production, environmental concerns, or any form of knowledge that goes unexchanged because of our global production systems. To a certain extent, these gaps can be alleviated by developing building practices around collaborative knowledge exchange.

EK Absent an expansive and detailed history of building as part of the history of architecture, do you know of interesting examples in architecture, including examples of so-called canonic architecture, which provide us with an understanding of the work of the actual builders and craftspeople?

JC There are three projects that come to mind immediately. The first is Anupama's installations and work at the 2016 Venice Biennale. This project was not only an installation but a showcase of the connections that bind construction and design. By this I mean her work highlighted the material and labor relations between developing ferrocement as a construction medium and the masons, who came from India, to work with it on-site. Kundoo speaks of duality as an underlying method to her work where design, construction, environmental awareness, labor equality, and knowledge sharing are each balanced and integral to the overall project goals.[6] This project fit within Alejandro Aravena's curatorial agenda for 2016 titled *Reporting from the Front*. His own work stands as another example—particularly the "incremental" housing in Quinta Monroy, Chile—of engagement that attempts to build agency within community to make their own choices concerning the design, construction techniques, and aesthetics of their own housing. The long-term success of projects like "incremental" are still being debated, but the strategic goals are worthy of study.[7] Lastly, a project like Francis Kéré's Gando Primary School is worth mentioning, as it considers both the method of local construction, in this case locally fired earthen bricks, as not only a local construction issue, but a potential for further

6   Nicholas Korody, "Previewing the 2016 Venice Biennale: Anupama Kundoo's 'Building Knowledge'," *Archinect*, May 26, 2016, https://archinect.com/features/article/149947194/ previewing-the-2016-venice-biennale-anupama-kundoo-s-building-knowledge.
7   See Sandra Carrasco and David O'Brien, "Revisit: Quinta Monroy by Elemental," *The Architectural Review*, January 4, 2021, https://www.architectural-review.com/buildings/housing/revisit-quinta-monroy-by-elemental.

development. In terms of building a relational strategy of design, Kéré developed techniques that required local materials and knowledge. It will be interesting to see, again, what sort of long-term impact this will have on the local community and if the techniques can be implemented beyond the schoolyard.

There are, of course, ways to critique all of these projects, and showcases of similar work like the Biennale or MoMA's *Small Scale, Big Change*, but for me the interesting part of a shift in discourse is not the immediate success of any one project, but the idea that the question of "canonical" architecture is moving so much that even the idea of a canon seems anachronistic to the ways architects practice and especially to the issues we need to deal with as a profession, as a planet. The shift of discourse shared amongst these projects understands each one as part of a relation between site, occupants, labor, capital, and the environment at multiple difference scales. The idea of a canon flattens; these projects expand.

EK In a conversation on "Changing the Subject: Race and Public Space," published in *Artforum*, Mabel O. Wilson stated that reports by humanitarian organizations including, among others, Amnesty International or Human Rights Watch, are concerned with questions of architecture and building. Wilson draws attention to how legal issues are "spatial, material, architectural, and urban issues." She describes that they led to developing a "number of tactics that architects could begin to think through and deploy."[8] Can you explain these tactics and elaborate how you are working on making these tactics public and used by the profession?

JC If we take the definition of architecture I presented earlier—broadly understood as a field of spatial practices, procedures, and discourses—then two outputs of this definition are the profession of architecture and the figure of the architect. But of course, that is not the only way in which these particular practices and knowledges can manifest in the world. Another version of architectural practice is that it can develop forms of representation that address a much broader set of interests beyond any particular building project. Of course, this is taken as a given in many architectural schools where diagramming, mapping, and other forms of visual representation are taught along with—or more often in preference to—more traditional means of architectural representation such as drafting and detailing. In the project you refer to, we asked what sorts of representational skills we as architects could bring to these reports written by human rights organizations.

Wilson and Rose, "Changing the Subject."

205   Drawing and Building

For us, we started with an interest in understanding architecture's role in terms of human rights and fair construction labor. And at a different, perhaps deeper level, we asked how architectural thinkers can use our knowledge of space to consider the myriad questions surrounding global construction. Global architecture takes place, as the name suggests, around the world— materials are produced and shipped around the world, architects design projects around the world, and workers are recruited and moved around the world. All of these materials and people coalesce at the job site. We began our investigation trying to understand and represent this process. But through reading the reports spatially we began to understand the political and urban strategies that segregate workers apart from any sort of urban life, that condition their migration status, that drive forms of spatial exploitation. We began to understand the spatial logics of worker housing and the transportation networks that bind them to the job site. For us, this links the practice of design with the practice of construction, the politics of migration, and the logistics of housing. Drawing together the glossy images of a World Cup stadium with crowded housing and wage exploitation requires new forms of visual representation, which is where architectural knowledge can be integrated into human rights work, field research, anthropology, and other forms of collaborative work. In addition to using the reports as base research material, we also met with the authors of the reports, did our own on-site research, and met with workers involved in the construction-migration process.

[EK] What are methods, that is, ways of doing research, you can think of to make architects understand both the knowledge and skills that building requires? What are methods you can think of to render transparent the labor conditions in the construction sector? What are ways in which architects can understand the labor conditions of construction sites of buildings they themselves designed?

[JC] I want to address these two questions together. The methods for research and the methods for making material supply and labor inequity more visible are similar: working with people and organizations focused on labor rights and advocacy. A running theme within this discussion is the need to build relationships and coalitional strategies to address issues of labor exploitation whether in producing architectural material, labor on-site, or hierarchies within the office. This strategy comes not only from our own workshops and discussions, but from the longer history of labor and political organizing. And much of this strategic thinking has been theorized by decades of action led by Black feminists.[9] At a very simply level, it is difficult to productively advocate for labor equity without understanding what equity means from the point of view of workers on-site or in the field. And the only way to understand that is by forming relationships with them. On another level, it is through open dialogue that knowledge can be exchanged and our skills as architects can be utilized towards real advocacy. This is the only way we can understand what representation means to those on-site. And it will likely mean shifting what we might understand as professional expertise. Or, more radically, it would mean that expertise is something that is relational, that it is held between people and now simply a matter of transmission. If subjectivities are understood to be constructed from social relations, so too should knowledge. At its most radical, this would require us to reorient our thinking towards constituents and clients to one conceived as mutual support and based on care rather than transfer or appropriation. Elke and Angelika, you have both written extensively on care and its spatial resonances, but I would just quote from *The Care Manifesto* that focusing on care means "embracing our interdependencies," which is what I/we are ultimately trying to achieve.[10]

EK Globally, construction laborers are a workforce exposed to physically demanding, often unsafe or exploitative labor conditions. Furthermore, the labor of building and construction is highly gendered and racialized and marked by class and caste. There has been a lot of transnational feminist activist organizing as well as feminist and race critical scholarship on the exploitative conditions of the invisibilized and feminized labor of cleaning, repair, and maintenance, which is, of course, most intimately connected to the physical condition of buildings, and therefore to architecture. Furthermore, the analytical concept of "global care chains" put forward by Arlie Russell Hochschild has not only raised awareness of the transnational dimension of caring labor and the compulsory mobility of a female workforce, which results in their own absence as carers in their own families, circles of friends, and communities. To my knowledge, there is no comparable development of organized activism and critical scholarship on the labor conditions in the building and construction sector. There is no equivalent analytical notion of "global building chains" and little attention has been paid to the consequences of the extraction of male people from their families, circles of friends, and communities. Could you think about the reasons behind this absence of activism and research? Could you also think about what the analysis of "global building chains" would mean for practicing architects

On thinking through coalition building and working towards alternative futures, the work of Angela Y. Davis, Mariame Kaba, and Ruth Wilson Gilmore has been particularly crucial. See Angela Y. Davis, *Freedom Is a Constant Struggle: Ferguson, Palestine, and the Foundations of a Movement* (Chicago: Haymarket Books, 2016); Mariame Kaba, *We Do This 'Til We Free Us: Abolitionist Organizing and Transforming Justice* (Chicago: Haymarket Books, 2021); Ruth Wilson Gilmore, *Abolition Geography: Essays Towards Liberation* (New York: Verso, 2022). 10 The Care Collective, *The Care Manifesto: The Politics of Interdependence* (New York: Verso, 2020).

and could you sketch out ways in which architects could become actively involved in changing the labor conditions in the building and construction sectors?

JC My first reaction is to remember the chapter in which Arlie Russell Hochschild defines global care chains and recalls the only profession noted for any of the people hiring Pilipino care workers was an architect. But beyond simple irony, it is worth recalling Hochschild's definition of global care chains as "a series of personal links between people across the globe based on the paid or unpaid work of caring."[11] It would seem that the first thing we need to do is not think of how architects work within a global supply chain—that part of architectural thinking seems clear—but to think of our work as a form of care. How does our work form links between people and how can we work to make sure those links are equitable? I also agree that folding in the work of feminist thinkers can help build conceptual and theoretical links that can shift architectural pedagogy and the way we approach the question of practice. I am thinking here of the work of Sara Ahmed, who links ideas of phenomenology—a discursive tradition that architects have been well-versed in for decades—with the politics of gender and race via affect. For Ahmed and others, the effects of the built environment on the body are not only sensorial but political, they are part of the structures that racialize and gender our bodies, that create inequalities. Ahmed's work has resonance, as it adds space and sensation to scholarship from Hochschild and Silvia Federici (among many others) that offers sharp critiques on the exploitative nature of care work as uncompensated labor crucial to the reproduction of capital.[12] If we can broaden our understanding of the relationship between bodily sensation and space, we can begin to bring in other discourses concerning labor, gender, and race.

To address your question about building supply chains, I might point to a few more concrete examples. There are initiatives at Grace Farms, Verité, and some of my own research with Phil Bernstein and Lou deBaca that are trying to address the question of labor exploitation within the architectural supply chain. For WBYA? it has been important to link with these efforts— and with people like Peggy Deamer who have been working on unionization and labor within the architecture office—to create a network of people and organizations concerned with labor at a material, site, and office scale. The

11   Arlie Russell Hochschild, "Global Care Chains and Emotional Surplus Value," in *Justice, Politics, and the Family*, eds. Daniel Engster and Tamara Metz (New York: Routledge, 2015), 250.

12   See Arlie Russell Hochschild and Anne Machung, *The Second Shift: Working Parents and the Revolution at Home* (New York: Viking Press, 1989); Silvia Federici, *Caliban and the Witch: Women, the Body and Primitive*

Accumulation (Brooklyn, NY: Autonomedia, 2004); Silvia Federici, *Wages Against Housework* (Bristol: Falling Wall Press and the Power of Women Collective, 1975).

efforts go in multiple directions, from the perspective of the profession to the academy, to concerns of the industry and global governance. Much work has been done in the legal sector in trying to enforce existing laws and in creating new legislation and transnational agreements. We want to connect with a broad array of people and organizations that are working towards similar goals to understand how the perspective of the architect and educator can contribute to their efforts.

EK WYBA? is organizing in the space of the transnational and the global, which is also the space in which global architecture operates. At the same time, architecture is always local, occupies a specific ground, is part of a location and thus of the political and legal system of the nation-state. Can you share with us how the tactics and strategies of your work can be applied at the level of the transnational, the global, the nation-state, and the local. Building on the previous work of the platform, what are the next steps you are envisioning and how do you see WYBA? developing in the future?

JC Over the years we have done workshops and exhibitions around the world. One question that routinely came up was: "What about labor conditions in New York?"—which is where we are all located. It is a good question and got us thinking about the next steps of our project in terms of working with local labor, migration, and migrant rights organizations at a local level. One thing that had always been a blinder was the presence of large labor unions. But labor unions only protect workers on union projects, and in New York there are many projects outside union labor. In one way, our work started global but has become more local.

Another, more broad and slightly obvious answer is to understand the limits of addressing any of these issues solely within the profession. We are all political beings along with being whatever we choose as a profession. We can put pressure on our professional organizations like the American Institute of Architects (AIA) or the U.S. Green Building Council (USGBC) to address human rights and labor. We can join with local organizations working for local communities. We can vote and protest. All these avenues are open and should be used to address something as complex, intertwined, and difficult as global labor exploitation. Our professional selves might only be able address these issues so far, but building relationships around shared goals and mutual respect can bring us much farther.

Life, Care, Maintenance
Essays

Homing as a Verb

Elke Krasny in conversation with Shumi Bose

Opening up the question of home in architecture, in the following exchange Elke Krasny and Shumi Bose think about home and homemaking practices in relation to architecture, housing, and the household. Understanding that the home is implicated in the economic conditions of the production of housing and aware of the fact that housing creates the conditions of homes and everyday householding, Krasny and Bose unpack a number of questions concerned with the notion of home in architecture with a specific interest in the impact of capital on home and housing, home and displacement, the idea of the family, as well as classed, gendered, and racialized dimensions of housing, homemaking, and householding. The two bring to this written conversation long-standing interests in housing, home, and the household: Shumi Bose was co-editor of the 2014 book *Real Estates: Life without Debt* and co-curator of the 2016 *Home Economics* exhibition at the British Pavilion at the Venice Biennale, and Elke Krasny co-curator and co-editor of the 2016 *In Reserve: The Household! Historic Models and Contemporary Positions from the Bauhaus*.[1] In this written exchange we will turn to two seminal texts on home and on housing, which were both not written by practicing architects, but in the contexts of feminist theory as liberation and historical materialist analysis as revolutionary praxis. These two texts are bell hooks' essay "Homeplace (a site of resistance)" and Friedrich [Frederick] Engel's book *The Housing Question*.[2] Finally, the exchange will turn to Anupama Kundoo's *Wall House*, using it as a specific example to think about the question of home in architecture.

Elke Krasny Can you share what first provoked your interest in the questions of home and housing and how you have worked on these concerns for more

---

1 Jack Self and Shumi Bose, eds., *Real Estates: Life Without Debt* (London: Bedford Press, 2014); Jack Self, Shumi Bose, and Finn Williams, eds., *Home Economics* (London: The Spaces, 2016); Regina Bittner and Elke Krasny, eds., *In Reserve: The Household! Historic Models and Contemporary Positions from the Bauhaus* (Leipzig: Spector Books, 2016).

2 bell hooks, "Homeplace (a site of resistance)," in *Yearning. Race, Gender, and Cultural Politics* (London: Routledge, 2015), 41–50; Frederick Engels, *The Housing Question* [1872] (New York: International Publishers, 2021).

than ten years now as an editor, curator, and researcher? I would like to invite you to speak about the motivations and aims behind *Real Estates: Life without Debt* and *Home Economics* and how you have pursued these questions since.

Shumi Bose Well, I think my focus on the idea of home would start, actually, long before either *Real Estates* or *Home Economics*. I grew up across several homes. I was born in the UK; my father worked as a doctor in contract positions, so we moved around the north of England through my early childhood. Then, my context changed quite drastically—from a small town in Yorkshire to the chaotic megalopolis of Calcutta, as it was then called. I was exposed to such different ways of living, firstly in the various hospital-provided accommodations; also as a minority person in England, I was alert to how a sense of "home" and community were formed beyond the immediate nuclear unit, through cultural and linguistic ties. In India too, while the nuclear home family might be more common now, families themselves are much more rhizomatic. We tend to live in clusters or across multiple generations. So my sense of home or what a home is was very elastic by the time I reached adolescence. Having moved back from now-Kolkata to the Peak District, I had become quite adept at making myself at home and thinking about what that means. I think that's possibly exacerbated as a child, as these moves happen without your control or agency.

I studied architecture at an art school called Central Saint Martins—which is incidentally where I now teach, though many things happened between those periods. At the time, my course was applying for professional accreditation, but they hadn't yet received it—and in fact, it didn't receive that validation in time. So I realized, halfway through, that I would not be graduating with a technically valid architectural degree. Obviously, that was frustrating. As a result, and drawing on the context of a megacity in the so-called developing world that I'd grown up in, I immediately became very dedicated to housing struggles and housing as an activity that may or may not involve architects. It was a rather defiant, teenage reaction. Having grown up in Calcutta, I was familiar with an urban fabric in which there's a lot of informal housing—we could say slum housing, or we could say vernacular housing—depending on what context and what fashion you care to follow. I was kind of like, well, who needs architects? How many people can actually afford an architect to build their home? Like, literally, how many homes are architect-designed and fuck that, basically. So from my second year onwards, all my research was around housing crises, starting with my first essay on this subject about redlining in Chicago and white flight in the face of Black migration coming up from the south, as well as Mario Cuomo's version of housing advocacy in New York—these historic urban cases, which I wasn't taught; I don't know how I sought them out, but it was about putting together

213   Homing as a Verb

the dynamics of economics, and race, property, and politics really act on each other.

My final project involved two years of field research, deeply embedded in the different typologies of slum housing or informal housing in Bombay, which was alien to me. I knew the texture; the terrain is not dissimilar to Kolkata, but as I don't speak Marathi or Hindi, I didn't have access in a meaningful way. But that was great, spending a long time in various informal neighborhoods, seeing people make themselves at home in a lot of different situations: often exploited, and just as often redolent with pride and agency; a lot of intention in how the spaces were designed, built, and set up. There are, of course, complex and nuanced spatial and economic politics: none of it involves an architect. It was all very validating for me—not to say that I wanted to become a slum architect, but to underline that spatial praxis and design thinking was visible across every inch of this place. None of it would meet code. There are dozens of serious problems, not least of them safety. Nonetheless, this was people making themselves at home at scale; deeply at home in the face of many obstacles—without the architectural training or whatever it was that I wasn't going to be accredited for having. At that time, I was unaware of bell hooks' "Homeplace," which would have been a perfect text, as it continues to be for me now, albeit in a shifted context. At the time, I was actually spurred by Heidegger's essay "Building, Dwelling, Thinking," a text that has been vastly misread over the years, not least by me.[3] As well as phenomenology, I was also interested in the potency of mythologies, the way people told stories about why and how they had the right to live in a particular spot. Even the late Anthony Vidler's writing around the uncanny, related to kin or kinship, and therefore familiarity and family in the home; this was an interest that had been percolating for a long time.

Skip forward by a decade, to when I started to work with Jack Self on projects about real estate and finance. Jack had initiated a really great student publication called *Fulcrum*; partly through conversations around that, we developed a common thread of interest in the relationships between architectural production and financial speculation. The amount of stuff that was being built in London seemed to have no correlation with the housing crisis that had reached a nadir at the time. Having lived in London for twenty-five years, it continues to be impossible to avoid the intersections of finance and architectural production. I'm speaking to you now from home, where I can't work without noise canceling headphones: the sound of real estate investment around me is deafening; the bond between money and bricks

3   Martin Heidegger, "Building, Dwelling, Thinking," transl. A. Hofstadter, in Poetry, *Language, Thought* (New York: Harper & Row, 1971): 143–62.

so patently obvious, tangible, overwhelming. Actually, I was shortlisted for a research proposal called #MONEY at the CCA (Canadian Centre for Architecture) in 2013, which stemmed from the idea that many aspects of design are decided in spreadsheets rather than on the drawing board. I remember being asked if I was a Marxist in the interview and I answered, not quite. Perhaps that was the wrong answer, but at the time I felt I had not digested enough of Marx to want to label myself as such.

That book—*Real Estates: Life without Debt*—allowed us to talk to lots of different people that we wanted to talk to about these issues; it was a blessing and a lovely thing to come out of it, and I'm grateful to Jack for that. Directly afterwards, and together with Finn Williams—planner and current city architect for Malmö—we made the application to curate the British Pavilion at the Venice Biennale for Architecture 2016, pitching *Home Economics*. This was another opportunity to explore and research ideas of home. As you might know, we used time as a universal lens or metric to think about different models of what can be considered home, as a matrix for organizing that exhibition: what is a home for hours, days, months, years, or decades. Rather than describe the specific forms and ideas of that particular exhibit here, I will say that the great pleasure and experiment was to think through the proposals made by our participants: by Jack himself, for the room for Hours; DOGMA and Black Square for Months; Ayr for Days; Julia King and Naked House for Years, and Hesselbrand for Decades. All had radically different proposals on what home might be, touching on political, social, cultural, and economic issues. At that time, I was most interested in Dr. Julia King's experimentation with Naked House; that proposal tried to privilege an awareness of usufruct over asset value. That is not restricted to functionality; it relates to beauty, to how you want to live—but not for the purpose of financial accumulation or speculation. Their model resists the "property ladder," playing into these dynamics between money and the built environment.

EK A lecture you gave at the Technical University of Vienna in the context of a program called *Wohngespräche* was announced with the following abstract:

> "We Are Family
> Home has long been the ground zero of architectural thought, combining as it does an immediacy of universal lived experience, with layers of political, socioeconomic and cultural specificity. If such a thing can be said to exist, the shape of the 'ideal family home' has been invented, attacked, morphed, crystallised and—more recently—looks set to collapse, under the intense societal pressures of global lockdown, recession and the erosion of binary gender values, among other things. This talk is a necessarily light skim through a conception of

'home' through the things that have continued to figure in the ever-shifting 'idea'—money, security and the most architectural of them all: family."[4]

Can you elaborate on the notion of the ideal family home and the family and how the home can perhaps be transformed into a site of resistance to heteropatriarchal normativity?

SB Since *Home Economics*, my research on this subject goes back to some of the origins that I mentioned earlier. Particularly during COVID, I began to notice how much of a constraint was posed by the nuclear family and the attendant family home. In the UK, the family home is definitely an aspiration of privacy and property; the maxim "a man's home is his castle" was basically enshrined in the Magna Carta. We don't have a lot of communal street life or even visual access into each other's homes. During COVID, there were exacerbated problems of isolation; particularly, there was a problem when children had to stay home, as that meant that parents couldn't work. Suddenly it became starkly clear that schools were enabling the economic function of the country by taking children out of the picture. Economic changes mean that increasingly, parents work. If caregivers were working from home during COVID, children really became a problem—even discussed in the news as a problem. This seemed mad: People are encouraged to have families and live in family homes; even the arrangements of streets in rows and estates of these very isolated, nuclear family homes—all served by schools that remove the problem for eight hours a day. It became very stark. It's not new, but it's not that old, either: this concept of the nuclear family that lives in a home, it's not more than 150–200 years old. We've become so attached to it, and I started to reflect that I myself didn't grow up in a nuclear home. There was an apartment in which my mum, my sister, and I lived, but there were several familial and even pseudo-familial homes around Kolkata where I could live without pre-arrangement or formality, through ties of kinship of one or another form. And I still feel that way—home is a very rhizomatic, dispersed condition which doesn't necessarily require any kind of biological or geographical tie. Many people raised me; many people fed me, bathed me, even slapped me. This situation where people were absolutely unable to function in their own private enclosures pushed me to question the hegemony of the nuclear family, particularly in housing, which has a lot of politically and socially conservative ideals embedded in it. For the last few years, it has been my privilege to explore these discussions with students

4   "Michael Obrist [feld72] in conversation with Shumi Bose about 'We are Family,'" Wohnbau und Entwerfen, TU Wien, June 7, 2022, https://wohnbau.tuwien.ac.at/de/wohngespraeche/ss-2022/shumi-bose-we-are-family.

at TU Wien; we have been exploring the work of family abolitionist Sophie Lewis and looking towards alternative social arrangements in LGBTQIA+ communities, as well as diverse cultural organizations of family, kinship, space, and property.

EK What makes a home a home? I have raised this distinctly broad, perhaps too broad, question here in order to think about economic and gendered dimensions of the production of housing and everyday householding and homemaking practices.

SB I guess I began to indicate this above, and it is of course a very hard question to answer, partly because it's subjective—and fleeting, also. Speaking personally, it implies a certain level of surrendering arms (I will come back to this), even blossoming into the fullness in one's creative and capable self, that one would hope to feel "at home." Thinking about the terms you raise, namely the economic and gendered dimensions to homemaking, hooks' essay "Homeplace" speaks to all of this. I'm thinking now of home as a place to rehearse alternative forms of being. Reading it feels—for others as well as myself, I'm sure—like coming home to a sister, to all the words one has felt in the body without articulation; I could quote great swaths of it here, despite coming to it relatively late in life.

Practically speaking—and in my privileged situation which lifts me above basic necessities—the main obstacle to *owning* a home, as property of my own, is a mortgage. As you know very well, the word mortgage links the idea of debt to death; *mort* and *gager*. Financially speaking, those are rather bleak and existential questions of surrender. How then to equate this to the liberated fullness that I envision?

When I think of the many places where I may continue to feel at home— unarguably, that hospitality and welcome is fostered by women. Certainly, and others have spoken much more eloquently about the gendered ways in which we have enacted homemaking. Homemaking and economics are connected through their etymology, at least in these Athenian foundational concepts. If the polis, the demos, or the name for the public or the citizens, the *oikos*, implied the realm and management of the domestic. I therefore have always inferred that *oikos* at least implies the realm of women, as women did not count in the public sphere. Of course, historically, women were not given power; the management of the domestic has not been accorded the conditions of labor and recognition, nor are women especially powerful in the offices of political economy, in the management of capital within nation-state scales of domestic product. Yet in my conception, *oikos* (and therefore many attendant notions of economy) implies a realm that includes women's agency, because in my experience it was women who ran the household. It's silly, maybe, but the etymological root became meaningful at least in my conception of things. Again, others have spoken much more eloquently about how that is enacted, and again I look to bell hooks' "Homeplace" as a touchstone among many others. Certainly, it was something we were thinking about during *Home Economics*, particularly through the research by Maria Giudici, Pier Vittorio, and Martino Tattara.

EK Globally, we witness the destruction of houses and the ruination of homes, what one might call "home-i-cide," because of wars and "unnatural disasters." Because of conditions of wars and climate catastrophe, because of conditions of mortgages and economic pressures, millions of people lose their homes, are displaced. What does this mean for architecture as a sector and for practicing architects? How do you address these questions in your work as an architectural educator?

SB You've hit on a very precise dissonance, right? Certainly, we tend to believe that one of the main functions of architecture is to shelter people. But what is there to say about the many massive ways in which people are being displaced and unhoused at the moment... it is beyond comprehension. We've touched on financial disenfranchisement, but I'm now thinking of recent events like the LA wildfires, as well as the intentional destruction or "home-i-cide," as you say, in Ukraine, in Gaza and other parts of Palestine, and many places beyond. The fact is that architecture, as a sector, doesn't have the agency to apply itself to these; as long as it remains a market-driven industry, folks still have to be paid. When I say folks, I'm partly thinking about the practitioners that my students will become. How can they apply themselves as architects to these massive instances of spatiocide? It's not a clear path. We are taught that the basic calling of architecture is to provide shelter, but as a profession, it's obviously not a basic calling; it could even be extraneous. We know that architects are not necessary to produce a built environment. Don't get me wrong; I continue to believe that there are many advantages in architectural study, and the discourse of an accredited discipline—but quite plainly, it's not required that industry orient itself critically, or towards humanitarian or liberatory causes. The industry is oriented towards market causes and predicates on having to be able to function that way. So as long as these humanitarian causes are not backed up by political will, it seems to me that architecture is handicapped by the absence of capital and other obstacles to apply its capacities to some of these planetary crises.

This is a dissonance that my students and I feel a lot, and we feel it together. My longest-running teaching position to date has been with the undergraduate cohort at UAL Central Saint Martins which is, at the time of writing, fully accredited and professionally validated. As I'm not an architect, I am not permitted to teach a design studio; I teach history and theory, which I adore. Our class becomes a space to have these critical discussions—not measured in productivity but rather in purpose. Acknowledging my own bias, I will say that these discussions veer into the political, the economic, and the postcolonial consequences of various histories or narratives that we're looking at. As a school, Central Saint Martins has been somewhat more socio-politically oriented rather than technologically or formally oriented; our students come to us imagining that they can make the world a better place, a more socially just place. They realize that they will be graduating, potentially, into a sector which does not apply itself to social or humanitarian causes with much regularity or commitment. We tend to see students become enthusiastic about community-led practices or participatory practices, even thinking about things like planning or policy: maybe further up the food chain is where they can make a critical difference, rather than in the design of facades. It's true that the path to bridge humanitarian concern and the application of architectural skills is hard to indicate in my class, and it's a conversation that we have openly. It's not a conflict that I can resolve; I try not to be dogmatic without masking my own un-simple position. That goes for lots of different political issues that have come up over the last decade and a half.

In any case, I do take teaching as the opportunity for all of us to practice critical conversations, to confront some of these conflicts and accountabilities before students hit the professional world. That's actually what we're doing, whether I am with first years or postgraduates. I'm not necessarily fixated in the strictly factual when it comes to history or theory; rather, we use the past and its loaded narratives as a gymnasium to address some of the ethical dilemmas that we face in our lives, in our careers—not a history of objects, but a series of demonstrations. The twentieth century alone holds many instances of so-called philanthropic forces, or perhaps benevolent states, which would support an architectural project. In as many instances, changing economic or political circumstances reverse those endeavors. These are the reasons to study history, to counter these kinds of dissonances that happen in the real world. I've also been teaching architecture students from Syracuse University, which has a program based in London. As such, we liberally use the fabric of London to illustrate some of the dissonances in what might need to happen and what actually happened. In terms of the much larger and intractable issues of international displacement, the main job I have is to support students in our conversations, rather than selling the possibility of heroic solutions.

EK The home is perhaps the best place to study that the personal is as much economic as it is political. Systemic conditions take shape in the home. How can the study of architecture help transform systemic conditions? How can the study of systemic conditions help transform architecture and consequently the ways in which homes and housing spatialize political and economic conditions of everyday life?

SB There's a lot of discussion about systemic thinking around. While we might live in the live-stream of these conversations, I need a bit more time to digest and reflect on the various implications made under this heading. Again, it's not a new frontier, but I do think that there are advantages of being mindful—to quote Donella Meadows—of the different places to intervene in a system. Architecture is a messy, willfully undisciplined field, right? We talk about the discipline of architecture, and we do separate into tribes: technicians, theorists, designers, historians, but it's an inglorious, messy, and fractious lot. We all know it; we will not even commit as to whether we belong to the arts and humanities, or the sciences. The very fact that architecture is a very undisciplined field brings together different systems of thinking, of value systems, of logic; of course, then there are different systems of pedagogy.

As a student of architecture, one has to navigate that terrain; one has to recognize affinity with some aspects and not with others—because nobody's good at everything. You also recognize systems of thought, of historiography. I was reading recently a conversation on the Cartesian perspective, which has dominated our understanding of space and time; a Lagrangian perspective—which traces dynamics of movement—would give us a completely different architecture. The study of architecture forces you to encounter certain things like that: how sound is measured, or how carbon costs are estimated, or how representational nuances hold meaning. Indeed, systems of meaning are among the most arcane and difficult to rationalize. Architectural training does expose you to a lot of complexity and contradiction, with a nod to Venturi; that alone is instructive. The twentieth century is littered with those who claim to have found the correct or superlative system, all of which have subsequently been found to be flawed. Yet we are drawn to invent systems, to take comfort in the structure offered by the very idea of a system. I think that's just a human instinct. Complex and beautiful systems are evidently present in nature and in ethics; certainly in this messy "discipline," you can encounter conflicts between them; we are aware that there are many differing and dynamic logics at play. My visceral suspicion around contemporary systems discourse is that I see in there, again, the instinct to take comfort in something that has order. It is the unwritten mission of architecture to provide order, but the truth of systems dynamics is that they are dynamic. The quest for order may be instinctual, but it's an ongoing quest in a world that I accept as being in flux. So I'm instinctively suspicious of perfectly crystalline ordering systems and the strenuous efforts to justify them.

To return to Donella Meadows, her 1997 essay "Leverage Points: Places to Intervene in a System" was pretty transformative. I read it during the

2020 lockdown, when we were thinking about racialized systems of oppression, and how to think about changing that which is really ingrained. Meadows' essay really makes a few things clear; crucially that there are various points of leverage across a system. At the time, I was finding it hard to post the black square. That aesthetic, momentary gesture of solidarity could not hold what I was feeling, nor represent the difficulty of the work ahead. But Meadows' essay helps to demonstrate that there are various points of leverage; if one finds oneself able to act at the scale of optics, that is also valid and important. If, in architectural education, we can really make space for these questions around the various points for intervention, that would be great. Then too, if we could realistically empower our students to address some agency beyond the market, they might have more freedom to think about these points to intervene. The cost of living is such that I cannot blame my students for thinking about the market; their financial burdens certainly inform how they arrive, when they arrive to study. While I can be optimistic about how the study of architecture opens one up to systemic thinking—actually offering a very wide range of points to intervene—I can't realistically suggest that all of those agencies are available to my students, not when they're operating in the current climate. This climate is not just one of financial, societal, and planetary precarity, but also the vociferous fear-mongering about that precarity; not only is everybody scared, but also deeply aware that they should be scared. This obviously shuts down any capacity for intersectional or cross-systemic thinking, because when you're scared, you just want to survive and look after yourself. The constant precarity—probably for all disciplines, but certainly for a messy, not-quite-necessary discipline like architecture—affects future practitioners in thinking about how and where they should use their agency.

EK Historically, the home is a deeply classed, gendered, and racialized space. How can architecture become relevant to undoing the classed, gendered, and racialized conditions of home and of housing more broadly?

A specific historical strand of feminism today often critically referred to as white feminism, civilizational feminism, or capitalist and lean-in feminism, has focused on liberating women from the home and the household. Black feminism in particular has foregrounded home as a site of care and resistance. In the seminal essay "Homeplace (A Site of Resistance)," feminist author and educator bell hooks states that a "critique of the sexist definition of service" is needed just as much as it is crucial to understand that "one's homeplace was the site where one could freely confront the issue of human-ization, where one could resist" the conditions of "racial apartheid" and "domination."[5] What is a critical feminist approach, feminist theory as

hooks, "Homeplace," 41–50.

practice of liberation, to the question of home in architecture today? How do you, how does one, bring such a feminist approach into architectural theory, teaching, and practice?

SB I feel extreme kinship with what you're describing as has been identified by Black feminists before me. This isn't something that I necessarily like to attest in intellectual or scholarly terms. I could say that the kinship that I feel is extremely instinctive, shared, and even inherited. As it emerges out through my teaching and approaches towards work, I find companionship and strength from the many luminaries who have walked before me, and to whom I am indebted—like bell hooks, June Jordan, Angela Davis, Audre Lorde. In contemporary architectural practice, I'm fortunate to be able to seek out and think together with people like Anupama Kundoo, Samia Henni, Anooradha Iyer Siddiqi, Esther Choi, Marie Louise Richards, and Anna Puigjaner; we multiply our strands reading across the works of transformative thinkers like Arundhati Roy, Sara Ahmed, and Anna Tsing, among many others.

Bringing together both the realms of the domestic, and the almost-defensible, private manner in which I hold the lessons of these scholars close to me, relates to the possibility for surrender that I alluded to earlier. Compared to the world of the polis or the demos, home is a place of surrender: not surrendering *to* something, but a surrendering of arms. When we talk about bell hooks' "Homeplace," I conjure a place where one can drop the guard that one is forced to hold up—particularly as a woman of color—in any space that is *not* home. This act of holding up a guard is ultimately so exhausting that to posit the home as a woman's place as problematic—as certain strands of first-wave feminism might have reasonably felt justified in doing—seems quite wrong-headed. It becomes simplistic, as it serves to remove significance from just what it takes to survive outside of the home and just how precious it is to have sanctuary. A space where perhaps one's own politics might matter a little bit more than those agreed upon by the demos, by those who are properly accredited, and their hubris outside. This seems to me something that I know, as I mentioned, more instinctively than intellectually, in my body.

In terms of how I bring that through in teaching, again, it's not necessarily something that would come through in theory—although many of the scholars mentioned above are treasured discoveries for my students in many of our discussions. Rather, it comes through in the way we pursue and structure our conversations, and in allowing the freedom to challenge both canonical knowledge and dogmatic assumptions. Certainly, over the last five or six years, I've been actively encouraging students to bring a bit more of themselves to the table. It's something I might need to practice, as well as preach! It also involves applying pressure to the system to allow for and recognize other ways of producing and exchanging knowledge; in the ossified traditions of teaching architecture, this is no small task. There are many instances in which we might demonstrate students' own experiences as valid sites of learning. The hope is that this empowers people to bring their own "systems" of thinking into the classroom, and to push these around. If feminism is to be understood broadly as a liberatory practice, then it feels right to liberate ourselves from certain orthodoxies—while still understanding and relating to canonical systems and their impacts, we can still challenge these with altered, even dynamic metrics of value and meaning.

The explicitly "corrective" modes of white feminism or first-wave feminism played into certain binaries; staying open harder is undoubtedly work. Allowing, in the classroom and in student progression, for that complexity—allowing for people to have different value systems and navigate for themselves—does feel like a form of feminist practice, rather than imposing a particular dogma or sovereignty. We could talk about reading lists and curricula but those are easier things to change. In terms of feminist practice, perhaps the most vital forum is the "classroom" in whatever shape that takes; it's the way that we make space for each other and trust each other with our critical discussions. That seems to me one place to act or point at which to intervene, by enabling experience-based, critical thinking. I don't tend to describe these as explicitly feminist practices—yet, to return to hooks' essay, one seeks a space where there is permission to test out things, and to resist dominant discourses or disciplinary orthodoxies. Perhaps this is how I make myself "at home" with a mode of teaching.

EK "Zur Wohnungsfrage," the original German title of Friedrich Engels' text is a bit different from its translation into English. The original title actually means the question of the apartment. The title addresses the individual housing unit and not the apartment block or mass housing. "Zur Wohnungs-frage" has inspired my thinking before. I have turned to this title before to think about the differences and connections between housing units, that is the built dimensions of architectural units, and the everyday practices of living and homemaking that are performed in the built environments of homes. In a contribution to *Arch+* 244, first published in German in 2021 and then translated into English in 2024, I tried to mobilize this distinction for my title.[6] My original essay was titled "Die Wohnfrage," which even though very close to "Die Wohnungsfrage," raises a different set of questions.

Elke Krasny, "Die Wohnfrage. Von den Maßstäben der Sorge." *Arch+* 54/244 (2021): 52–55; Elke Krasny, "The Housing Question is the Question of Living: On Scales of Care" in *Arch+ Vienna – The End of Housing (as a Typology)*, eds. Anh-Linh Ngo et al. (Leipzig: Spector Books, 2024), 42–45.

My title asks about all the activities people perform in their apartments, in their homes, the activities which, in the broadest sense, are translated into "living" in English. One can say that the question of where you live gets very close to the connections between the place of living and the activities needed for living. In order to stay close to my intent, the English translation of the title of my essay is "The Housing Question is the Question of Living." I have explained this in some detail in order to show how closely connected the conditions of living are to the conditions of housing. What, then, if we bring this question to the home to ask the following: In what ways is the question of home the question of living?

SB I feel like I might repeat what has been said previously, in terms of the spaces for rehearsal and non-performance that I think of when I essentialize an idea of home, as opposed to living. Living—and I should not be shy here to specify my position as a woman of color—often requires so much front, so much energy, so many performances, even unto oneself. I was framing it another way, thinking about a mode of living as something over which one has greater authorship than one might over the prosaic conditions of home, or shelter. For instance, to what extent is authorship necessary to make oneself feel at home? That prompted bigger questions, like how do you measure authorship? For instance, is it only authorship if I bash a hole through the wall or change the layout of the house in a plan—or is it equally authorship that I make up different stories or invent little rituals that I do in different parts of the house? So I do that authorship by living, right? I have places where I like to sit. I have places where I know some good thoughts occurred to me. I know the place from which you can see foxes. These are not things that the architect has inscribed onto the house. That's something I've inscribed onto it. I know this isn't a perfect answer, but I have faith in the ways we have of inscribing ourselves onto space and, by extension, the way we see the world and where we might feel at home within it.

EK "The Question of Home" is a reference to Friedrich Engels' seminal text *The Housing Question*.[7] Engels provided his analysis of housing in the 1870s, at the heyday of the formation of colonial imperial capitalism. This formation also needs to be understood as spatialization. At the time, there was an extreme shortage of housing resulting from industrialization's hunger for working bodies. With people leaving their homes and moving to cities in order to become workers in factories, this new class of the urban proletariat was faced with a housing crisis and with extreme rents. In Engels' analysis

7   Frederick Engels, *The Housing Question* [1872] (New York: International Publishers, 2021).

this was not a problem of housing so much, but rather a problem of the capitalist mode of production. How can one make this problem of housing a problem of architecture and architects? How can we relate Engels' analysis to concerns of displacement, dispossession, and debt today?

SB I find it very difficult to imagine living outside of the city, so I live in London, paying alarming amounts of rent to prop up this system. I am still a subject of Engels' analysis, part of the urban proletariat who is faced with the housing crisis and extreme rent, so we're still there. Engels says it's not a problem of housing, but more of a capitalist mode of production, meaning that if the modes of production could be more distributed, then we wouldn't need that. Yet the concentration of cultural capital is why I'm here. To be clear, the concentration of cultural production is absolutely the thing that persuades me to keep paying my extortionate rent, bidding goodbye to the prospect of secure home ownership. I teach in an art school—across several, actually. I find myself in the cultural sector of the economy, also through my work with museums and galleries: all part of what Jameson described as an endless logic of capital, swallowing all forms of cultural production. When my partner suggests that we leave the city, I panic: I feel the things that I do only hold value in the city, or perhaps I require the throng and the intensity of dialogues and systems to hold my own resonance. Then too, as a woman of color I feel much safer in the city; kinship and solidarity are much easier to find. Yet on paper, it doesn't make much sense to perpetuate my living arrangements, especially in relation to conversations about mortgages and debt.

The title I suggested for this conversation comes from the Colin Ward quote; actually, a chapter title in one of his books: Housing is a verb, meaning that it's not an object to be produced, but that it is rather a program to be enacted by various actors. Ward was an anarchist—a planner and an anarchist—and has been quite influential in thinking about belonging and rights to the city. He seems like a relevant person to bring up in response to Engels, and perhaps his anarchist position tells you something about the messiness through which I think architecture might find some salvation. I'm not saying that it's necessary to leave the architectural discipline and get involved in politics or finance in order to address these issues of dispossession and displacement. A little promiscuity perhaps, a broadening of literacy in various areas, not least legal and labor protections, sociology, and science. I'm not breaking new ground here but there are still places where disciplinary autonomy is valued. Such archaicism has undoubtedly produced interesting meditations; in terms of broader planetary agency, however, architects may need to rethink the remit of our discipline as perceived. I'm not a practicing architect, so I want to advocate for the profession more than I want to critique it. But in order to keep momentum, or even agency—if we're to believe Colin Ward and the notion that housing is a verb, a word of action—we must acknowledge that architecture is neither a self-starting discipline nor can it ever be autonomous.

EK A specific strand of architectural history, in particular modern architectural history, has been produced through singling out houses as canonic objects. This tradition of "iconic houses," very often also the homes of famous architects, is currently being reproduced and continued via social media platforms such as Instagram. The iconicity, read visuality, of houses becomes their signature trait. Both of us had the honor and the privilege to work with the *Wall House* by Anupama Kundoo, which is a home the architect created for herself, for family, and also for working. How does one escape the traps of iconicity and visuality when working with houses that shape and redefine architecture? How would you describe the *Wall House* from the perspective of the question of home? What does one make of the fact that the *Wall House* is designed by and for an architect, and, at the same time not this architect's house, as neither land nor houses can be owned in Auroville? What does the *Wall House* bring to the question of living, and living otherwise?

SB With the *Wall House*, I have to think of the process in which I encountered it, and indeed of the process of its becoming. So I should confess that I have never actually visited Auroville—ideally, I'd visit a building before saying too much about it. Yet I can say that I have experienced the *Wall House*, at least part of its spatiality, because we did recreate parts of it at full scale for the Venice Biennale in 2012, on which I worked as an assistant curator under the directorship of David Chipperfield. If I were to identify the particular moments of pride and joy in my professional history, then persuading Anupama Kundoo to be part of our exhibition ranks high among them.[8] We had some very candid conversations; we both took issue with the word "vernacular," especially when it came to the framing of Anu's work. While she often borrows deeply from very situated knowledge and regional understandings of material, it seemed a rather gross simplification when referring to her practice. When I discussed this with Anupama in 2011, she was adamant in defining hers as a modernist approach. She expressed this in terms of her understanding of materials, technologies, and her desire to efficiently deploy these to achieve various functions of use and beauty; she saw this as not so different from the manner of working proliferated by modernist architects. Yet it seemed that her context as somebody trained

8   I would note that while academic conventions of respect would suggest that I refer to Anupama Kundoo using her surname, our friendship obliges me to use the more familiar "Anu." – S.B.

in the global South would invariably elicit the use of this word "vernacular." Besides being quite a sensitive and inventive architect, Anu is a really wonderful engineer; it was her total command of the technical, financial, and practical consequences of rebuilding her home—a fairly bold move, involving the movement of material from South India to Venice—which convinced and reassured Sir David of her caliber; Anu tells that story much better than I can here. In any case, I am bound to think of the *Wall House* in terms of how it is put together. The reality of rebuilding it in Venice involved not only tons of bricks arriving by boat, but also a team of highly skilled craftspeople and builders from South India, who instructed students from the University of Queensland in Brisbane and the IUAV in Venice. Across the installation, construction teams included South Indian craftspeople together with students, sharing knowledge and expertise across various traditions. Not to be romantic, but they really were eating and sleeping together, sharing information, and speaking across technologies. I recall it taking shape as a process of understanding, a product of experience and familiarity with materials and techniques, really in process. This is perhaps at odds with the suggestion that it is an icon, as I think of icons as rather coherent—so easy to grasp as to become a replicable image. The *Wall House* was not designed to be an icon, yet in the unusual manner in which it takes its shape, it has an iconic value.

Returning to the question of home, my reading of Anupama's *Wall House* aligns with a dynamic understanding of hom-ing or the act of making oneself at home. This is a series of experiments that the architect has trialed, tested, and then composed; I believe it is an ongoing site of experimentation in forms of life. There are so many elements of that house—from the perforated concrete to the inlaid terracotta bowls; the vaulted roof made of locally produced components to the use of ferrocement; the technical and formal experiments that have been perhaps trialed elsewhere—arranged in response to the way in which the inhabitant wishes to set out their life, and testifies to their depth of knowledge. Anupama's somewhat autodidactic professional trajectory has seen her experiment with so many materials and technologies of construction, indeed partly through the many one-to-one building tests developed in Auroville. That is partly as a result of the singular entity that is Auroville, which allows for such experimentation precisely because rather than private ownership, it is stewarded by a larger entity that responds to the needs of its community. As such, the *Wall House* is this opera of lived experience as well as experiment. I find it easier to crystallize its attitude than it is to read this house as an icon, despite the fact that it has, of course, many beautifully intentional, memorable, and recognizable features.

As to whether this is the architect's house, perhaps this is a question of how we value spatial authorship as opposed to property ownership... Allow me to recount an anecdote that has stayed with me since the curatorial period of *Home Economics*; this came from Rachel Bagenal, one of the cofounders of the not-for-profit developer Naked House, and her experience working in the housing department for the London Borough of Hackney. She shared a seemingly quotidian story about a council tenant who had been in his residence for a number of years, but who had no prospect of owning it; the property is owned by the municipality. The tenant had nonetheless installed polished marble flooring in a part of his home. Now, this person had no vested interest; that is to say there was no real potential for financial gain or profit through this significant material investment. Rather, he installed it simply because he wanted to live with it, to enjoy it. This too aligns with our earlier discussion around ownership, in the sense that I believe that we inscribe ownership through the act of living in a particular space, rather than through outright possession. Home is all the spaces in which I identify and inscribe my own patterns of living, in which I can read modes of life that are in some part authored or constructed by me, regardless of ownership. Anupama, too, has lived in myriad experimental spaces, many of them self-built. Going back to "Homeplace," the bell hooks essay which has threaded through this conversation, the text describes the act of establishing a homeplace as a claim to agency.[8] hooks writes of it as an act that "elevated our spirits" and "kept us from despair, and that taught some of us to be revolutionaries." This goes back to our notion of rehearsal, and the fact that domestic space allows us to rehearse the forms of life. As a composition of Anu's practice, knowledge, and experience, I see the house as a space of rehearsal for enacting forms of life—which very much confirms it as the architect's house in this ownership and authorship, without necessarily dealing with those material aspects of property or land. Now, those elements of land and property have many fundamental and critical discourses attached to them. But in terms of making home, it's this dynamic process in which the experiment of living can be rehearsed.

9 hooks, 41–50.

On Maintenance

Elke Krasny in conversation with Shannon Mattern

Architecture, most broadly understood, only endures because of acts of maintenance ranging from daily scrubbing and cleaning to facility management and large-scale repair work. Yet, the importance of the work of maintenance only seems to come into view when the negligent maintenance of buildings causes injuries or even deaths of people or when the meticulous and precise work of restoration is celebrated as it maintains valued landmark buildings and architectural icons, often protected by heritage laws. Until quite recently, maintenance was completely neglected in the history and theory of architecture. It only appeared in the news when buildings made headlines because of maintenance catastrophes or when a building was spectacularly saved through restoration. One exception is architect Hilary Sample's 2016 book *Maintenance Architecture*.[1] Shannon Mattern's 2018 essay, "Maintenance and Care. A working guide to the repair of rust, dust, cracks, and corrupted code in our cities, our homes, and our social relations,"[2] expanded the notion of maintenance even beyond individual buildings and brought maintenance as a lens to urban environments and social relations. In relation to understanding abundance of architecture and abundance in architecture, maintenance is key. Maintenance, as one can argue, keeps alive and thus creates architectural abundance. Maintenance can also become a form of resistance to the capitalist speed of construction cycles and its disastrous impact on accelerating climate ruination. Acknowledging maintenance also means acknowledging the labors and knowledge of all those who invest their work, their time, and their expertise into keeping buildings alive and ready to use. The following research conversation on maintenance with interdisciplinary scholar Shannon Mattern was conducted via email by Elke Krasny.

EK I would like to begin this written conversation on maintenance in relation to critical architectural and spatial practices today with what can be referred to as an eye-opening maintenance experience of architecture. When researching the context of Anupama Kundoo's built work in Puducherry,

---

1 Hilary Sample, *Maintenance Architecture* (Cambridge, MA: The MIT Press, 2018).

2 Shannon Mattern, "Maintenance and Care," *Places Journal*, November 2018, https://doi.org/ 10.22269/181120.

Angelika Fitz and I had the opportunity to visit *Golconde*, which is India's first modernist building. Mirra Alfassa, referred to as "The Mother," invited architect Antonin Raymond, a Czech-American architect who primarily worked in Tokyo, to design this building, which serves as a dormitory for the members of the spiritual commune Sri Aurobindo Ashram. Today, this building, a reinforced concrete structure completed in 1945, which made the building seventy-nine years old at the time we visited it, is pristinely and meticulously maintained. This includes not only infrastructural maintenance and technological and facility management, but also everyday material maintenance and care. In the building's lower level, I noticed a line made of paving stones. Each of the stones had a slightly different size, there were little spaces between the stones, and, curiously, each of the stones was numbered. I asked our tour guide about these numbers. She explained that the numbers were written with white chalk on the surface of the stones by the cleaners. They regularly clean the stones, and, equally, if not more importantly, they also clean the spaces underneath the stones. Numbering them helps to put the stones back in the right order. Such a dedication to maintaining a building, a modernist building considered an architectural icon, is extraordinary and impressive. It made me think of the attentiveness needed to understand the maintenance needs of a building, and also opened up a number of questions in relation to the knowledge, labors, and ethics of maintenance, which I would like to share with you.

SM I am not sure if you wanted me to respond to this opening anecdote, Elke, but I will note that it made me reflect on an article I recently published about the history, politics, and aesthetics of the repair manual—and whether the genre of the manual is equally applicable to gadgets, larger structures, and expansive social or ecological systems. In that article I talked about the value of what philosopher Ivan Illich calls "convivial" objects and structures that invite repair, and that make readily intelligible—often through their form and composition—their operative logics and instructions for their own repair.[3] In the anecdote you have shared here, it is clear that *Golconde*'s cleaners have partnered with the building to ensure that its "manual" is written directly on the structure itself. In a sense, *Golconde* is its own embodied maintenance diagram!

EK Maintenance, in the context of *Golconde*, appears at different scales, different levels of intensity, and different areas of expertise. There is the everyday maintenance of cleaning, there is infrastructural maintenance, and there is technological innovation and maintenance. I would like to

3   Ivan Illich, *Tools for Conviviality*
(London: Calder & Boyars, 1973).

invite you to reflect upon scales of maintenance and what they bring to a building, what they perform for maintaining architecture, and what kind of labor and knowledge is needed to identify and understand the maintenance needs of a building.

SM Vents, spigots, switches, plugs, and control panels are our interfaces to larger building systems. Ideally, each time we turn the knob or flip the switch, we would think about the pipes and wires that connect us to those architectural systems—and to the municipal utilities and global networks that bring data and power to our homes, as well as those that flush trash and stormwater away. We would also recall that all the nodes and links at each layer of those systems require maintenance. But such cross-scalar conscious-ness often presents too great a cognitive load: We can't always contemplate, each time we clean a toilet or put out the trash, the labor and expertise expended at the extreme ends of our infrastructural systems. And as so many of our architectural apparatae are computerized and wired into automated systems, it becomes impossible for us not only to ensure the smooth operation of the system as a whole, but even, in some cases, to take responsibility for the nodes in our homes. This is why it is increasingly important for us to ensure that our buildings are constructed of convivial, sustainable materials and technologies that lend themselves to immediate, local maintenance—and that we also care about how those local nodes are connected to larger systems and supply chains, which would also, ideally, lend themselves to maintenance.

EK *Golconde* also made Angelika and I think of the modernist promise of forever, or perhaps even forever young, that was represented and materialized by modernist architecture. In the twentieth century, concrete came to be viewed as the right material, the material of choice, in order to build for eternity. Modernist architecture joined together the two claims for contem-poraneity, of now-ness, and of permanent future, of unchanged future existence. There is a rift, a gap between what these buildings represent and stand for, and how they materialize this promise as they age, and often times do not age well, over time.

Now, modernist buildings, as all buildings, are dependent upon their material condition in order to exist, and to exist well. Many of these buildings show signs of aging and even neglect or decay. At the same time, the materials used for these buildings, in particular concrete and steel, render obvious that the material choices of modernism were problematic, as they resulted in causing environmental and climate ruination. What does this mean for a new understanding and new practices of maintenance? What are your suggestions for understanding maintenance differently?

SM If we link this question to your previous query—about scales of maintenance—we might consider how cross-scalar thinking could inform our choice of building materials. How can we select materials that balance our immediate—as in both temporally and spatially proximate—and distributed needs for maintenance, that balance local ease of upkeep with commitments to ecological conservation, for instance? How can we balance the demands on local cleaning staff with the burdens placed on the crews charged with clean-up or remediation where our building materials are extracted, harvested, fabricated, or recycled?

It is also important to determine what degrees and kinds of degradation are inevitable, or even desirable. Geographer Caitlin DeSilvey proposes that we practice "curated decay," which involves a collaboration with natural processes.[4] More recently, Kiel Moe and Daniel Friedman have proposed that we shift our focus from "maintenance" to "tending," which, as they describe it, "accepts, anticipates, and designs in consonance with inevitable change — and it understands this change as a desirable expression of material properties, site dynamics, inter-species coexistence, and the behavior of buildings and their contexts over time."[5] In other words, it requires cross-scalar sensitivity. Thus, "curated delay" and "tending" are not simply matters of resigning ourselves to unavoidable deterioration or absolving ourselves of the responsibility of care. To the contrary, Moe and Friedman say, such approaches require "assiduous attention: observing the full bio-geophysical circumstances that influence how something exists or appears in the world"[6]— and, I would add, how it fades away.

EK *Golconde*, which is now almost eighty years old, made me think of how humans age and how we relate to processes of aging in relation to maintenance. A human being about to celebrate their eightieth birthday is not expected to have the body of a forty-year-old person or to move like a twenty-year-old person. It is understood that a human being who has lived for eighty years has other needs than a human being who is very young. How can this thought be helpful to think about age and buildings differently? How can needs that are specific to aging buildings be diagnosed and understood in order to develop maintenance practices that are different from the norms, in particular norms of capital?

SM "Curated decay" and "tending" incorporate a sensitivity to how maintenance needs evolve as a building ages. We might also supplement architects'

---

4 Caitlin DeSilvey, *Curated Decay* (Minneapolis, MN: University of Minnesota Press, 2017).

5 Kiel Moe and Daniel S. Friedman, "Tending Building,"

Places Journal, February 2024, https://placesjournal.org/article/tending-building-an-ethic-of-repair-in-architecture/.

6 Ibid.

standard approach to "lifecycle analysis," which assesses a building's environmental impact throughout its life, with archivists' understanding of a record's lifecycle, which considers their responsibilities to material from its creation through its decay or destruction. Aging media necessitate different strategies of care—and these evolving needs are ideally anticipated at the time a record is made or a collection is acquired. A similarly longitudinal approach can be applied to architecture.

What's more, if we think about architecture and archives together, we can also appreciate how buildings themselves are historical records and integral components of cultural heritage. They age along with the communities that live with them, and they come to embody and scaffold the accumulated wisdom of those communities. They carry the material traces of their entwined lives. The epistemological and experiential depth that comes with age merits sensitive strategies for maintenance, too.

^{EK} Thinking about aging buildings and maintenance also made me think of a number of other dimensions of maintenance. What is the cost of maintenance? Or, more specifically, how do we understand the cost of maintenance in terms of labor, environment, and climate? How do we place the cost of maintenance in relation to the value of maintenance?

^{SM} Keeping with our cultural heritage metaphors, buildings—like rare books and archival materials—circulate within multiple economies, each of which defines and operationalizes "cost" and "value" in different ways. Buildings are investments, they are public goods, they are artifacts of cultural heritage, they are social infrastructures, they are embodiments of community and family memory. These different identities, and the economies within which they resonate, can sometimes work at cross purposes. Investing in the upkeep of a structure might enhance its market value and that of other properties on the block, which can benefit local property owners but cost local renters their capacity to stay. Investing in the maintenance of an energy-inefficient structure—whose upkeep requires the labor and carbon-intensive logistical deployment of multiple specialists and voluminous resources—can exact significant environmental costs. Maintaining a building with significant historical value or community meaning might require large investments of capital and labor and offer little *measurable* return on that investment—but it could be of incalculable symbolic and ethical value. Maintenance requires balancing these multiple economic considerations, which itself requires acknowledgment that, in some economies, *value* is immeasurable in quantitative terms.

^{EK} If maintenance adds value to buildings, how is maintenance valued? Why is maintenance often badly paid and considered menial labor or cheap

labor? Do you see differences and hierarchies within the kinds of labors needed for maintenance? How do you see local differences in labor cost reflected in how buildings are being maintained and cared for?

SM The subjects *to* which, locations *in* which, and the scales *at* which maintenance is applied often determine its social and financial values. Social reproduction—itself a form of social maintenance that has historically been a form of feminized labor—is typically unwaged. We might pay someone a couple hundred dollars to fix our laptop. We would probably pay a plumber or HVAC technician significantly more to fix our domestic building systems. And we would pay engineering firms hundreds of thousands, if not millions of dollars, to maintain our bridges and airplanes. These valuations are often based on (questionable) assumptions regarding the skills necessitated by and stakes of the operation.

EK In the local context of Puducherry, Angelika and I observed rituals of celebration and pride connected to the labors of maintenance needed in the home. Women who clean their homes draw a mandala in front of their houses on the surface of the sidewalk or the street to show to others, to the public, that the daily work of maintaining and cleaning their houses is finished. Anupama also shared with us the fact that the women, after having finished the cleaning their homes, adorn themselves by putting some flowers in their hair. Can you think of rituals of maintenance that show pride in this work which is often considered menial work?

SM Self-care and -improvement culture has transformed the seemingly "menial" work of bodily upkeep into a ritual of pride and self-affirmation. Yet even those values have different political and moral valences within different communities. This past semester two students in my "Local Media" class focused their final projects on African-American hair and nail care. Barbers, stylists, and "nail techs"—and I do think it is significant that these artisans refer to themselves as "technicians"—situate their time-intensive work within celebratory, affirming social rituals. And those care workers share the outcomes of their work with great pride on their social media accounts and salon walls.

Sometimes repair technicians and cleaning staff will place signed cards or seals on, or wrap paper bands around, mended objects and perfectly plumped hotel pillows to mark their work and signal its readiness for use. The owner then has the pleasure of peeling off the seal, or tearing the band, as a symbol of rebirth. I do wonder, though, about these and other practices— folding the end of the toilet paper into a little point, placing artfully folded towels on the bathroom counter. Are they self-directed expressions of pride, or are they compulsory acts of affective labor, a corporate directive that obligates underpaid, overworked employees to perform their dedication for guests, who might then supplement their below-minimum-wage paychecks with a tip?

EK Maintenance is central in relation to the contemporary paradigm of sustainability in architecture. Sometimes, maintenance is cost-intensive, requires technological innovation, and is labor-intensive. Sometimes, maintenance is not aligned with sustainability. Could you think of examples of this?

SM I think some of my previous responses already address this question. Maintaining massive hydroelectric dams can exacerbate and perpetuate the devastation of riparian ecosystems. Maintaining highways and city streets can mean de-prioritizing public transit, bike, and pedestrian infrastructure, and public space. And under the current (as of Spring 2024) New York City mayor, maintaining a well-equipped and compensated police force means undervaluing parks and libraries.

EK To complicate matters, I propose thinking about how maintenance is valued differently in relation to different types of buildings. Some buildings are valued more than others. Economic value hinges on maintenance. Symbolic and cultural value, even the value in global architectural history, is measured in and reflected through the status quo maintenance.

What is the value of maintenance and how do we value buildings through their maintenance? Listed buildings are valued through maintenance. Other buildings are neglected. Introducing the concept of maintenance justice and rights to maintenance here, I would like to invite you to think about the politics of maintenance and the social, cultural, and economic values of maintenance and how they complement, contradict, and complicate each other. Should all buildings be treated equally? Should all buildings have equal maintenance rights? Who should decide over the right to maintenance in architecture, a right to maintenance beyond concerns of heritage and protected monuments?

SM Again, I think my response to the previous question about costs and values touches on these issues. I would add only that these competing economies of "value" typically determine which buildings are *worthy* of maintenance—and certain of those economies carry more weight than others! Historical preservationists, real estate developers, global cultural heritage organizations, and other such entities typically determine which structures will be maintained. Sometimes, community associations and activist organizations can exercise influence, too. As for who *should* determine maintenance priorities: again, we have to balance the different, often competing priorities of these overlapping economies. Yet it is clear that market economic values eclipse other considerations. We need to recalibrate this calculus so other equally meaningful values—which often defy calculation and reveal themselves longitudinally—can be given their due.

EK We can understand neglect of buildings as the intentional withholding of maintenance. Such neglect is one of the ways through which the violence of capital acts on buildings. Can you think of local or international examples of such intentional neglect of maintenance? Can you think of political organizing and new pedagogies in architecture in order to counteract such intentional withholding of maintenance which, in its extreme forms, can lead to the abandonment and destruction of buildings and domicide? The neglect of maintenance also presents a risk to the lives of inhabitants and users of buildings. Can you think of examples where a lack of maintenance puts inhabitants or workers at risk or even cost them their lives?

SM The intentional failure to maintain safe working conditions and labor rights in construction and the building trades certainly puts architecture *workers'* lives in danger. Withholding maintenance—of housing, public utilities, social infrastructures, and so forth—can then be deployed as a means of passive redlining, of tacitly effecting eminent domain and pushing populations from areas that gradually become unlivable. Failure to contain and maintain abject zones—like extraction sites, industrial farms, and landfills—likewise threatens those who live in close proximity.

At the scale of the gadget: planned obsolescence often manifests as a refusal to repair gadgets after a certain number of years, thus compelling consumers to upgrade—and flushing their outmoded equipment into global waste streams, which create ecological maintenance challenges in terrains far removed from the Apple Store. As more and more urban infrastructures and building systems are networked into digital systems and outsourced to tech vendors, the maintenance of their hardware and software is integral to the upkeep of buildings and cities.

Design pedagogy should cultivate concern about labor rights and various dimensions of social justice. Students should be introduced to projects and collectives like Who Builds Your Architecture? and The Architecture Lobby. They should be encouraged to think about the larger supply chains and waste streams within which they work. They should also engage with local environmental and digital justice advocates and familiarize themselves with the field methods and community organizing strategies they use in their work.

EK So far, I have been thinking about maintenance in relation to existing buildings, to buildings that are already here. What if we begin thinking about the maintenance of buildings in relation to the design process and transforming existing buildings or building new architectures? Can you think of architects who have designed and planned buildings based on requirements of maintenance, in material, technological, and infrastructural terms, but also in terms of everyday cleaning and repair? What would such maintenance architecture do differently? What are important ways of thinking with maintenance in order to design otherwise? Can you give some concrete examples of how maintenance requirements and needs could become different conceptual starting points for designing?

SM We can draw inspiration from landscape architects who work with remediated terrains like brownfields and architects who focus on adaptive reuse. Particular building types—including, for instance, laboratories, libraries, and data centers—require attunement to needs for technical maintenance. Labs, commercial and industrial kitchens, hotels, and hospitals ideally facilitate everyday cleaning. Creating spaces to accommodate such upkeep requires involving maintenance workers and cleaners in the design process, observing them doing their work in a variety of spaces, allowing them to perform their expertise and narrate their processes, and inviting them to reflect on how their existing work environment helps and hinders their work—and how an improved environment could make their work more efficient, effective, safe, fulfilling, and empowering.

EK Very often, maintenance is thought to maintain buildings in their original state, or as close as possible to how they were when they were first constructed. What about letting processes of change and transformation become part of maintenance? What would it require to think architecture through aging and weathering and make these processes part of maintenance without maintaining or restoring buildings as originals? Could we think of new forms and critical contemporary practices of maintenance architecture? Can you think of examples? How do you view the responsibility of architects in relation to maintenance when thinking about the conditions of labor and the impact of architecture on the environment?

SM Critical historic preservationists are already thinking in these terms. They take into consideration the spirit or essence of a project; the designer's motivation and vision; evolving ecological, socioeconomic, and political contexts; new ethical obligations; the shifting availability or renewability of materials; and so forth. Our earlier discussion of "curated decay" and "tending" represent additional approaches to designing for maintenance.

EK Care and maintenance have become central concerns in contemporary architectural discourse and practice. In 2016, Angelika and I started working on a project called *Care+Repair*, which then led to an edited volume titled *Critical Care. Architecture and Urbanism for a Broken Planet*. In 2018, your seminal essay "Maintenance and Care" was published in *Places Journal*. Why do you think that politics and ethics of care and politics and ethics of maintenance have become central themes in architecture today? What has changed over the last ten years since architecture and urbanism have turned to concerns of care and maintenance? What can we learn from the last decade of critical engagement with maintenance and care?

SM As I noted in my "Maintenance and Care" piece—which I intended to serve as a literary "environmental scan" of relevant work across myriad fields of study and practice—we have seen an explosion of critical work and activism around maintenance over the past decade or more. The decline of infrastructures funded and constructed after World War II—structures that were then over sixty years old—drove home the repercussions of our inattention to maintenance. More recently, we witnessed the dangers of Silicon Valley's ascendance. Its fetishization of innovation, and the willful historical ignorance that undergirds its boundless hubris yield both the risk of repeating historical mistakes and ignorance of, or disinterest in, the value of maintaining basic civic infrastructures. Even more recently, the resurgence of authoritarianism and historical revisionism, along with deliberate attacks on our public institutions and infrastructures, have again reminded us of what is at stake when we fail to maintain all the hard and soft systems that hold our society together.

Since the proliferation of maintenance-related work in the design realm, we have seen more interest in social justice, labor politics, building lifecycles, supply chains, climate and carbon footprints, and healthy materials. Not all of these new or strengthened commitments were *inspired* by the work on maintenance, but these simultaneous, complementary concerns are part of a broader ethical sensibility.

And while this strengthened focus on maintenance has helped to challenge the uncritical valorization of innovation, maintenance and care have themselves become, in some cases, a fetish, an empty orthodoxy, a performative aesthetic: It is pastels and succulents and land acknowledgments. It is important that, in this age of converging climatic, technological, economic, and political crises, we rebuild a broken world that can withstand shock and insulate those who are most vulnerable—a world that facilitates the maintenance of our most fundamental, essential infrastructures.

Feminist Practices and Architectures of Care

Elke Krasny in conversation with Rupali Gupte

The following text is an interview with Rupali Gupte, an architect, urbanist, and educator with a focus on feminist practices of care and the role of gender in architecture and the built environment. Starting from the shared interest in feminist practices and in widening the understanding of the concept of care in spatial and material terms beyond Western-centered traditions of ethics and theorizing, the interview foregrounds multidimensional and multidisciplinary practices in architecture and urbanism, including different ways of teaching and learning and redefining architectural pedagogies. Emphasizing spatial and pedagogical practices that resist compulsory neoliberal capitalism, the focus is on care, inhabitation, land rights of Indigenous communities, and responses to monsoon conditions and climate change across South Asia.

Elke Krasny You have, for a long time, been interested in care in relation to architecture and urbanism. What sparked your interest in care? What does the notion of care bring to the understanding and making of architecture that other concepts such as sustainability, resilience, or degrowth, to name just a few of the contemporary keywords, do not entail?

Rupali Gupte A group of us realized very early on that the discipline of architecture cannot be seen in isolation. It needs a multidisciplinary approach. Our practice started bringing together architecture, art, and urban studies. Cities and their lived relationships became important to understand architecture. But art became an important mediator to ask new questions about what we were seeing and experiencing. In the mid-2000s we formed an architecture and urbanism collective called CRIT (Collective Research Initiative Trust – https://crit.in). More recently, two of us have been consolidating our works and thoughts through a multidisciplinary practice called Bard Studio (https://bardstudio.in). Along with some other colleagues we also started an architecture school called the School of Environment and Architecture (SEA) (https://sea.edu.in). Through all these consolidations, questions of care have been central to our thinking, as they allow architects to think in multidisciplinary ways. We hope to shift the idea of architecture as a cartographically contained space to start thinking of it as "inhabitation" in more relational ways. This is hinged on an understanding that spatial imaginations, institutional forms, and lived experiences for humans and more-than-human forms are all linked.

EK You are invested in innovating and redefining architectural pedagogies. Can you describe when and why the School of Architecture and Environment was founded, the teaching methodologies you have developed, and the specific interest in care, which was also part of the school's program.

RG We founded the School of Environment and Architecture (SEA) in 2014. The founders came with various interests and from diverse practices: conservation, landscape design, housing activism, art, etc. We were keen on reformulating architectural pedagogy to make it relevant for contemporary times. The idea of care was very important for this. In 2019 I did a studio at SEA called "What Is a Clinic? Architecture of Care." This was part of a series of studio projects we offered every year to second-year undergraduate students. Instead of taking a program as a given, we trained students to ask ontological questions about an architectural program. The students traced the program's genealogy, the spatial type that evolved vis-à-vis this program, and asked what a new type could be for this program in the contemporary context and how the program could evolve around questions of spatial justice. Care became an important rubric to shift the idea of the institution of the clinic from its medicalized idea to that of embodied social relations. The focus helped students shift the idea of the clinic from questions embedded in the standards and efficiency of a clinic and its workings to ideas of well-being embedded in questions of care and its spatialization. The idea of care extends to other studios, with the third year addressing questions of the environment and the fourth year dealing with questions of gender, labor, etc., as a part of the investigations on emerging urbanisms in second cities in India. Care helps to repoliticize questions around the environment that have shifted from the politics of reclaiming land by Indigenous groups in India in the early 1960s to the recent hijack by corporate capitalism as they aggressively push trends in greening and carbon credits to inflate their markets. Care also helps in thinking of emerging urbanism in new ways as we shift from neutral ideas of urban design that has a generic "public" at its center, to starting to understand how these are implicated in questions of difference.

At SEA, friendships and solidarities become important to rejig its institutional structures. We see the school as a set of practices and students as companions in the journey who are trained to ask long questions and to set up their own longue durée practices. Instead of a lecture-based form of teaching, we like to build the pedagogy around conversations. We like to see the production of knowledge as a collaborative process rather than an individualized one. Care becomes the basic unit for tying people together.

EK Thinking about care and social reproduction in the specific context of India and South Asia more broadly, what are the most significant specifics and how do they come to bear on architecture and urbanism?

RG At SEA we have a research cluster on South Asian Architecture and Urbanism, which I lead. We have been trying to build an archive of spatial practices in South Asia, which we believe can help shift the theorization of space for us. Through our multidisciplinary practice called Bard Studio, we have been writing on urban form and its affordances in South Asia. To analyze urban form in South Asia we employ the term "transactional capacities," which we coined in an essay we wrote a few years ago in *e-flux Journal* called "It Takes so Much for a City to Happen,"[1] further articulated recently in a paper for *Public Culture* called "Small Forces."[2] This framework, we argue, can be used to theorize an architecture not only of South Asia but also from South Asia, in order to reimagine spatial logics in the world. Transactional capacity builds on the term "affordance" used by the psychologist James Gibson.[3] Take the example of two streets: one street affords only a rapid movement of people, the other one affords them the opportunity to linger, watch, shop, meet, etc. The affordance of urban form produces a transactional possibility where human beings are not only able to derive utility for buying, selling, inspecting, etc., but also of pleasure, safety, security, and care. The urban form also impacts transactions between human beings—they are able to watch, meet, talk, exchange, etc., with each other. The affordance of urban form is its "transactional capacity," the capacity to allow flows of bodies, commodities, money, ideas, imaginations, and environment through it: the higher the flow, the higher the transactional capacity. The urban form of the second street that affords multiple transactional capacities is porous, corroded, and blurred, allowing for multiple exchanges and occupancies. As opposed to this, the first street has defined and clarified edges like boundary walls that do not allow transactions and are bound by proprietary logics. The second street has higher transactional capacities. Transactional capacities are further defined as densities, number of activities, networks, transactions, care, livelihoods, cultural settling, security, accommodation of diversity, imaginations, etc. The idea of care is inherent to the idea of transactional capacities. Architecture in South Asia abounds in transactional capacities.

Rupali Gupte and Prasad Shetty, It Takes so Much for a City to Happen," *e-flux Journal* no. 65 May 2015), https://www.e-flux. com/journal/65/ 336404/ it-takes-so-much-for-a-city-to-happen/.

2 Rupali Gupte and Prasad Shetty, "Small Forces," *Public Culture, Urbanism beyond the City* 34, no. 3 (98), (September 1, 2022): 537–62, https://doi.org/ 10.1215/08992363-9937424.

3 James Gibson, *The Ecological Approach to Visual Perception* (Boston: Houghton Mifflin, 1979).

EK More recently, the understanding of care was expanded to include not only social care and dimensions of social reproduction and maintenance, but to pertain to environmental care, planetary care, and climate care. How does this play out in the local context of India? How does environmental care relate to dynamics of accelerated urbanization and the industrialization of the rural? What does urban planning and architectural designing with the environment and the climate mean in the local context?

RG Urbanization and industrialization are not a problem. It's the precluding of an alternative modernity that has the possibilities of allowing spatial thinking that works with ideas of commoning, collectivization, multiple shared tenures, and impermanence. However, a point to be noted here is that while we do face the dangers of rapid modernization unleashed by capitalist processes, the politics on the ground in India, (as well as most of South Asia), makes for a patchy urbanization where the rural and the urban coexist, and the obstinate practices of people that are in sync with ecological conditions keep coming back like a multi-headed hydra to contend with this capture. This is actually an interesting situation, unlike the West, where this process is a lot more "successful," but also a lot more violent. Visions of architectural designs with the environment and the climate in focus, when reduced to the visions of one person or one homogeneous group of people, tend to be equally problematic, as they erase many more claims on the ground. In India, for instance, we find many lands where multiple tenures exist at the same time. The same piece of land tilled by a farmer in fair weather is flooded in the monsoon, allowing the fisherfolk to use it for fishing. The ambiguity of tenure has allowed multiple claims as well as a complex economic relationship that is in tandem with ecological cycles. A process of modernization that believes in one vision tends to erase these complexities and relationships. In Bangladesh, some of our field work, as well as Marina Tabassum's study of prefabricated houses,[4] show that in a shifting land and water situation, a whole ecosystem of carpenters has evolved, who make beautiful prefabricated houses out of wood and tin that people can buy in a market called the *ghorer haat* or house market.[5] These are ways in which architecture has been responding to questions of climate change and complex ecological terrains, but these are relational ideas that do not come from a singular plan.

4 Marina Tabassum, *Prefabricated Houses of Bangladesh*, Sharjah Architecture Triennial, 2019.
5 Rupali Gupte, "Of Corrosions, Continuums, Refractions, Seepages and Entanglements: Towards an Architecture of Life," *Inside Space Surface Object* 3, no. 1 (2023): 8–27.

Prefabricated houses in Munshiganj in Bangladesh that negotiate the fluid land and water condition
Photos: Rupali Gupte

EK Can you give some examples of caring architecture and caring urbanism in the local context of India and South Asia more broadly? What are methods used to produce caring architecture and caring urbanism? What distinguishes these architectures? What sets them apart from architecture as business as usual?

RG As mentioned above, we use the term "transactional capacities" to evaluate architecture. To give you an example, consider Zaobawadi, a chawl in Mumbai. The chawl is a particular housing type that evolved in Mumbai at two points in its history. The first was during the mercantile economy when the East India Company invited traders from neighboring parts to facilitate its trade. Traders came in large numbers to set up their enterprises in the inner city. Around the port where they settled were orchards and plantations. Plantation owners found it lucrative to build housing for these traders. The first chawls in Mumbai were built here. The second time was in the 1850s when cotton textile mills were moved to the colony from Britain. This is when cotton textile mills were set up in Mumbai. The mill owners built chawls for the workers who came from the hinterland to work in the mills. A chawl generally has one or two rooms strung along one or more corridors with common toilets. The tenement in Zaobawadi is a twenty-

Zaobawadi Chawl, a housing project
with high transactional capacities
Photo: Rupali Gupte and Sunil Thakkar

five-square-meter space. The houses, however, are never perceived as small, because there are wide corridors where much of life spills out. There are bridges that connect parallel corridors, where people are seen hanging out. One resident told us they were able to survive COVID only because they lived in such a building. They pointed to a multi-story tower next door, which a neighboring chawl was redeveloped into. They said they would have felt trapped and suffocated if their building was also redeveloped into this form. Although the houses in the tower were bigger than the chawl tenements, there was a sense of alienation that the apartment created. The chawl for the residents, on the other hand, felt like one large house. In the absence of social security, it is the form of the house that allows the inhabitants to watch out for each other and the architecture provides the transactional capacity to be able to do so. This is an architecture of care, one that has high transactional capacities. South Asia is full of many such examples of architectures of care.

EK Imaginaries, as well as affective and spiritual understandings of care, but also the material conditions of care, have to do with the meanings this word holds. In my mother language, which is German, to care not only means to take care of someone or of something, but also means to worry.

Zaobawadi Chawl, a housing project
with high transactional capacities
Photos: Rupali Gupte and Sunil Thakkar

I would like to invite you to explain how different languages spoken across India carry different meanings of care and thus result in different ontologies and cosmologies of caring relations. How do these understandings of care play out in the understanding of social and environmental interrelatedness and interdependencies?

RG Care can be translated into many words. In Marathi, my mother tongue, it is *kalji*, which incidentally also means "to worry." But it is also *purna laksha*, full attention, an attention to detail, as opposed to standardized or universal solutions. It can also be *savadhanata*, or "alertness, vigilance, watchfulness." This calls for an attentiveness to people and things around, as opposed to the narcissism of individualized societies. It can also be *khabardari*, which translates as "caution." This would mean caution in using resources, to prevent over-consumption and over-exploitation. Colonial education seems to have truncated many ways of thinking of the materiality of our inhabitations. For example, the ephemeral construction processes that we have developed over years of cultural consolidations in South Asia are often termed crude and impermanent in modern discourse. A close attention to the glossary of terms around inhabitation in local languages opens new epistemic thinking around inhabitation that is much more attuned to ideas of care. A house in coastal Maharashtra, for instance, is made of multiple concentric spatial layers. The outermost is called the *aangan*, the court which is the most public. The next layer is often a long verandah called the *padvi*, which is semi-public. This is a space where, through a tacit agreement with the neighborhood, friends and acquaintances can come and sit and don't have to be formally invited to do so. The next layer is the *osri*, which is where old people are often seen spending hours hanging out, waiting for people to stop by. The innermost area is called the *ghar*, which is the place of storage. The kitchen is often part of the *padvi* at the rear, connected to the *ghar*. This is a space connected to the yard with plenty of room to move around. Most of life is spent outdoors, as the climate permits. These nuanced ideas of inhabitation have changed through government funding structures and new aspirational models of construction into a standardized idea of the house, tied to ideas of property, permanence, and privacy. These have in turn more fully changed the ways we inhabit.

EK Many thinkers and theorists, but also architectural and urban practitioners, have foregrounded that care ethics have a specific relation to responsibility. How do you see the responsibility of architecture and architects today in light of the conditions of the global present?

RG Architectural practices today are often caught in operational logistics, where to survive they have to feed into an extractive logic of development.

All they care about is serving the client. But the client as a concept is far beyond the person who pays for the project; it includes all those people and the various species of plants and organisms that get affected by the architectural project. By default, an architect is a custodian of the environment and culture. For this, the approach of any given practice needs to be much more multidisciplinary. This may also necessitate an organizational restructuring of offices and studios beyond the patron-dependent nature of practice.

EK Caring, understood as work, and care ethics as a specific way of relating to the world, have been central to some strands of feminist theory and practice. How do you see the relationships between feminisms, care, architecture, and urbanism? Are there feminist practices in contemporary Indian architecture and urbanism that you view as specific answers to the challenges and responsibilities of care?

RG A theorization of architecture and urbanism requires being inflected with feminist thinking to unsettle some of the settled ways of spatial thinking that we have normalized. We need a world making that is infused with ideas of care, and feminist thinking will have to show this way forward. My fieldwork in two recent publications, a chapter titled "Women's Practices in Homemaking Beyond Policies and Programmes" in a book called *Gender and the Indian City: Revisioning Design and Planning*,[6] and in a paper I jointly wrote with Megha Rajguru, titled "Radical Homemaking in Mumbai, India and Brighton, United Kingdom: rearticulating design and policy in housing,"[7] showed that women's practices in homemaking are involved with repair and retrofit, and more in tune with lived relationships as opposed to extractivist practices provided as solutions by the current market. Unlike making new things, repairing things is much closer to the idea of care—it is a continuous process and needs to have a deeper relationship between the caretaker and that which is cared for. Women have played a central role in repairing the built environment, not as a project or a contract, but as part of everyday life.

Rupali Gupte, "Women's Practices of Homemaking, Beyond Policies and Programmes," in *Gender and the Indian City: Revisioning Design and Planning*, ed. Madhavi Desai (New Delhi: South Asia Press, 2022).
Megha Rajguru and Rupali Gupte, "Radical Homemaking in Mumbai, India and Brighton, United Kingdom: rearticulating design and policy in housing,"

Journal of Housing and the Built Environment (2019), https://doi.org/10.1007/ s10901-024-10151-4.

EK Can you give some examples of critical feminist spatial practices in India and South Asia which you feel are most important in counteracting capital-centric urbanization and the climate catastrophe?

RG There are several examples of critical feminist spatial practices in India and South Asia which are extremely important in counteracting capital-centric urbanization and climate catastrophe. My research, however, has shown that one needs to expand the scope of fieldwork to practices beyond what is happening in professional architectural circles. While there are interesting practices in the realm of sustainable architecture that many women architects are engaged in, when seen through the frameworks of political economy these often tend to be second homes and some elite institutions which have much smaller impacts. The research has shown interesting cases such as the role of women in the municipal bureaucracy who work with small contractors to install individual toilets in self-built settlements, thus improving habitation conditions, creating dignified living, and in turn stealthily countering NGOs which, in pursuit of international funding, end up making large sanitation infrastructures that eventually break down. Or in other instances I have seen tribal women countering state bureaucracies that refuse to fund what they call kutcha (impermanent) houses, houses made with wattle and daub, by tactically taking these funds to build some parts of their houses as pukka (or permanent) in government vocabulary, but then creating extensions in wattle and daub and other impermanent materials that they have expertise in, and modifying the standard homes that emerge through these frameworks to create spaces for their lived experiences. In one instance, a tribal woman modified her standard kitchen into a kitchen verandah, where many more people could participate in cooking, as opposed to the standardized space where only she could work. Modernization processes entrenched in capitalism often operate through modern regulatory frameworks that erase the multiple possibilities of inhabitations. We need to learn from the lived experiences of women to rethink the theorization of space and the coordinates we set for ourselves in what we value in architecture.

EK When you think about the future of architecture and the future because of architecture, what comes to mind? What are the most urgent concerns? What are the most critical practices?

RG In another recent paper titled "Of Disintegrations, Immersions, Scattering, Shifting and Flowing: Towards a Pedagogy of Life," which I presented at a conference at Cornell University in New York called *The Next Monsoon: Climate Change and Contemporary Cultural Production in South Asia*,[8] I argue that ideas of property, permanence, and privacy have been the cornerstones of our spatial thinking that has deep roots in colonial spatial epistemology. We need to learn from practices in South Asia and from feminist practices that revolve around impermanence, ones that are not wedded to private property and are interested instead in spaces of collectivization, of networked space, and spaces of multiple tenures.

Being attentive to minor practices through which women participate in world making is important for us to build future trajectories in a world riddled with economic crises and climate disasters. At the same time, feminist scholars like Vandana Shiva, from her early theoretical work *Staying Alive*[9] to a later volume on ecofeminism co-edited with Maria Mies,[10] have pointed out the link between patriarchy and environmental degradation and have critiqued modern science and development as projects of male, Western origin. They also point to women's agencies in creating alternative forms of knowledge and modes of living. They draw on ecofeminist structures of knowledge to build a new ethics for future living. However, some of the ecofeminist arguments have been critiqued as being caste blind. Many scholars have drawn on writings such as those of Jyotiba Phule to draw on the intersection of Dalit and environmental histories in order to point to the social dimensions of a just future.[11] At the School of Environment and Architecture (SEA), we have courses on Ethics and on Repair and Retrofit that deal with these questions. This course is a reworking of the Mumbai University syllabus that asks us to teach Professional Practice. Unfortunately in the university syllabus as well as in the practicing world of architecture, Professional Practice is rooted in professional ethics that supports the idea of universal progress and is unattentive to the fact that these knowledge forms are not gender- and caste-neutral. These courses have further led to studios where students have worked with communities to create dignified inhabitations. We hope the new generation of architects equipped with a new ethical framework and diverse forms of knowledge is able to create a better, more spatially just future.

Rupali Gupte, "Of Disintegrations, Immersions, Scattering, Shifting and Flowing: Towards a Pedagogy of Life," *The Next Monsoon: Climate Change and Contemporary Cultural Production in South Asia*, eds. Iftikhar Dadi, Sonal Khullar, Sarah Betsky, and Rupali Gupte (forthcoming).

9   Vandana Shiva, *Staying Alive: Women, Ecology and Survival in India* (New Delhi: Kali for Women, 1998).

10   Vandana Shiva and Maria Mies, *Ecofeminism* (London, UK, and New York: Zed Books, 1993).

11   Mukul Sharma, *Caste and Nature: Dalits and Indian Environmental Politics* (New Delhi:

Oxford University Press, 2017) and V.M. Ravi Kumar, "Non-Brahmanism and Nature: An Intellectual Environmental History of Jyotirao Phule." Scope IX, no. II (2019): 98–110, https://scope-journal.com/ assets/uploads/ doc/94b6a-98-110.13284.pdf.

Appendix

Acknowledgments

We would like to begin by acknowledging the abundance of knowledge, energy, enthusiasm, dedication, and insistence that we have experienced during the process of writing, editing, and conversing with the contributing authors and, above all, with architect Anupama Kundoo, whose practice inspired us to introduce the notion of abundance in architectural discourse in the first place.

Our dialogue with the architect Anupama Kundoo began in 2018, when we were working on the exhibition and the edited volume *Critical Care. Architecture and Urbanism for a Broken Planet* (The MIT Press, 2019). At the time we were, and we still are, interested in how architecture can be understood and practiced as care. Our aim is to continue to contribute and to expand the understanding of care in architecture. Seeing how Anupama Kundoo practices in complex and insistent ways under contradictory conditions, we decided to continue our exploration of care through her work and to dedicate a book and an exhibition to her practice. Following care leads to new concepts, such as abundance. During our curatorial research visit to Anupama Kundoo's built work in South India, we began to understand that abundance is the lens through which her practice is best captured, and we also stayed committed to our interest in care. We see abundance as an extension of care, and we are most grateful to Anupama Kundoo for allowing us to understand this. We cannot thank Anupama enough for her hospitality, for her generosity in sharing her work, and for many, many hours of conversations dedicated to mutual learning. Our embodied experience of Anupama Kundoo's lively architecture not only led us to the theoretical concept of "abundance" but has left a lifelong impression.

A book is always a collaborative work, and this is particularly the case with this format of an extended monograph, which creates space for themes and advocates alternatives. We thank the authors whose critical scholarship exposes the systemic conditions of modernist and contemporary architecture practice including colonial, extractive, neoliberal, and patriarchal realities. We are thankful to the Architekturzentrum Wien with its dedicated and experienced staff, and, of course, to the core team working on the book and the exhibition. We thank Karin Lux, managing director at Architekturzentrum Wien, for her commitment to this project and her wonderful support throughout.

We had the pleasure of working with various team members from Anupama Kundoo's studios in Puducherry, Mumbai, and Berlin. We would like to thank Sonali Phadnis for the excursions she made with us and the insights into everyday life in Auroville; Nishanti Srinivasan and Shreshta Gopalakrishnan for spending time together at the Wall House; Yashoda Joshi and Keerthana Jayaseelan for additional support from the Mumbai office; May Lange, Alba Sans Morcillo, Manuel San Miguel, and Laura Ranzi in Berlin for tracking all the details of the exhibition design; Ambika for delicious food, fresh flowers, and a glance at the maintenance of the Wall House; many Aurovilians for a variety of conversations; Kumar and his team for taking us to a quarry; and to Amra and Linda for making it possible for us to visit Golconde.

Thanks to the dedicated staff at the MIT Press for their openness to a book format that redefines the canonical, male- and white-centered format of the monograph and makes the monograph a space for themes that we all care about, and especially to Victoria Hindley for her trust and guidance, to Gabriela Bueno Gibbs for support, and to Kate Elwell for advice on production. We are most grateful to all the contributors to this book: Ranjit Hoskote, Madhavi Desai, Peggy Deamer, Laurie Parsons,

Charlotte Malterre-Barthes, Jordan Carver, Shumi Bose, Shannon Mattern, and Rupali Gupte. Working with the book and exhibition team has not only been inspirational, but it has also been rewarding and fun. We are most grateful to Agnes Wyskitensky for her meticulous work as project coordinator. For the second time, we were able to benefit from her experience, her accuracy, and her thoughtfulness. Brian Dorsey was always there for translations, language editing, and proofreading whether the authors met deadlines or not. Lisa Kusebauch supplemented the careful proofreading. We thank Alexander Schuh for his beautiful graphic design for the book and the exhibition, and Anupama Kundoo for her exhibition design which manages to be both stunning and soothing at the same time.

We would like to thank the experienced team at the Architekturzentrum Wien for making the book and the exhibition possible. We thank Maria Falkner for coordinating e-meetings, meetings in person, for transcribing interviews, for organizing our travels and finding lost suitcases. We thank Andreas Kurz, as production manager of the exhibition, for his tireless search for local, feasible, and sustainable solutions, as well as Philipp Aschenberger for constructing prototypes and coordinating the workshop team. Thanks to Katharina Ritter for supervising the program coordination, Anne Wübben for developing the educational offer, Lene Benz for organizing the accompanying program, Suzanne Kriszenecky for arranging the excursions, and Ines Purtauf and Alexandra Viehhauser for providing the communication.

We thank all the supporters and funders who have made the book and the exhibition possible: the public funding partners of the Architekturzentrum Wien—the Cultural Affairs Department of the City of Vienna, the Urban Development and Planning Department of the City of Vienna, and the Arts and Culture Division of the Federal Ministry for Arts, Culture, the Civil Service and Sport—and all the members of the Architecture Lounge of the Architekturzentrum Wien.

Angelika and Elke are most grateful to each other for their friendship, their ongoing inspiring collaboration, and their mutual support throughout. This book is dedicated to all those who use their imagination to reflect and practice architecture otherwise. It advocates for an architecture based on the premise that there is enough for all. Let's work with and for abundance together.

About Anupama Kundoo

Founder and Director of Anupama Kundoo
Architects
Berlin, Germany, Mumbai and Puducherry, India

*1967 in Pune, India

1990
First professional office in Auroville, India

Education

2005–2008
Ph.D. at the Technische Universität, Berlin,
  Germany "Building with Fire. Baked-Insitu
  Mud Houses of India: Evolution and Analysis of
  Ray Meeker's Experiments"

1997
Research Fellowship "Urban Eco-Community:
  Design and Analysis for Sustainability," Vastu
  Shilpa Foundation, Ahmedabad

1984–1989
Bachelor Degree at Sir J. J. College of
  Architecture, University of Mumbai

Awards

2022
Global Award for Sustainable Architecture, under
  UNESCO patronage

2021
RIBA Charles Jencks Award for Architecture
  Theory and Practice
Building Sense Now Global Award, German
  Sustainable Building Council (DGNB)
Auguste Perret Prize for Architectural
  Technology, International Union of Architects
  (UIA)

2013
Arc Vision Prize, Honorable Mention
V. D. Joshi Award, Best Ferrocement Structure,
  Ferrocement Society of India

2003
Architect of the Year Award, Category Group
  Housing, JK, India

2001
A+D Awards, Honorable Mention in "Young
  Enthused Architect Category"

2000
Indian Architect & Builder Award, Architect of
  the Future

1999
Architect of the Year Award, Category Young
  Architect, Focus State Tamil Nadu, JK Cement,
  India

Built Work

Public Buildings

2023
People and Nature Centre, Keystone Foundation, Kotagiri, India (ongoing)

2022
Auroville Main Town Hall, Auroville, India (ongoing)

2021
Amba Seifenmanufaktur, Ketzin, Germany (ongoing)
Ruta Pais Pavilion, Pomaire, Chile (ongoing)

2019
Sharana Daycare Facility, Puducherry, India

2018
Library Nandalal Sewa Samithi, Puducherry, India

2012
Guest House, Keystone Foundation, Kotagiri, India

2009
Tribal Crafts Center, Keystone Foundation, Kotagiri, India

2008
Honey-processing Unit, Keystone Foundation, Kotagiri, India
Watch tower, Botanical Gardens, Auroville, India

2007
Sports Facilities, New Creation, Auroville, India
Incense Factory, Mereville Trust, Auroville, India

2005
Mitra Youth Hostel, Auroville, India
Multimedia Centre, Town Hall Complex, Auroville, India

2004
Workshops and toilet blocks, Auroville Village Action Group, Auroville, India

2003
Abri Transport Service, Auroville, India
Auroville Centre for Urban Research, Town Hall Complex, Auroville, India

Mountain Apiculture Center; Environmental Development Unit; Marketing and Production Unit; Training and Networking Unit, Keystone Foundation, Kotagiri, India

2002
Gems Resort, Tiruvannamalai, India
Sub-Health Center, Rayapudupakkam, India

2001
Auroville Institute of Applied Technology, Auroville, India
Completion and Renovation BN Auditorium, Auroville, India

2000
Village Action Center, Auroville Village Action Group, Auroville, India
Sub-Health Centers, Thiruvai, Poothurai, and Aprampetu, India
Multipurpose Hall S.A.W.C.H.U., Auroville, India
Child-Line Centre and Life-Line Centre, Tiruvannamalai, India

1998
Animal Dispensary, Dayakara Trust, Auroville, India

1997
Mechanical Training Center, Auroville, India

1996
Community Kitchen, Aurogreen Kitchen, Auroville, India

Housing

2015
Line 10, Auroville, India (ongoing)
Full Fill Homes, Chennai and Auroville, India

2014
Terra Amata International Zone, Auroville, India

2013
Light Housing Prototype, Sonepat, India
Light Housing Prototype, Auroville, India

2008
Volontariat Homes for Homeless Children, Puducherry, India

2005
PARSN: Housing Complex, Coimbatore, India

2003
Creativity Co-Housing, Auroville, India
SECURE: Senior Citizens User-Friendly Housing,
   Visakhapatnam Urban Development Authority,
   Visakhapatnam, India
Sangamam (Phase 1 and 2), Auroville, India

2002
Promesse Staff Quarters, Auroville, India

Residences

2023
Residence Siethoff, Sundern, Germany (ongoing)

2022
Naya Bazaar, Pune, India
Verve, Ahmedabad, India

2016
Residence Pratima Joshi, Kotagiri, India
Residence Rajiv Raman, Kotagiri, India
Residence Gautam Chatterjee, Kotagiri, India
Shah Houses, Brahmangarh, India
Residence Caretakers, Brahmangarh, India

2015
Residence Bonheur, Puducherry, India

2012
Residence Shammy Jacob (Phase 2), Chennai,
   India

2004
Sneh and Pratim's House, Kotagiri, India
Vivek's House, Puducherry, India

2003
Reverend Mulley's House, Kotagiri, India
Anita's House, Kotagiri, India
House for Paul and Claudine, Auroville, India
Care Taker's House, Residence Spirit Sense,
   Auroville, India

2002
Mathew's House, Kotagiri, India

2001
House for Kireet Joshi, Auroville
House for Krishan Myer, Auroville, India
Residence Balasubramaniam, Chennai, India
Srinivasa Murthy's House, Puducherry, India
Residence Spirit Sense, Auroville, India

2000
Wall House, Auroville, India

1999
House for Karen and Gerald, Auroville, India
Courtine's House, near Puducherry, India
Mathew's House, Kotagiri, India

1998
Residence Shammy Jacob (Phase 1), Chennai,
   India
Residence Hemant Divya, Auroville, India
Ried House, Puducherry, India

1997
Yoga Hall in Petite Ferme, Auroville, India

1996
Kolam Studio Residence, Petite Ferme, Auroville,
   India

1993
House Prototypes for Yoga Resort, Mulshi, India

1992
Residence Pierre Tran, Auroville, India

1990
Hut Petite Ferme, Auroville, India

Urban Design and Planning Projects

2024
Auroville City for 50,000 residents, in
   collaboration with Auroville Town
   Development Council as Head of Urban Design

2018
Line of Goodwill, Auroville, India

2015
"Inverse Functions," African City Prototype for
   200,000 people

2010
Auroville City Centre, Habitat Area for 1,500
   residents, Auroville, India

2007
City Centre, Auroville, India

2005
Adyar Eco-Park, Concept Stage, Chennai, India

2004
Administrative Zone, Auroville, India

2002
Perspective Plan 2025, Auroville 50,000 inhabitants (in collaboration with Roger Anger and AV Groups), Auroville, India

1998
Bharat Nivas Campus, International Zone, Auroville, India

Installations

2025
German Pavilion *Shelf Life*, International Kolkata Book Fair, Kolkata, India

2017
Set Design, Q Berlin Questions, Schiller Theater, Berlin, Germany

2015
Samskara: Made in India, IGNCA, New Delhi, India

2014
Unbound, The Library of Lost Books, BCN Re.Set, Barcelona, Spain

Exhibitions

2025
Abundance Not Capital. Anupama Kundoo, September 11, 2025 – February 16, 2026, Architekturzentrum Wien, Vienna, Austria

2024
Material Acts: Experimentation in Architecture and Design, Craft Contemporary, September 28, 2024 – January 5, 2025, Los Angeles, US

2022
Co-Creation. Architecture is Collaboration, May 4 – September 30, 2022, Roca Gallery, Barcelona, Spain
Visionaries, Co-curated with Anastassia Smirnova and Caroline Voet, October 1 – December 4, 2022, Trienal de Arquitectura de Lisboa, Lisbon, Portugal

2021
Good News. Women in Architecture, December 16, 2021 – October 23, 2022, MAXXI National Museum of XXI Century Arts, Rome, Italy

2020
Anupama Kundoo – Taking Time, The Architect's Studio, October 8, 2020 – January 31, 2021, Louisiana Museum of Modern Art, Humlebæk, Denmark

2019
Bauhaus Festival *Architektur Radikal*, May 31, – June 2, 2016, Bauhaus Museum Dessau, Germany
Critical Care. Architecture and Urbanism for a Broken Planet, April 24, – September 9, 2019, Architekturzentrum Wien, Vienna, Austria
Reflex Bauhaus, February 18, 2019 – January 17, 2021, Pinakothek der Moderne, Munich, Germany

2017
Building Knowledge, Building Community, September 8 – October 21, 2017, Architektur Galerie Berlin, Germany

2016
"Building Knowledge: An Inventory of Strategies," 15th edition of La Biennale di Venezia – *Reporting from the Front*, May 28 – November 27, 2016, curated by Alejandro Aravena
Anupama Kundoo: High-speed Housing, March 31 – June 18, 2016, ROCA London Gallery, London, UK

2014
Unbound. The Library of Lost Books, BCN Re.Set, June – September 2014, organized by Fundació Enric Miralles, Barcelona, Spain
Samskara: Made in India, February 10 – 28, 2014, IGNCA, New Delhi

2012
"Feel the Ground: Wall House One to One," 13th edition of La Biennale di Venezia – *Common Ground*, August 29 – November 25, 2012, curated by David Chipperfield

Academic Teaching and Research

From 2024 onwards

Professor for Architectural Design, Head of Department/Chair of "Making Matters," Architecture and Design Methods, Technische Universität, Berlin, Germany

2024

Norman R. Foster Visiting Professor, Yale University, New Haven, US

2018–2024

Professor for Design Studio, Fachhochschule Potsdam, Potsdam, Germany

2023

Visiting Professor, Advance Design Studio, GSAPP, Columbia University, New York, US

2020

William B. and Charlotte Shephard Davenport Visiting Professor, Yale University, New Haven, US

2017–2018

Professor, Design Studio, IE University, Segovia/Madrid, Spain

2014–2017

Professor, Chair for Affordable Habitat, Universidad Camilo José Cela (UCJC), Madrid, Spain

2012–2014

Senior Lecturer for Architectural Design, Environmental Technologies and Material Sciences
University of Queensland, Brisbane, Australia

2011

Assistant Professor, School of Constructed Environments, Parsons, The New School of Design, New York, US

Publications (in Chronological Order)

Edited Volumes, Authored Books and Book Chapters

Line of Goodwill: Urban Eco-Communities as Prototypes for Sustainable Living. IRGE Insitut für Raumkonzeptionen und Grundlagen des Entwerfens, University of Stuttgart, 2019.

"Rethinking Materiality. Constructing under Climate Change." In *Make City. A Compendium of Urban Alternatives*, edited by Francesca Ferguson. Berlin: JOVIS, 2019, 270–76.

Kundoo, Anupama, and Yashoda Joshi. *AVPNY Auroville & Pondicherry Architectural Travel Guide*, Barcelona: Altrim Publishers, 2019.

"Foreword." In Meeker, Ray. *Building with Fire*. Ahmedabad: CEPT Publications, 2018.

"Affordable Housing: Rethinking Affordability in Economic and Environmental Terms in India." In *Inclusive Urbanization Rethinking Policy, Practice and Research in the Age of Climate Change*, edited by Krishna Shrestha, Hemant Ojha, Phil McManus, Anna Rubbo, Krishna Kumar Dhote. New York/London: Routledge, 2015.

Kundoo, Anupama, Brian McGrath, Atch Sreshthaputra, David Robson, Scott Drake. "Sufficiency, Balance and Harmony: Ecological Architecture from an Asian Perspective." *Nakhara Journal of Environmental Design and Planning*, vol. 8, Chulalongkorn, 2012.

Wissen bauen, Gemeinschaft bauen. Building Knowledge, Building Community. Brakel: FSB, 2017.

Roger Anger: Research on Beauty. Recherche sur la beauté. Architecture 1953–2008. Berlin: JOVIS Verlag, 2009.

Sustainable Building. Design Manual, Volumes 1 and 2. European Commission Project: 'Strengthening Capacities for Planning and Implementation', in partnership with the municipalities of London and the State of Haryana in India. Barcelona: Institute of Energy Catalunya, 2004.

Journal and Magazine Articles

"Human Time as a Resource. Twelve Strategies for Rethinking Urban Materiality," *The Plan Journal* 6, no. 2 (2021): 305–22. https://doi.org/10.15274/tpj.2021.06.02.1.

"Prendre le Temps (Taking Time)." *Tracés*, 3512, Berne (September 2021).

"Roger Anger, Against the Dictatorship of the Curtain Wall." AA 429 – *Ornament* (March 2019).

"Fifty years of Auroville: A laboratory city to steer the common future of human society." *ARCH+* 232, "An Atlas of Commoning" (2018): 195–201.

"Anupama Kundoo. A call for Action." *Boletín Académico*, no. 8, Universidade da Coruña (2018): 11–24.

"Ferrocement: Environmentally, Economically and Socially a Highly Promising Technology." *Detail*, no. 6 (2018): 18–25.

"Exhibiting Architecture in Full-Scale: Wall House, One to One at the 13th Architecture Biennale, Venice 2012." *Tekton* 1, no. 1 (2014): 96–105.

"Proyecto y Material: Wall House." *Palimpsesto*, no. 11, Cátedra Blanca ETSA Barcelona, Barcelona (October 2014): 8–9.

"Hornos Habitados: Orphanage in Pondicherry, India." *Arquitectura Viva*, no. 161, Madrid (March 2014): 48–51.

"Green building strategies for a rapidly urbanising India." *Survey of the Environment* (2012): 72–75.

"Urban development: Options for urbanization." *Survey of the Environment* (2008): 94–98.

Conference Papers

Kundoo, Anupama, Arndt Goldack, and Mike Schlaich. *Ferrocement Solutions for Affordable Housing Prototypes in India*. 11th International Symposium on Ferrocement and Textile Reinforced Concrete, 3rd ICTRC, Aachen, 2015.

Kundoo, Anupama, and VV Rangarao. *Form Development and Ferrocement: A Synthesis of Science and Art*, Second National Conference on Ferrocement, Pune, July 13–14, 2013.

"New Building Approaches rather than New Building Materials." *JA Journal of Architecture* 01, no. 02, The Research Cell of Chandigarh College of Architecture, 2012, 25.

The Plasticity of Ferrocement, Tenth International Conference on Ferrocement FERRO X, Habana, Cuba, October 15–17, 2012.

The Plasticity of Ferrocement: Its Potential for Architectural Applications and Influence on Architectural Form, FS 2011 National Conference, Pune, 2011

Reception of Anupama Kundoo's Work in Literature and Media

"Fired-on-site Masonry. Anupama Kundoo." In *Material Acts, Experimentation in Architecture and Design*, edited by Kate Yeh Chiu and Jia Yi Gu. Los Angeles: Craft Contemporary, 2024, 214–15.

Contal, Marie-Hélène, and Jana Revedin, eds. *Sustainable Design. Vol. 10: The Territory: Threat or Opportunity?* Paris: Cite de l'Architecture et du Patrimoine, 2023.

Srivathsan, A. "Revisit: Wall House in Auroville, India by Anupama Kundoo." *The Architectural Review*, January 18, 2023. https://www.architectural-review.com/essays/revisit/revisit-wall-house-auroville-india.

Kapil, Nisha. "Anupama Kundoo: Redefining the Principles of Architecture." *Architectural + Design*, January 2022. https://www.architectureplusdesign.in/ad-exclusives/anupama-kundoo-redefining-the-principles-of-architecture/.

Advani, Rajesh. "Conversations: Envisioning the Possibilities of Our Environment Through the Repository of Unbuilt by Sameep Padora & Anupama Kundoo." In *Unbuilt 2.0 – Architecture of Future Collectives*, edited by Gautam Bhatia. New Delhi: Architecture Live, 2021, 93–104.

Schwitalla, Ursula. "Anupama Kundoo." In *Women in Architecture. Past, Present, and Future*, edited by idem. Berlin: Hatje Cantz, 2021, 120–23.

Bose, Shumi. "Content creator. Anupama Kundoo on architecture that builds happiness." *Wallpaper* * (April 2021): 164–73.

McGuirk, Justin, ed. *Waste Age: Catalogue of the Exhibition at the Design Museum.* London: Design Museum, 2021.

Fitz, Angelika. "Volontariat Home for Homeless Children, Pondicherry, India, 2010, By Anupama Kundoo." In *Critical Care. Architecture and Urbanism for A Broken Planet*, edited by Angelika Fitz, Elke Krasny, and Architekturzentrum Wien. Cambridge, MA: The MIT Press, 2019, 226–31.

Fernández-Galiano, Luis. "Kéré and Kundoo in Dialogue." *C Architecture and Everything Else*, no. 13 (2019): 56–67.

Puglisi, Luigi Prestinenza. "L'Architettura Sostenibile di Anupama Kundoo." *Greenbuilding Magazin*, no. 25 (November 2019): 4–7.

Mossin, N., S. Stilling, T. Chevalier Bøjstrup, V. G. Larsen, A. Blegvad, M. Lotz, and L. Rose, eds. *An Architecture Guide to the UN 17 Sustainable Development Goals*. 1st ed. Copenhagen: KADK 2018.

Oris Magazine, ed. *Oris House of Architecture Opens Its Doors!* Zagreb: Oris House of Architecture, 2015.

Louis, Simone. "Guardians of the Green." *VERVE Magazine* 23, no. 8, August 2015.

Mehta, Meghna. "Reviving the Derelict." *Indian Architect & Builder* 28, no. 10, Jasubai, Mumbai (June 2015): 62–67.

Baratta, Adolfo F. L. "Uso non convenzionale di prodotti tradizionali. La Wall House." *Costruire in Laterizio*, no. 162, anno XXVIII, Milan (April 2015): 52–59.

Louis, Maria. "Austerity Drive." *Architect and Interiors India* (Women's Day Special) 6, no. 12, March 2015.

Fairs, Marcus, ed. *Dezeen Book of Interviews*. United Kingdom: Dezeen Limited, 2014.

Lepik, Andres. "Anupama Kundoo." In *Arquitectura Necesaria/ Necessary Architecture*, edited by Luis Fernández-Galiano. Madrid: Fundación Arquitectura y Sociedad, 2014, 38–49.

Dalvi, Smita. "Wall House: One to One." *Oris Magazine*, no. 89, Zagreb, December 2014.

Obiol, Cecília. "Rethinking Materiality. Buildings Voids with Less Resources. Excerpts from a Lecture by Anupama Kundoo." *Palimpsesto*, no. 11 (October 2014): 4–5. https://doi.org/10.5821/palimpsesto.11.3754.

Crosas i Armengol, Carles. "Diálogos entrecruzados con Anupama Kundoo." *Palimpsesto*, no. 11, Cátedra Blanca ETSA Barcelona, Barcelona (October 2014): 5. https://doi.org/10.5821/palimpsesto.11.3726.

Avenia, Gabriella, and Shahmen Suku. "An Interview with Anupama Kundoo." *D/zine*, Issue 2, Brisbane (September 2014): 18–21.

Balestra, Filipe. "Anupama from Auroville." FORM Nordic Architecture and Design, 2/2014, Stockholm (March 2014): 46–48.

Trzcińska, Milena, and Łukasz Stępnik. "Eksperiment i odpowiedzialość. Rozmowa z Anupamą Kundoo." *RZUT Kwartalnik Architektoniczny*, RZUT+3, Warsaw (January 2014): 32–37.

Albrecht, Benno, ed. *Africa: Big Chance Big Change: Catalogue of the Exhibition at the Triennale di Milano*. Milan: Triennale di Milano, 2014.

Colegio de Arquitectos del Ecuador, ed. *BAQ 2014: De la Casa a la Ciudad, de la Ciudad a la Casa: Catálogo Académico de la XIX Bienal Panamericana de Arquitectura de Quito*. Quito: Colegio de Arquitectos del Ecuador, 2014.

Foro Cultura, ed. *Foro de la Cultura, Innovación para un Cambio Social: Catalogue of the Congress*. Burgos: Foro Cultura, 2014.

Scenari Immobiliari, ed. *22º Forum Scenari: Catalogue of the Congress*. Santa Margherita Ligure: Scenari Immobiliari, 2014.

Fernández-Galiano, Luis, ed. *The Architect is Present: Catalogue of the Exhibition at Museo ICO*. Madrid: Museo ICO, 2014.

The University of Queensland, ed. *UQ. Prospectus 2014*. Brisbane: The University of Queensland, 2014.

Chan, William. "Building Common Ground at the Venice Biennale." *The Window*, New Delhi, February 2013.

Teller, Juergen. *Common Ground: In Photographs*. Venice: Marsilio Editori, 2013.

Italcementi Group, ed. *ArcVISION Prize 2013 'Women and Architecture': Catalogue of Finalist Projects*. Venice: Italcementi Group, 2013.

Bielefelder Kunstverein, ed. *Neue Bescheidenheit: Architektur in Zeiten der Verknappung: Catalogue of the Exhibition*. Bielefeld: Bielefelder Kunstverein, 2013.

The University of Queensland, ed. *UQ. Prospectus 2013*. Brisbane: The University of Queensland, 2013.

"Wall House Indien/Italien." *TEGL*, Copenhagen (December 2012): 30–37.

Hall, Min. "Feel the Ground." *BLOCK: The Broadsheet of the Auckland Branch of the New Zealand Institute of Architects*, Auckland, November 2012.

Pritchard, Owen. "Venice, The Wall House." *International Design, Architecture & Culture* (ICON), no. 113. Media 10 Limited, United Kingdom, November 2012.

La Biennale di Venezia, ed. *Wall House: Making and Remaking, Anupama Kundoo: Catalogue of the Installation at the 13th International Architecture Exhibition*. Venice: La Biennale di Venezia, 2012.

La Biennale di Venezia, ed. *Common Ground: Biennale Architettura Guide*. Venice: La Biennale di Venezia, 2012.

Capuani, Monica. "Mattone su Mattone." *Casamica* (*Corriere della Sera* Design Magazine), no. 5, Milano, October 2012.

Högner, Bärbel. "Es fehlt in Indien an Diskussionen über Architektur." *Modulør*, no. 7. Urdorf: Boll Verlag, October 2012.

Tipnis, Aishwarya. *Vernacular Traditions: Contemporary Architecture*. New Delhi: The Energy and Resources Institute, 2012.

Think Brick Australia, ed. *Think Brick Awards 2012: Commemorative Booklet*. St. Leonards NSW: Think Brick Australia, 2012.

Mehrotra, Rahul. *Architecture In India: Since 1990*. Mumbai: Pictor Publishing, 2011.

Rössl, Stefania. *Architettura Contemporanea: India*. Milan: Motta Architettura, 2009.

Editors of Phaidon Press, eds. *The Phaidon Atlas of 21st Century World Architecture*. London: Phaidon Press, 2008.

Shah, Jagan. *Contemporary Indian Architecture*. New Delhi: Roli & Jansen, 2008.

Barthel, Elena. "Beyond Johnny. An Observation Post for the Botanic Garden of Auroville, India 2007, March." *Macramè. Trame e ritagli dell'urbanistica 2*. Florence: Firenze University Press, 2008, 155–66.

Mathewson, Casey. *International Houses Atlas: World Atlas of Contemporary Houses*. Cologne: Feierabend Unique Books, 2007.

Feuer, Katharina. *Young Asian Architects*. Cologne, London, New York: DAAB Publishing, 2006.

Arnold, Thomas, Paul Grundei, Claire Karsenty, Elke Knöß, eds. *Architektur Rausch: A Position on Architectural Design*. Berlin: Jovis, 2005.

London, Geoffrey. *Houses for the 21st Century*. Sydney: Pesaro Publishing, 2004.

Editors of the Phaidon Press, eds. *World Atlas on Contemporary Architecture*. London: Phaidon Press, 2004.

Auroville Communication Centre. *Auroville Architecture: Towards New Forms for a New Consciousness*. Auroville: Prisma, 2004.

Ngo, Dung. *World House Now: Contemporary Architectural Directions*. New York: Universe Publishing, 2003.

Powell, Robert. *The New Asian House*. Singapore: Select Publishing, 2001.

Somaya, Brinda, and Urvashi Mehta. *Women in Architecture 2000 Plus, Focus: South-East Asia*. Mumbai: Hecar Foundation, 2000.

About the Authors

Shumi Bose

Shumi Bose is an academic, curator, and editor in the field of architecture and architectural history. She is Senior Lecturer in Architecture at UAL Central Saint Martins in London and also teaches at the Royal College of Art, Syracuse University, and the Technische Universität Wien.

Bose is Chief Editor of *KoozArch*, and contributes regularly to books and periodicals including *Log*, *PIN-UP*, and *Wallpaper**. She has curated widely, including at the Venice Biennale of Architecture, the Victoria and Albert Museum, and the Royal Institute of British Architects. She is a founding member of Architects for Gaza and the critical reading group Unsettled Subjects. In 2020 she founded Holdspace, a platform for extracurricular discussions in architectural education, and she currently serves as trustee for the Architecture Foundation.

Jordan Carver

Jordan H. Carver is a transdisciplinary scholar, designer, and critic at the Yale School of Architecture. He works across architecture, race, sovereignty, nationalism, politics, and abolition. He is the author of *Spaces of Disappearance: The Architecture of Extraordinary Rendition* (UR, 2018), co-author of *America Recovered* (Actar, 2019), and his writing has been published in *The Avery Review, Volume, Thresholds*, and *PLAT*, among other publications. He is a founding editor of *The Avery Review*, and a core member of Who Builds Your Architecture? Jordan holds a doctorate in American Studies from New York University and advanced architecture degrees from Columbia University GSAPP.

Peggy Deamer

Peggy Deamer is Professor Emerita of Yale University's School of Architecture. She has also taught at The Cooper Union, Parsons, Princeton University, Barnard College, and The School of Architecture and Planning at Auckland University. She has lectured widely on issues related to labor, design, and subjectivity, and organized events and publications that emphasize the misunderstood worth of architectural workers. She is the principal in the firm of Deamer, Studio. She is a founding member of the Architecture Lobby, a group advocating for the value of architectural design and labor. She is the editor of *Architecture and Capitalism: 1845 to the Present* (Routledge, 2014) and *The Architect as Worker: Immaterial Labor, the Creative Class, and the Politics of Design* (Bloomsbury, 2016), the author of *Architecture and Labor* (Routledge, 2020), and the co-author with six other women of *The Organizers' Guide to Architecture Education* (Routledge, 2024).

Madhavi Desai

Madhavi Desai is an architect, researcher, writer, and teacher. She was an adjunct faculty member at CEPT University, Ahmedabad (1986–2018). She has had Research Fellowships from ICSSR and SARAI, Delhi, the Aga Khan Program for Islamic Architecture, MIT, and the Getty Foundation, USA. She is a co-founder of Women Architects Forum and the Feminist Collective in Architecture. She is the co-author of *Architecture and Independence: The Search for Identity, India 1880 to 1980* (Oxford University Press, 1997, 2022), *Architectural Heritage of Gujarat: Interpretation, Appreciation, Values* (Gujarat Government, 2012), and *The Bungalow in Twentieth Century India* (Ashgate, 2012). She is the editor of *Gender and the Built Environment in India* (Zubaan 2007, 2023), and *Gender and the Indian City* (South Asia Press, 2022). She is the author of *Traditional Architecture: House Form of the Islamic Community of the Bohras in Gujarat* (Council of Architecture, 2007), and *Women Architects and Modernism in India* (Routledge, 2017).

Rupali Gupte

Rupali Gupte is an architect, urbanist, and artist based in Mumbai. She is a founding member and currently serves as a Professor and Director at the School of Environment and Architecture (sea.edu.in). Along with Prasad Shetty, she is a partner at Bard Studio, Mumbai (bardstudio.in). She was one of the co-founders of the urban research network CRIT and has recently been a senior research fellow at the University of Brighton. Her work includes research on South Asian architecture and urbanism with a focus on urban culture, housing, urban form, tactical practices, gender, and space. This work often crosses disciplinary boundaries and takes different forms—writings, drawings, mixed-media works, teaching, walks, and spatial interventions. It has been shown around the world, including at the 56th Venice Art Biennale, Manifesta 7, the São Paulo Biennale of Architecture, the 1st Seoul Biennale, MACBA Barcelona, MAAT Museum Lisbon, Project 88 Mumbai, the Dhaka Art Summit, and the Kiran Nadar Museum of Art.

Ranjit Hoskote

Ranjit Hoskote is a poet, cultural theorist, and independent curator. His collections of poetry include *Vanishing Acts* (2006), *Central Time* (2014), *Jonahwhale* (2018), *Hunchprose* (2021), and *Icelight* (2023). Hoskote has been a fellow of the International Writing Program, University of Iowa (1995), associate fellow of Sarai-CSDS at the Centre for the Study of Developing Societies, Delhi (2008), writer-in-residence at Villa Waldberta, Munich (2003) and the Polish Institute, Berlin (2010), and researcher-in-residence at BAK/basis voor actuele kunst, Utrecht (2010 and 2013). He was a contributor to BAK's long-term *Former West* research project. He curated India's first-ever national pavilion at the Venice Biennale (2011) and was co-curator, with Okwui Enwezor and Hyunjin Kim, of the 7th Gwangju Biennale. With Rahul Mehrotra and Kaiwan Mehta, he co-curated the benchmark exhibition *State of Architecture* (National Gallery of Modern Art, Mumbai, 2016). Hoskote has served on the Jury of the Venice Biennale (2015) and is a founding member of the Advisory Board of the Bergen Assembly, Norway.

Charlotte Malterre-Barthes

Charlotte Malterre-Barthes is an architect, urban designer, and Assistant Professor at the Swiss Federal Institute of Technology-Lausanne EPFL, where she leads RIOT, a research laboratory focused on driving systemic change across architecture and the construction industry. Her interests encompass urbanization, material extraction, climate emergency, and social justice. In 2020, she launched the initiative 'A Global Moratorium on New Construction' at the Harvard Graduate School of Design (publication, Sternberg/The MIT Press, 2025). She is a founding member of the activist networks Parity Group (Meret Oppenheim Prize, 2023) and the Parity Front, and holds a Ph.D. from ETH Zurich. Her award-winning publications include *On Architecture and the Greenfield* and *On Architecture and Greenwashing* (both Hatje Cantz, 2024), *Migrant Marseille* (Perenthèses, 2022, Ruby Press, 2020), *Eileen Gray: A House under the Sun* (Dargaud, 2020, Nobrow, 2019), and *Housing Cairo* (Ruby Press, 2016). She has co-curated exhibitions globally, including the 12th International Architecture Biennale of São Paulo (2019), and has exhibited at various institutions as well as architecture biennials in Venice, Seoul, Shenzhen, and Tbilisi.

Shannon Mattern

Shannon Mattern is the Penn Presidential Compact Professor of Media Studies at the University of Pennsylvania and the Director of Creative Research and Practice at the Metropolitan New York Library Council. From 2004 to 2022, she served in the Department of Anthropology and the School of Media Studies at The New School in New York. Her writing and teaching focus on media architectures and information infrastructures. She has written books about libraries, maps, and urban intelligence, and contributes a column about urban data and mediated spaces to *Places Journal*. You can find her at wordsinspace.net.

Laurie Parsons

Laurie Parsons is a Reader in Human Geography at Royal Holloway, University of London. His work explores the nexus of climate change and the global economy, exposing the hidden environmental impacts of global production and the unequal landscape of exposure to climate change impacts. It examines how climate change is shaped by social, political, and economic systems, highlighting the inequalities that amplify its effects through the lens of pre-existing local and global precarities. In 2020, his project *Blood Bricks* was awarded the Times Higher Education Prize for Research Project of the Year, and he has continued to write widely on this nexus since. His books include *Carbon Colonialism: How Rich Countries Export Climate Breakdown* (Manchester University Press, 2023, awarded the Association of American Publishers prize for Economics book of the year in 2024), *Climate Change in the Global Workplace* (Routledge, 2021), and *Going Nowhere Fast: Inequality in the Age of Translocality* (Oxford University Press, 2020).

About the Editors

Angelika Fitz

Angelika Fitz is the Director of the Architektur-zentrum Wien. Since the late 1990s, she has worked as a curator and author in the fields of architecture, art, and urbanism. She focuses on the social dimensions of architecture, planetary and feminist perspectives. In 2022 she was awarded the Julius Posener Prize for Architectural Theory. Her curatorial and editorial projects include Austria's contribution to the São Paulo Biennial, *Capital & Karma* at the Kunsthalle Wien, the international travelling exhibitions *Weltstadt* and *Actopolis*, and, with the Architekturzentrum Wien, *Assemble. How to Build*, and *Downtown Denise Scott Brown*, the first comprehensive show on Scott Brown's work. Her most recent exhibitions and publications include *Hot Questions. Cold Storage* on the permanent collection of the Az W, *Critical Care. Architecture for a Broken Planet*, co-edited with Elke Krasny and published by the MIT Press, as is her book *Yasmeen Lari. Architecture for the Future*, co-edited with Elke Krasny and Marvi Mazhar, 2023.

Elke Krasny

Elke Krasny is Professor at the Academy of Fine Arts Vienna. Krasny focuses on concerns of care, reproductive labor, social and environmental justice, commemorative practices and transnational feminisms in architecture, infrastructures, urbanism, and the arts. Krasny was a fellow at the CCA Canadian Centre for Architecture. Her curatorial work on *Hands-on Urbanism* was shown at the 2012 Venice Biennale for Architecture. Together with Angelika Fitz she edited *Critical Care. Architecture and Urbanism for a Broken Planet* (The MIT Press, 2019). Together with Lara Perry she edited *Curating as Feminist Organizing* (Routledge, 2023) and *Curating with Care* (Routledge, 2023). Her book *Living with an Infected Planet. Covid-19, Feminism, and the Global Frontline of Care* (transcript publishers, 2023) focuses on militarized care essentialism and feminist recovery plans in pandemic times. Together with Urska Jurman, Krasny convenes the group *Ecologies of Care* focusing on gendered and racialized dimensions of public space, colonial and contaminated heritage, infrastructures under pressure, and new imaginaries for environmental rights.

Architekturzentrum Wien

The Architekturzentrum Wien is the Austrian museum of architecture. Located at Museums-Quartier in the heart of Vienna, the Architekturzentrum Wien exhibits, discusses, and researches the ways in which architecture and urban development shape the daily life of each one of us. The broad program of the Architekturzentrum Wien is seen as a bridge between the specialist world and everyday experts. What can architecture do? This is a question of great relevance to all of us. The program comprises more than 500 events per year, ranging from international exhibitions, symposia, workshops, and lectures to guided tours, city expeditions, film series, and hands-on formats. The museum's facilities include a unique collection on Austrian architecture of the 20th and 21st centuries and a public architecture library.

Public funding for Architekturzentrum Wien (AzW)

☰ Bundesministerium
Kunst, Kultur,
öffentlicher Dienst und Sport

AzW is supported by

ARCHITECTURE LOUNGE
Architekturzentrum Wien

The Architecture Lounge at the AzW is an important platform for the exchange of ideas between architecture, business, and politics.

Architecture Lounge Members:
BDN Fleissner & Partner
Bundesimmobiliengesellschaft m.b.H.
Buwog Group
EGW Erste gemeinn. Wohnungsgesellschaft
Gesiba, Gemeinn. Siedlungs- & Bau AG
Gewog – Neue Heimat
Grohe Ges.m.b.H.
iC Projektentwicklung
Immobilien Privatstiftung
Kallco Development GmbH
Kallinger Projekte GmbH
Mischek Bauträger Service GmbH
Neues Leben Gemeinn. Bau-, Wohn- und Siedlungsgen.
Österreichisches Volkswohnungswerk
Sozialbau AG
Strabag Real Estate GmbH
Swisspearl Österreich GmbH
Vasko+Partner Ingenieure
WBV – GPA Wohnbauv. f. Privatangestellte
WKÖ – Fachverband Steine-Keramik
Wien 3420 Aspern Development AG
Wienerberger Österreich GmbH
wohnfonds_wien
WSE Wiener Standortentwicklung GmbH

Imprint

Co-published by Architekturzentrum Wien
and the MIT Press
© 2025 Architekturzentrum Wien
All texts © the authors
Images, plans, and drawings: © the creators.
Image credits are provided alongside the visual
material.

All rights reserved. No part of this publication may be
used to train artificial intelligence systems or
reproduced, stored in a retrieval system or
transmitted in any form or by any means, electronic,
mechanical, photocopying or otherwise, without the
written permission of the publisher.

Library of Congress Control Number: 2024951419
ISBN: 978-0-262-55312-4

Editors: Angelika Fitz, Elke Krasny,
and Architekturzentrum Wien
Editorial Assistant and Project Coordination:
Agnes Wyskitensky
Graphic Design: Alexander Ach Schuh
Proofreading: Brian Dorsey
Translations (German–English): Brian Dorsey
27–41, 43–55, 57–69, 83–93

Front Cover: Production of terracotta pots, Auroville,
India. Photo: Andreas Deffner
Back Cover: Anupama Kundoo, *Wall House*, 2000,
Auroville, India. Photo: Javier Callejas
Paper: Salzer Design White 1.5 100g
Printed and bound by Gerin Druck GmbH, Austria

This book is published on the occasion of the exhibition
Abundance Not Capital. Anupama Kundoo
(September 11, 2025–February 16, 2026)
at the Architekturzentrum Wien.

Director: Angelika Fitz
Executive Director: Karin Lux
Curators: Angelika Fitz, Elke Krasny
Curatorial Assistant and Project Coordination:
Agnes Wyskitensky
Exhibition Design: Anupama Kundoo Architects
Exhibition Graphic Design: Alexander Ach Schuh
Production: Andreas Kurz and Philipp Aschenberger

Architekturzentrum Wien,
Museumsplatz 1, 1070 Vienna
www.azw.at

The MIT Press
Cambridge, MA 02142
mitpress.mit.edu